Contents

Acknowledgements

I have learned a great deal through talking over the years with many early years practitioners, playworkers and parents. An equally valuable source of learning has been the many children whom I have watched and played with, including my own son and daughter. Full thanks to everyone would produce a very long list. So I will restrict myself to individuals who have been directly helpful for the content of this book.

I would especially like to thank: Paul Bonel (Head, Playwork Unit, Sprito) for help in understanding playwork as a tradition and as an area of good practice; Jacqui Cousins (Early Years Consultant) for insights into children's learning and the impact of adult anxiety on that potential; Peter Elfer (Senior Lecturer, University of Surrey Roehampton) and Dorothy Selleck (Early Years Advisor, Hammersmith and Fulham) for their knowledge and insights into very young children; Penny Mukherji (Tutor at City and Islington College, and author) for her helpful comments on the first draft of this book; Marjorie Ouvry (Early Years Consultant) for her understanding of outdoor play and helping me make sense of Margaret McMillan; Ann Robinson (previously Information Officer of the Early Childhood Unit) whose information search skills have been invaluable for many of my books; and Wendy Titman (Consultant) for her understanding of children's play in school grounds.

Most photos were taken from a range of settings in London, Stoke-on-Trent and Bridgwater. Many thanks go to the staff, children and parents of Abacus Nursery, Balham Nursery School, Bridgwater Early Excellence Centre, Cherubs Day Nursery, Newtec Day Nursery, Ravenstone Primary School, Saplings Nursery, St Peter's Nursery Class and Staffordshire University Day Nursery. Other photos come from my family collection. The photographs (except page 18) were taken by Lance Lindon or by myself. Many thanks to Lance for using his skills on the scanner to reproduce and tidy up many of the images.

The case studies in the book were developed from real people and places but the names and details have been changed to preserve confidentiality. Excerpts from the diary of my own children are taken from what I observed and wrote at the time. I thank Drew and Tanith for their permission to quote from this personal material, as well as use photos of their childhood. The photos from the 1950s are from my own childhood.

The author and publishers wish to thank the following for permission to reproduce their material: Format Photographers for the cover photographs; Brennan Linsley/Associated Press for the photograph on page 18.

Understanding Children's Play

Jennie Lindon

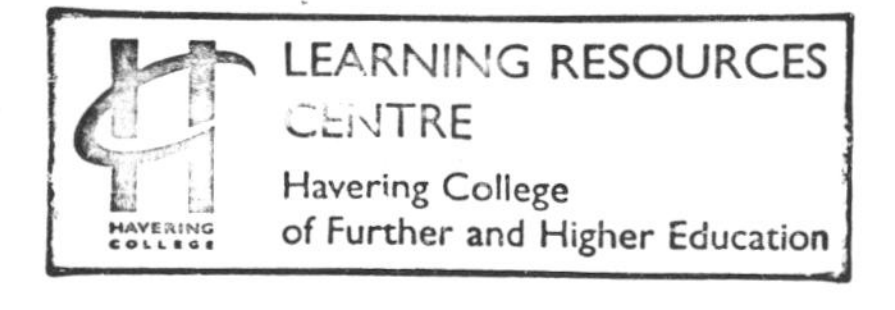

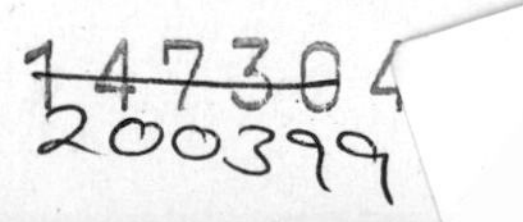

Published in 2001 by:
Nelson Thornes Ltd
Delta Place
27 Bath Road
CHELTENHAM
GL53 7TH
United Kingdom

01 02 03 04 05 / 10 9 8 7 6 5 4 3 2 1

A catalogue record for this book is available from the British Library

ISBN 0 7487 3970 X

Illustrations by Jane Bottomley
Page make-up by Northern Phototypesetting Co. Ltd

Printed and bound in Great Britain by The Bath Press.

Introduction

This book aims to help you to extend your understanding of children's play and to reflect on some of the assumptions and beliefs about play that inform your work with children from very young ages through to older children.

The traditions of early years and of playwork in the UK place a strong emphasis on the value of children's play as part of their learning and personal development through childhood. This perspective is not necessarily shared throughout society and many social changes have combined to restrict children's easy access to play space and play materials. Yet it is important to recognise that practitioners do not completely agree among themselves over how children learn through play and especially the nature of positive adult involvement in play.

This book is written to support early years and playwork practitioners. You could be at the beginning of your career or an experienced practitioner, who also supports students or less experienced colleagues. You may be undertaking qualifications in early years or playwork and this book especially supports vocational qualifications at NVQ Level 3, the diplomas offered by CACHE and BTEC-Edexcel. Students undertaking HND or Early Childhood Degrees will also find the book relevant to making those essential links between theory and informed practice.

This book draws on theory and research about children's play and its role in development and learning. The point of such material is to help you stand back from what you already know and to come afresh to your observations of children at play. We all need to make the effort to see how the cultural and social context affects our adult views and therefore how we enable children to play.

In this book you will find a range of activities, short examples, case studies and invitations to think about an issue. Please use these suggestions to make links between the ideas and your own practice in any of the early years and playwork settings. You can undertake many of these suggestions on your own, but most will be even more useful if you share ideas in discussion with colleagues or your fellow students.

ABOUT THE AUTHOR

Jennie Lindon, B.A., M.Phil., C.Psychol. is a Chartered Psychologist who runs her own business as a trainer, consultant and writer. Jennie has specialised in working with services for children and their families. She has considerable experience working with practitioners from all the different types of early years and playwork provision.

DEDICATION

To Ann Robinson – with sincere thanks for all your help over the years

CHAPTER 1

Play around the world

PREVIEW

The key topics covered in this chapter are:

- What is play?
- Have children always played?
- Do children play within all cultures?
- What prevents children's play?
- Play within society.

The word 'play' is a major feature of many discussions within early years and playwork in the UK. The value of children's play is taken as an agreed fact, although there are discussions, and sometimes arguments, about how children learn through play and the appropriate role for adults. Yet, how much do we really know about children's play? To what extent are we restricted, as well as supported, by our own cultural and social context, and indeed our own childhood memories? The aim of this first chapter is to explore play and children's playful activities in a broad framework of time and place, well beyond the four countries of the UK at the beginning of the twenty-first century.

DEFINITION

reflective practitioner a phrase that describes an alert professional, in early years and playwork, who is willing to think as well as act. Reflective practitioners are ready to re-consider as well as explain their current approach, values and priorities in work with children

WHAT IS PLAY?

Good practice for any practitioners closely involved with children is to step back sometimes from what seems 'normal' or 'obvious' to us in children's play, learning and their development. This stepping back is part of being a **reflective practitioner**, where you are ready and willing to consider your approach and preferred practice with children. However experienced early years and playwork professionals may be, no person can ever say that she or he has nothing further to learn. There will always be new ideas, a fresh angle on an existing idea and valuable food for thought about daily practice.

A working definition of play

There is no concise definition of play that could possibly cover all the features that people include when they use the word. Furthermore, as this book describes, early years and playwork practitioners do not all agree about the nature of play and where to draw the boundaries. So the working definition that guides this book is as follows.

- Play includes a range of activities, undertaken for their own interest, enjoyment or the satisfaction that results. Play activities are not essential to meet basic physical survival needs, although they appear to support psychological wellbeing, the learning of physical skills and intellectual stimulation. A playful quality in activities is shown by the exercise of choice, enjoyable repetition and invitation to others to join the play. Chosen play may look serious and players may show great absorption in the activity. Although play is usually used to describe the activities of children from babyhood, there is no reason to stop using the word for similar, playful pursuits enjoyed by teenagers or even adults.

Most children like playing with natural materials

Questions to consider

There are many questions one could ask about play and how children play. You might like to return to this list after reading each chapter, not just after this first chapter.

- What is play? What makes a child's activity into play rather than something else?

- When are activities undertaken by children not play or not playful in character?
- Why do children play? Do they inevitably play or can circumstances restrict or prevent children from playing?
- Is play universal within current societies around the world? Do all children play in all societies? In what ways does the pattern or extent of their play seem to differ?
- Have children always played throughout history? How did they play and to what extent is our current view of play any different?
- How recent are the ideas that children learn through play? Do they only learn through play or are there other positive routes to learning in early childhood?
- Do children need to play? Is their development undermined in any way if they are not able to play?
- When do children start to play? For instance, do babies play?
- When does play stop? For instance, do older children and young people still play; do adults ever play?
- Do all children play? What about children who are very sick or disabled – do they still play, do they want to play and do they need to play?
- What do adults think about play? How have adults explained play through developmental theory and research?
- How have adults studied play, what have they discovered and what appear to be the adult assumptions?
- What do children think about play and how do they talk about play activities?
- How do young people and adults recall the play of their childhood and what can we learn from these reminiscences?

HAVE CHILDREN ALWAYS PLAYED?

Although you need to be cautious about interpretation of historical material, it does seem that children have played in many past societies around the world, so long as their lives permitted some leisure.

The value of a historical perspective

Taking a historical perspective is as valuable as a cross-cultural viewpoint (see page 10). A sense of history, recent and longer ago, helps you to stand outside your own time and place, if only for a short while. Insights into what play, and the rest of children's lives, may have been like in other eras and other societies can highlight that children and childhood exist within a broader social context. It is also important that we do not become self-important or arrogant, believing that we have all the knowledge and the absolutely correct approach to children's play and their learning. Play, playthings, games and even learning through play are not an invention of twenty-first-century Europe or the United States.

TRY THIS!

How would you put together a historical record of your own childhood and play?

- For instance, what toys and books do you still have in your possession?
- Do you have a photographic or diary record that would support your descriptions of 'how I used to play?'
- What kind of memories come to the surface and to what extent do you realise that they are a selection of how you and your friends probably spent your days?
- In what way are your memories a match, or mis-match, with what your parents or siblings (if you have them) recall?

There is a number of different sources of historical evidence for building a picture of whether and how children played in previous eras. Some possibilities include:

- playthings and any play materials that have lasted from earlier times
- visual material from paintings, engravings or illustrations on decorative items like vases
- written accounts of childhood and play, perhaps within autobiographical and biographical accounts of family life.

A note on dating

This book uses the more recently developed abbreviation BCE, standing for Before Common Era rather than BC. The latter stands for Before Christ, so it is inappropriate for a multi-faith society or for cultures past or present whose traditions are not Christian.

Playthings from previous centuries

Archaeologists often study ancient societies by uncovering towns that have been buried in earth or sand. These explorations are called archaeological digs. The teams sometimes find evidence that suggests children from these lost, often ancient, societies had play materials.

Archaeologists and historians have to be cautious about interpretation, especially if items are found in tombs or burial mounds. Small figures or models are not necessarily playthings. A small doll-type figure buried with a child may appear to be a toy to modern eyes, but the 'doll' could have had a spiritual significance of which modern observers have no understanding. The significance of items can also change over time — see the description of Kachina dolls on page 10.

Doll figures

A small coarsely woven rag doll was found in the tomb of a child dating from about 300 BCE in Egypt. Additionally, what appear to be dolls, made from two pieces of bamboo, with black wool hair and unbaked dry clay at the end of each plait, have been found in Egypt and other parts of Africa dating from a wide span of centuries. Small figures in the British Museum date from around 2000 BCE.

Wheeled toys

In a dig in Central America of one of the cultures existing prior to the arrival of Europeans, archaeologists found what seems to be a toy cart with wheels. This find is especially striking since the society where it was found does not appear, from other evidence, to have used wheels in full-size vehicles for adult use. A Greek wine jug of the fifth century BCE (2,400 years ago) shows a small boy pulling what looks like a toy wagon or chariot.

Baby rattles

Rattles for babies have a very long history and often have been more than a plaything. Different cultures have seen the rattle as assisting the teething process, but some rattles seem to have had spiritual significance as well. Rattles have been found adapted from natural objects like gourds and everyday items. In Ancient Greece, earthenware feeding bottles have been

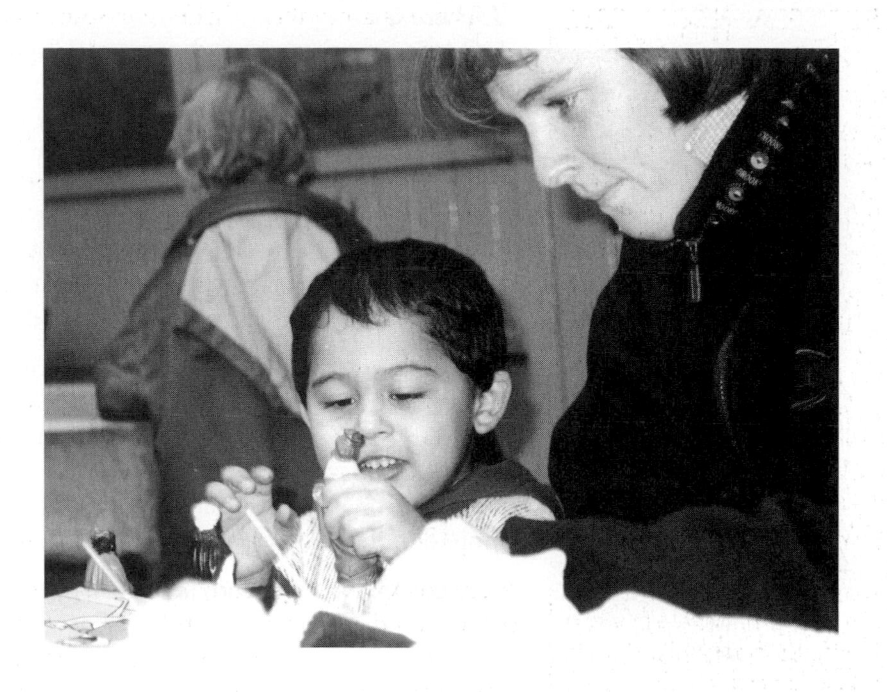

A contemporary use of small figures

found containing pebbles and the assumption is that these were designed to be rattles.

During the Middle Ages in Europe, coral teething sticks were often added to the end of rattles because it was believed that coral contained supernatural qualities to ward off evil and that it stopped bleeding gums. By the eighteenth century, coral was being replaced by ivory and mother-of-pearl. Teething rings and hollow, mass-produced rattles came into fashion by the second half of the nineteenth century.

Mechanical toys

Toys that move mechanically, known as automata, are known from as early as the second century BCE. However, they seem to have been mainly adult playthings, until they reached a high popularity in the nineteenth century and were made for children too. Many different ways were found to create the movement.

Wooden playthings

Wooden toys appear to have been made for children in Eastern Europe for many centuries. In Russia, for instance, some toy making evolved from making religious souvenirs for pilgrims. Wooden toys and dolls have been made in many parts of India since the fourteenth century and examples have survived of little figures, animals and wheeled transport.

Toy soldiers

A few toy soldiers have survived from Europe of the Middle Ages. Most examples that still exist are metal versions made from the eighteenth century onwards, mainly in Germany, which was a thriving centre of toy manufacture. Forts have been made to accompany play with the soldiers since the eighteenth century.

Toy horses

Hobbyhorses existed long before rocking horses, and the latter can be tracked back to the seventeenth century. Hobbyhorses are a horse's head attached to a pole, with or without wheels and are ridden astride by children. They are mentioned in writings that survive from classical Greek and Roman authors and were definitely popular from the Middle Ages in Europe.

From contemporary illustrations, children seem to have had fun with hobbyhorses, but the adult aim was that of preparing boys in particular for riding. Hobbyhorses can be seen in illustrations from Europe of the fifteenth century and appear to have been popular in China for centuries, appearing on Chinese ceramics, such as bowls.

Jigsaw puzzles

Jigsaw puzzles date from the late eighteenth century when they were first known as 'dissected puzzles' and were made with a deliberate instructional aim. Learning through play is not a new idea and this concept is discussed in more detail from page 140.

Games and play activities

Children's games are less easy to document, since very simple games equipment fell apart through enthusiastic use. String swings and skipping ropes, bits of wood for bats or stilts break up over time. The games equipment may not last, so the evidence that children have played games has to come mainly from visual and written records.

Illustrations on household items and other visual material from Ancient Greece show that children in that society played games using balls, tops and hoops. In China, a thousand years ago during China's Sung dynasty period, a painter showed *A Hundred Children at Play* and included children riding hobbyhorses, juggling and apparently dressing up as grown-ups.

A painting, centuries later and halfway across the world from the East, – *Children's Games* by the sixteenth-century Flemish artist Pieter Breughel the Elder – shows many forms of play that would be familiar to us now. Children are having a tug-of-war, a pretend wedding, rolling hoops and two girls are playing a game that looks like jacks.

A wooden engraving from the mid-sixteenth century shows a little girl with a doll and toy kitchen utensils. Another engraving dating from 1625 was used to illustrate a 1665 edition of the poem 'Kinder-spel' ('Children's play') by Jacob Cats. There are images of children playing at skipping, bowling hoops, spinning tops, flying kites and girls playing house with kitchen equipment. Both these illustrations are in the Victoria and Albert Picture Library, and reproduced in *Dolls' House Furniture* by Halina Pasierbska (Shire Books 1998).

Do playthings last?

More recent historical times can be documented by the playthings that have survived in personal collections and then housed in museums. However, such collections, as rich as they are, do not portray the full picture.

The guide from the Bethnal Green Museum (East London) points out that this collection has playthings that date mainly from the time when toy making had become a craft that adults did to make a living, rather than parents making playthings for their own children. The large-scale production

TRY THIS!

If possible, ask older members of your family (ideally grandparents or great uncles and aunts) to tell you about their play and playthings. How many of their toys and games still exist?

I remember my grandmother, who was a child in the first decade of the twentieth century, describing her great distress when she took her new doll to bed and woke in the morning to find that the wax material had melted so much as to distort the doll beyond recognition. She could tell me about this much-loved doll, but it was long gone.

of toys in Europe began in Germany in the sixteenth century and was a craft industry mainly using wood. Production expanded tremendously in the nineteenth century.

Some cheap fairground toys were of value to children in the nineteenth and twentieth centuries, but have rarely survived. Metal toys have a greater chance of lasting than paper or wood. Dolls and other kinds of representations of people or children seem to be an enduring form of plaything. However, the material used in the past could bring unexpected drawbacks and lead to the toy's demise.

THINK ABOUT IT

When considering the possible history of play and historical artefacts, it is important to realise that much-loved play materials may not last, to be gazed at in museums by later generations.

For instance, the actor Mark Hamill, Luke Skywalker in the original 'Star Wars Trilogy', was interviewed when the first set of 'Star Wars' toys became collectors' items for adults. His own children had been given a complete set of the figures, had played enthusiastically with them and characters like Princess Leia were now seriously the worse for wear. As teenagers, their semi-serious reaction was that their father should have told them the toys would be valuable one day: 'Why did you let us play with them, Dad!'

Adult pursuits and children's play

There can be movement over time within society between adults' and children's pursuits.

Games and playthings

As Iona and Peter Opie (1997) have documented, some games start out as adult amusements and move into the childhood sphere. They point to five-stones as an example and the Bethnal Green Museum of Childhood shows how a range of board games were initially used as much, or more, by adults than by children. The earliest dolls' houses, called at first baby houses, were made for adults. Some exquisitely crafted dolls and the early mechanical toys were also initially made for adult enthusiasts and not for children's play. Items tend to last if they were made for and kept by adults, which removes them from a history of children's play, but opens the perspective that adults with leisure have frequently relished playthings.

Adult chants to nursery rhymes

Some children's games and rhymes have long histories and a fair number have their origins in events of relevance to the adult world. Some rhymes that are now associated with children started life as satirical adult street chants about contemporary people, for instance 'I'm the King of the Castle' (Colonel Cockburn who fought Oliver Cromwell) or 'The Grand Old Duke of York' (Frederick, second son of George the Third).

Some rhymes were definitely rude in their original versions and were tidied up for children during the nineteenth century. 'Lavender's Blue' was first printed in the 1670s as 'The Kind Country Lovers' and included

Dolls' houses have a very long history

> **TRY THIS!**
>
> You could plan and undertake a project with the children on play and playthings from the past. The following are possibilities.
>
> - Visit a specialist toy or childhood museum, if one is close to you. Alternatively general museums sometimes have toy and play sections.
> - Talk with parents and see what toys they may still have from their childhood that could be carefully displayed.
> - If you and the children become interested in a particular kind of play material, Shire Publications offer a wide range of short books focused on particular kinds of playthings as part of a list for adult collectibles and antiques. Titles on, for instance, dolls, rocking horses or constructional toys, are a good source of information on the historical background.

some decidedly adult ideas about how to keep warm at night. Some rhymes, such as 'Lucy Locket', were about courtesans or the less up-market prostitutes.

There is not always agreement about the origins of what is now a children's song, nor an easy way to settle such adult disputes. A common explanation of the game and song of 'Ring-a-ring-a-roses' is that it started with a chant from the time of the Black Death. The smell of flowers was thought to ward off the evil and 'all fall down' refers to sudden death. On the other hand, some social historians claim the plague has nothing to do with the rhyme.

Chants and songs were passed on orally for generations, so there is often room for argument. Understandable concern arose among early years practitioners when it was proposed that 'Baa Baa Black Sheep' had its origins in slavery. However, some historical explanations of the song are related to ordinary commerce and not to the slave trade at all.

Written accounts of play

An alternative window onto the world of children's play is through any written accounts that survive. Some historical writers are not very interested in children or family life and the best sources tend to be in social history: bringing together source material or autobiographical accounts. One such personal account was written by Molly Hughes. She offers a detailed insight into a past childhood in *A London Child of the 1870s* (first published in 1934, Oxford University Press).

TRY THIS!

There remains a cross-over area between the absorbing interests and hobbies pursued by adults and children's play. Have a look at the magazine displays in the larger books and newsagent shops. You will find specialist hobby magazines for adult dolls' house enthusiasts, model railway collectors and adult play with model cars and aeroplanes. What else can you find? Some of these keen collectors and players also attend specialist fairs and conferences. Shall we call this activity 'adults at play'?

Molly Hughes was raised in a middle-class family with four older brothers. Her avowed aim in writing about her childhood was to show that Victorian children did not have such a dull time as many people suppose:

> It is true that we had few toys, few magazines, few outside entertainments and few means of getting about … For us, a large box of bricks was the foundation of all our doings. It served for railway stations, docks, forts, towers and every kind of house. Another box of bricks, thin and flat with dove-tailed edges, enabled us to build long walls around our cities. Some two dozen soldiers, red for English and blue for French, mostly wounded and disarmed, carried our grand manoeuvres on specimens of granite and quartz arranged on the mantelpiece and were easily mobilised anywhere. A packing case did for a shop, where goods of all kinds were sold for marbles or shells or foreign stamps. The whole room was occasionally the sea … We had several remains of ninepins and plenty of marbles. (Pages 3–4.)

Some further historical accounts are described from page 19 onwards.

CASE STUDY

A toy display

The team at Stoneway nursery school was keen to bring history alive for the children. The local history displays in the library had helped the children to understand how the streets and traffic had changed over the decades. Now the nursery team was interested to explore with children how some parts of life do not change that much.

The idea for a display of toys developed when Jerry was so enthusiastic about how his granddad had let Jerry play carefully with his Dinky™ cars. The children were keen and two of them dictated a letter to parents explaining the plan. They then illustrated and photocopied the final draft, with the support of an adult.

Many of the families were equally interested in contributing to a display. Even precious playthings were loaned when adults felt reassured that they would be safe. The children understood about taking care and were intrigued that all these grown-ups had played as children. Conversations flourished and not only among the children. Adults gathered by the display to reminisce.

1. Nursery teams find that children can take care with special displays, if they are prepared. In what ways do you think children could be helped?
2. What possibilities could you see for a display in your own setting?
3. Perhaps you are fortunate to work in an ethnically diverse area. As well as a perspective of recent social history, how might your display also reflect play in different cultures?

✔ PROGRESS CHECK

1 Suggest two ways in which your current practice could be enhanced by a historical perspective on play and playthings.
2 Look for two examples of how what we would regard as children's pursuits started as an adult interest or activity.
3 Explain why we need to be cautious about reaching conclusions about playthings or play from societies that are unfamiliar to us.

DO CHILDREN PLAY WITHIN ALL CULTURES?

It is very tempting to see the world through the lens of your own cultural experience, whatever that may be. Many child development texts and books about play used to be written exclusively from a European and North American perspective. Authors assumed that the rest of the world operated in much the same way, or was the source of interesting, slightly quaint anecdotes. To some extent, this bias can still be found, less blatant perhaps but still present.

More books now have a better cross-cultural perspective, but they are still often shaped by the culture of the writer(s). For example, books about play and development written by authors from the United States often include a section discussing Little League baseball. This game, and the social rituals surrounding it for both children and adults, is an activity of great cultural significance in the US, but of limited direct interest to readers from other cultures (see page 86).

Of course you will be grounded in your own culture, but your work with children will be more rounded if you recognise that perspectives on play do vary. In every setting, you will be able to extend children's experience beyond their own back yard. If you live and work in a diverse area, then you reflect all the cultures of children who attend your setting.

Understanding play outside your own culture

Understanding the details of everyday life can be just as tricky across contemporary cultures as when you take a historical perspective, either within or outside your own culture. Some of the examples earlier in this chapter are from societies outside Europe. The further removed in time and distance, the more likely it is that anyone can make inaccurate assumptions about any aspect of a culture. Children, childhood and play are no exception.

The meaning of dolls and other figures

Dolls and puppets have been used in many different ways within European societies and not always for children or for their play. Further afield, meanings may be outside our daily experience.

A good example comes from the Kachina dolls. They are now made for tourists by Hopi Indians in Arizona and New Mexico. Yet, in the early twentieth century these carved and painted wooden figures of masked dancers were of spiritual significance. They represented Kachinas, the spirits who controlled nature and the weather. The figures were used with children, but with an instructional purpose to enable them to understand the religious beliefs of their society.

Some doll-like figures seem to have had mainly a play purpose for children in a range of American Indian and Central American cultures. However, a dual purpose involving religious instruction also seems to have been quite common. Some toys in Mexico are still sold in connection with specific religious festivals and saints' days, although many are now more generally available.

Traditional dolls in China and Japan usually seem to have had ceremonial and sometimes spiritual significance. They have been given to children, but not always with a play function in mind. In Japan, for instance, great emphasis has been placed on the value of dolls to help children to learn about Japanese history, cultural pursuits and human endeavour. The Girls' and Boys' Festival dolls are linked with two separate festivals, one for each sex. The dolls are designed to teach heroism and valour to the boys. The girls are instructed in the preservation of Japanese culture, including the importance of history and the royal family. Both boys and girls are given an appropriate doll each year and the collection is displayed in an orderly way.

Puppet and shadow puppet play has had a long history of communicating morality tales and stories of religious significance in many cultures. The traditions can be tracked through societies in Europe, China, India and the Far East and the tradition is still current.

In some cultures, dolls are not welcome because of a religious prohibition on human images. Dressing up, much beloved in the UK, would be inappropriate in those cultures for whom certain kinds of pretend dressing bring bad luck. For instance, in parts of Southern Africa it would be considered unlucky for the entire family if a little girl dressed up as a pretend bride.

GOOD PRACTICE

The examples in this section are a timely reminder about having conversations with parents from a culture other than your own.

- You need to understand the meaning and symbolism of items that may seem playful to you.
- A doll may be for display and not for playing; a puppet play may have spiritual significance.
- Bear in mind that the reverse of what you expect may happen. An item with clear meaning to you, or an important cultural event, may not be fully understood by parents or colleagues from a different background.
- Good practice will be to talk, to listen and to give other people the benefit of the doubt if they misunderstand or do not know something that seems obvious to you.

A good guideline for everyone is 'don't assume – ask'.

Play in diverse cultures

Descriptions of children's activities from a wide range of contemporary cultures suggest that play and playful childhood activities are part of all human societies. Observers from cultures outside that being studied always have to exercise caution. It is far too easy to misinterpret or to place the values and meaning of our own culture on activities we do not understand. However, there is enough descriptive evidence to conclude that children's play is not restricted to societies in the Western or Northern hemispheres, nor to industrialised countries.

Play as part of socialisation

All play unfolds within a social and cultural setting. Adults draw the boundaries around what they feel to be appropriate, as well as views about how children, boys and girls, should grow up into properly behaved men and women. Play is therefore part of the **socialisation** process. This word describes how children are enabled to take on the outlook and behaviour preferred in their society.

> **DEFINITION**
>
> **socialisation** the process by which children learn what is expected of them in terms of behaviour and attitudes within their society, or social and cultural group

Whiting and Edwards (1988) looked for shared as well as diverse features between cultures. They drew from Whiting's earlier 'Six Cultures Study' and they were interested in children's naturally occurring social behaviour, not specifically their play. Their observations highlight that children start out with potentials, that are then shaped by adults. The older generation is not necessarily reflective about their own behaviour; it seems the right way to act. The cultural forces operate through:

- adults' expectations of children
- what adults give children most opportunity to practise
- which behaviours adults make meaningful for children in terms of the central cultural goals and values.

Whiting and Edwards concluded from the data from many societies that both boys and girls were disposed to respond in a nurturant way to 'lap children' (under-one-year-olds), in a dependent way towards adults and in a playful and challenging way to child companions. Adults then set boys and girls on different paths, sometimes very different, by allowing them varied amounts of autonomy in daily life, giving them a different pattern of responsibilities and limiting the company they kept.

Play does not need toys

Children certainly do not need manufactured toys in order to play and they show their creativity in many different cultural settings. Clare Elliott (1992) describes the Chama and Guarayu children of the Bolivian jungle:

> [they] spend many hours creatively shaping toys from raw materials. Papaya and banana leaves are used for umbrellas and playhouse roofs. Large soft leaves are used as toy cups; these may also be pressed against the teeth and popped like bubble gum. Juice from the kwasoxa tree is blown into durable 'soap' bubbles. Small reeds are cut in different lengths and cut on one side to make variously toned whistles. Pet birds and monkeys also occupy their attention. (Page 16.)

Many children build and create, often reflecting adult activities that they observe. Tony Fairman describes the constructional activities he observed of boys in Africa:

TRY THIS!

Tony Fairman's description of the African boys and their lorry constructions may strike happy childhood memories in some readers of European backgrounds. In my own childhood we spent a considerable amount of time building and playing with go-carts. This absorption led us to regular searches for planks, orange boxes (a lightweight form of wooden box) and old pram wheels. The necessity of the latter we learned through bitter experience when an especially elegant upper construction failed because the small wooden wheels split on first trial.

As you read through this section, look for connections with the play you remember from your own childhood and memories that you can encourage from adults who are older than you.

- Make the links to what you know about children's play now. In your own setting, or in a public play park, observe children at play with natural materials.
- See what they do in the garden or with basic recycled materials such as cardboard boxes or a big bag of autumn leaves.
- How do children use and re-use the basic materials? What does the cardboard box or a collection of leaves become?
- What can the play perhaps tell you about the learning opportunities of materials that can be used in many different ways?

A successful go-cart, 1950s style

> [they] spend a lot of their spare time making and driving wire lorries. It is a highly skilled job. You need lots of wire of different sorts ... some small bean tins, or lids of jars, any bits of coloured plastic for windscreens, headlights, winkers etc, other bits of tin. Those are the easy things you need. You also need lots of time, lots of patience and endless skill. All lorries can be steered and the best ones can carry things. (Page 115.)

Audrey Curtis (1994) drew together her own observations with those of other researchers in parts of Africa and Sri Lanka. She describes children playing with any materials that came to hand. They use discarded household objects like used baskets, old gourds and cardboard cartons. Empty Coca-Cola™ cans make drums and small cartons converted into pull-push toys. Girls pretend to cook using left over grain and leaves. Boys in parts of Africa make home-made sling slots out of tree branches to practise catching birds and snakes. Girls carry corn cobs or plastic dolls slung over their backs like their mothers.

Curtis comments on the uninformed remarks of outsiders who felt children's play was possibly limited:

> When some researchers commented that African girls had few dolls, it was pointed out to them that they did not need dolls as they had the young members of the family to practise on. (Page 31.)

A view that children learn only within a play context has limited the perspective of some European observers and commentators. This issue is raised again on page 105 in the context of pretend play.

Play can co-exist with chores

Audrey Curtis points out that in the UK we have fewer children per family than in previous generations. Much of children's pretend domestic play seems to arise because they are not expected, or are actually discouraged, from trying to help in the daily routine.

Tina Bruce (1994) identifies the unwise confusion in some European commentators who seem to equate chores with removing the innocence of childhood. She comments:

> There is a strongly held view in Europe and North America that a high level of child labour is an infringement and abuse of children's rights, with an undertone that this is cruel and oppressive. There is an equally strongly held view that formal schooling is a sign of an advanced society. (Page 195.)

Bruce points out that families who expect children to help with chores or family work are not taking an oppressive line equivalent to putting children to work in factories. Children in agricultural and hunter-gatherer societies learn by watching, socialising, playing and slowly doing. They are proud of skills they learn and are part of important daily life. They also still find time to play.

THINK ABOUT IT

It would be unwise to idealise more rural societies, but the observations that children learn through being part of daily life are a reminder that young children in contemporary Britain are often very removed from daily routines.

Observation of children in Western societies shows how much they often want to be part of daily routines in their family home or early years settings. They will happily take a small part of an adult activity and are keen to learn within a real daily context as well as to recycle the experience through their play.

See also the discussion about the play ethos from page 142.

Children like helping out

Children taking care of each other

Melvin Konner (1991) observed play in some hunter-gatherer communities and comments upon the predominance of the 'multi-age play group'. The Western idea that children play with peers close in age does not apply in these communities. The idea should also be approached with some caution as given in Western societies (see page 55). Konner describes the mixed-sex social groups of siblings and cousins who can range from late infancy to adolescence but may break down into smaller groups with a narrower age band:

> Infants begin to join in from the time they can walk, and the sight of a toddler edging away from his mother to more or less throw himself on a pile of wrestling two- to five-year-olds is not uncommon. Two-year-olds who are better walkers will follow the group around and, if they have wandered from the village camp, will be carried by older children when they tire ... children are not assigned the task of taking care of infants; and mothers are always in shouting (or crying) distance ... but there is care, protection and teaching ... and older children are learning infant and child care. (Page 314.)

The main activity of the group of children is a form of self-directed play that nevertheless often includes watching and imitating adult work activities. The children sometimes play at subsistence activities like food gathering but on other occasions their activity actually produces edible tid-bits, such as the snails or honey that Baka children collect.

TRY THIS!

The children from hunter-gatherer societies are learning skills that they will apply directly in adulthood. Yet food gathering can be part of enjoyable childhood activities in Western societies.

In what ways can you engage in food gathering expeditions with the children (not shopping)?

- Are there patches of freely growing fruit like blackberries on a local common or park? Go picking with the children in the autumn. You could make a pie or muffins with some of your crop, as well as enjoy eating them as fresh fruit.
- Can you grow fruit or vegetables in your garden?
- Do you know someone with a vegetable plot or an allotment? Can you arrange several visits over the growing season?

Games with rules

There are many examples of children in different cultures playing games with clearly understand rules and some of these games seem to have lasted for centuries.

Tony Fairman describes 'Tin touch' played in some African countries. One team of children builds a tower of tins while the other team, standing at an agreed distance, throws balls at the builders and their tower. Builders are out when they are hit by a ball and the winners are the team who builds the whole tower most often before their team is all out.

Gyles Brandreth (1984) describes 'Gora', a team game from India with a very long history. One team links arms in the middle of the designated playing area and the line starts to rotate, chanting 'Go-ra, go-ra' until the leader shouts 'Off!' The team members break away and run for the finishing line that they have to reach without being caught by the waiting members of the opposing team. The 'Dragon Heads and Tails' game from China is fun for children but also important in a culture where dragons have great spiritual significance.

✔ PROGRESS CHECK

1. **Give three examples of how children's satisfied play does not need conventional toys.**
2. **Find two examples of how play, games and spiritual significance may be interlinked within children's learning.**
3. **Explain how children's play and learning practical daily skills might co-exist in some societies.**

WHAT PREVENTS CHILDREN'S PLAY?

Extreme social conditions can make it impossible for children to play. Yet, sometimes playfulness survives, also perhaps as a way for children to deal with harsh circumstances.

Play under stressful circumstances

Apparently, children in the nineteenth-century slave plantations of the southern United States still played traditional games from their original cultures and some newly devised games. One such game was 'Hide the Switch'. One child would hide a willow switch that the other children had to find. The finder then ran after the others, trying to hit them. Clare Elliott (1992) describes the game as a means for the slave children to deal with and gain some level of control over the ever-present danger of flogging. She also suggests from source material that the children's games were overwhelmingly co-operative. Their play avoided competition in which a child could be eliminated from the game and reflected the vital community spirit that sustained the highly stressful life under slavery at that time.

War and conflict

It is likely that children's play has always picked up the echoes of what they know, or think, is happening in the adult part of their society. Children are often more aware of dramatic local and national conflict than adults believe.

Playing with soldiers, especially for boys, was regarded as a natural reflection of the decades in which British armies were engaged in many different countries around the globe. Children's games in the first part of the twentieth century sometimes included re-runs of battles of which they had heard adults talk. There is a photograph of boys in pitched pretend battle, complete with sticks and Union Jack flag in Nicholas Bentley's *Edwardian Album* (1974, Cardinal).

EXAMPLE

A 1950s' childhood

During my own 1950s' childhood, the Second World War was very real to us, because many adults spoke about it, sometimes as far as we were concerned at boring length. Living as I did on the south coast of England, one of my childhood fears was of invasion from the sea.

In our pretend games that required competing groups of children, one division we used was English versus Germans and themes of escape, hiding and capture were important features. The War did not dominate our games by any sense; Peter Pan versus the pirates and Robin Hood versus the Sheriff of Nottingham were equally significant.

1. Think back to your own childhood and talk about the topic with friends or colleagues. Can you recall ways in which local or national events entered your play?
2. What differences do you find from adults whose childhood was in different decades or lived in varied parts of the country?

Northern Ireland

More than one generation has now been raised in Northern Ireland through what this mixed community calls the Troubles. Some adults would undoubtedly like to believe that children are unaware of the continued stresses caused by the long history of animosity between the two Christian groups of

TRY THIS!

Save the Children has published an account that shows that play and social relations under conditions of conflict have been everyday life for children within Northern Ireland.

- You could obtain a copy of **Do You See What I See: young people's experience of the Troubles in their own words and photographs** (SCF, 1998).
- How do you think these young people's childhoods have been shaped by the divisions in their society?
- Why might adults find it hard to accept that children are aware of the dissension?

Readers who live and work in Northern Ireland will experience this discussion far more personally than readers in other parts of the UK.

Protestants and Catholics. Many early years practitioners and playworkers have recognised that the symbols, attitudes and persistent divisions in this society are reflected in children's play content and themes, and in many friendship patterns (see also page 40).

Children whose childhood is lost

Some children experience such extreme pressures in their lives that any chance to play is removed.

Children who work

Within any society, past or present, when families need children to sustain the household income, then they tend to become involved either in work or in the necessary childcare of younger children from an early age. Playtime can co-exist with a low level of family chores (see page 14). However, children will have neither the energy nor the spare time to be playful, when their waking hours are filled with responsibilities. They will also be tired and in poor health.

Child labour is a major feature of some families' lives around the world. The Anti-Slavery Society estimated in the 1990s that as many as 200 million children were working, often under dangerous conditions and with no hope of release. (Some organisations estimate lower numbers, but still in the millions.) Children work in agriculture, on the sugar plantations in Brazil and the rubber plantations in Malaysia. They work as child prostitutes or are coerced into child pornography in Thailand, the Philippines and South Korea. Children work in various industries, including brick making and crafts such as carpet making in Morocco and India and textiles in Bangladesh. Children are preferred not just because they are cheap; their small fingers are valued as more dextrous for some crafts.

Dealing with the realities of child labour is a more complex issue than many Western commentators often recognise. Children and their families are sometimes trapped in a form of indentured labour that is little different from slavery. Some are working alongside their parents, desperately needed hands in a family enterprise or small holding. The children's earnings can be vital to family survival, and passionate Western opponents have to identify how the family will manage in changed circumstances.

Children at war

Children lose their childhood and often their lives by being forced to work as fighters. When children are drawn completely into the war experience, their childhood leaves no space or time for play.

Training and using children to fight is not a new phenomenon. Napoleon's armies had young drummer boys who were the first to fall because they led the army. The German Hitlerjugend squad that defended Berlin in 1945 was made up of twelve-year-old boys. In contemporary Britain, sixteen-year-old boys are still allowed to join the Royal Navy and in 2000 there were just under 5,000 soldiers in the British Army who were younger than eighteen years.

The last decades of the 20th century have seen an increase in the deliberate use of children rather than young teenagers. It is estimated that there are at least 300,000 child soldiers or guerrillas, boys as well as girls. These children are mostly no older than twelve years and often as young as

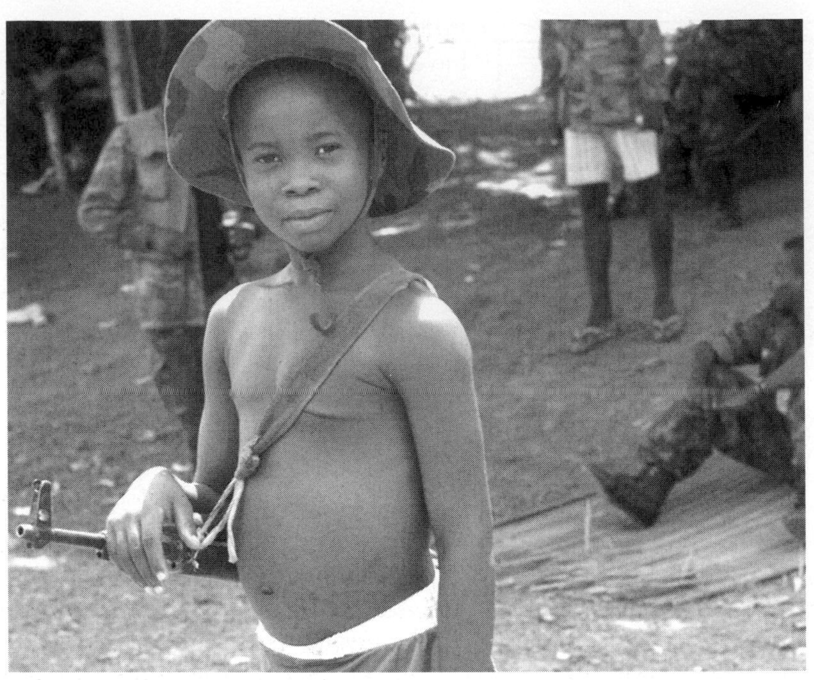

Child soldiers do not play

seven years (source: 'The children recruited to be killers' in *The Week* 29 July 2000). Children were used in the Iran-Iraq War of the 1980s and are active in parts of Africa, such as the Sudan, Uganda, Ethiopia and Sierra Leone and, in another region of the world, El Salvador.

Generally, the boys are taken to turn into child soldiers and the girls for a form of domestic indentured labour that often includes sexual abuse. All the children have lost their childhood years. Even if they are found and removed from the war zone, their emotional adjustment can be extremely difficult.

Refugee children

Other children have their homes, family life and childhood destroyed by the effects of war. There are considerable numbers of children world-wide who have months or years of displacement. They experience scenes of violence and traumatic loss that are hard for adults to understand, whose lives have been tranquil in comparison. Children can continue to play even under harsh conditions but any return to more peaceful play activities is unlikely without careful help and recognition of how much children have to cope with emotionally.

TRY THIS!

The organisation Save the Children has a range of publications and visual material relating to the experiences of children involved in armed conflict and whose families are refugees.

- The material will offer you and your colleagues an insight into different experiences of childhood under great stress.
- If you work with older children, in school or as a playworker, the material may also be useful to introduce with sensitivity to children, for them to understand that other boys and girls live very different lives.
- Contact the SCF publications department on 020 7703 5400, or write to 17 Grove Road, London SE5 8RD.

✔ PROGRESS CHECK

1 Find two examples of play under stressful situations.

2 Briefly describe two kinds of circumstances that could remove all chance for play in childhood.

PLAY WITHIN SOCIETY

Children do not exist separately from the society of which they are a part. They are the younger members of the population and they will grow into the next generation. In every society, over time and place, there are prevailing attitudes about what is childhood and how children should be treated. These views, and the behaviour that supports them, will seem to be the normal and best way to adults in the society.

Contrasting methods of raising or educating children tend to be seen against the backdrop of what is familiar to adults. Of course, approaches change over time and there is more diversity within some societies than appears obvious to outsiders. The main point to bear in mind is that children are part of their families and they are all affected by the social conditions and beliefs of the time.

Childhood and adult outlooks

During the 1990s, a number of sociologists, such as Berry Mayall, became interested in the **sociology of childhood**. They developed and described the ideas of a **social construction of childhood**. By this they meant that the whole idea of childhood, the usual experience of these years and the predominant images of children in any society, are neither universal nor fixed within a single society over time.

Adults bring their attitudes, philosophical and religious beliefs to bear on how they see children. Economic pressures, for an entire society or families who are under the greatest stress, exert an influence on how children are viewed. The extent to which children's labour is crucial to family survival will shape how far the years of childhood are significantly different from the adult years, including how long the childhood years are allowed to be.

Views of children and childhood

Children's play has a long and detailed history, but this activity has not always been regarded with enthusiasm by adults. One of the strongest influences on play has been the prevailing social view about the nature of children. Are children viewed as young humans in the making who need support and guidance? Or are they individuals whose negative potential needs to be restricted and firmly re-directed?

Changing views of children in the UK

Christina Hardyment (1995) described the changing views in Europe of how children should be treated, from 1750 up to the end of the twentieth century. Her examples of advice to parents are a timely reminder that opinion has changed dramatically and continues to circle. Hardyment also shows that experts can disagree, even within the same decades. She also reminds her readers that families do not always follow the advice of their time. So reading advice manuals of another era does not give an accurate description of what all parents actually did with their children.

Children as naturally bad?

Joan Perkins (1993) describes some of the changes over several decades within upper-class families living in England. During the 1800s, many families were influenced by the Christian-derived doctrine of original sin, that claimed

DEFINITIONS

sociology of childhood a branch of the discipline of sociology that has focused on children and childhood in the context of social groups and society as a whole

social construction of childhood the idea that there is neither an absolute, nor a universal image of a child and childhood. The image is created by social attitudes

TRY THIS!

Gather a small portfolio of public images of children and childhood from current magazines and newspapers. What range of images do you find?

- Are children portrayed as innocents in need of protection or as tearaways?
- Are they described as instruments of 'pester power' to get their parents to buy a brand of biscuits or designer clothing?
- What do children have to do in order to hit the newspaper headlines? Can they just be ordinary children or do they have to be extraordinary? Perhaps tragic tots battling illness, brave little angels or evil little beasts?
- What does the range of images say about our society and how it promotes the idea of children and the years of childhood?

children were born with a strong tendency to be evil. Children's lives therefore had to be strongly controlled by parents, a nurse or governess, in order to force them towards virtue. An associated belief was that play was a form of laziness and a dangerous temptation towards sin, as indeed was any activity other than work and religious devotion. The conviction that children and their play were potentially wicked went hand in hand with an enthusiasm for physical punishment as a necessary corrective. This approach is summed up by the deeply unpleasant childcare advice of 'spare the rod and spoil the child'.

Even when the very negative adult view of play had softened, there were clear restrictions applied to Sundays. The Noah's Ark sets of boat and animal figures became popular during the late eighteenth and then the nineteenth centuries. Because of the religious associations of the story, these were one of the few toys deemed appropriate for Sunday play for Victorian children.

During the second half of the 1800s, the nurseries of upper-class families were becoming more comfortable. There was more evidence of playthings such as dolls, dolls' houses, clockwork toys, toy animals, puzzles and bricks. Joan Perkins points out that children from poor families did not have the toys and recreation of their upper-class peers:

> The informal games of the street and field provided the enjoyment of their short childhoods. They made dolls from straw or rags, used an orange box for a doll's house, old rope for skipping, hoops from barrels for hoop-la, made a see saw from an old plank and some bricks, and a swing from rope hitched to a tree. (Page 20.)

THINK ABOUT IT

The approach that children are naturally bad still finds echoes in contemporary UK society. Adults, who are keen to use hitting in order to direct children's behaviour, will sometimes claim they only use a 'loving discipline' necessary for the child's own wellbeing. In some cases, this encouragement to violence continues to be presented as consistent with divine guidance.

Skittles as a game has been around for a long time

Marketing of children's playthings

The commercial production of playthings is not simply a creation of the late twentieth century, although the range and aggressive marketing has expanded significantly. The production of dolls and soft toys linked with books and cartoons started in earnest in the 1920s and 1930s with Christopher Robin and Pooh dolls, Peter Pan and Wendy and Mickey Mouse. (See, for instance, Pauline Cockrill's *Teddy Bears and Soft Toys*, Shire Books, 1997.)

A growing commercial interest in children's play and their learning has brought ever greater pressure on parents to buy playthings. Some merchandising linked with films and videos aims to tap into what the media call 'pester power': the persuasive impact of children who nag their parents to buy the latest collectible or 'must have' toy.

Another strand of marketing from the early twentieth century has been to convince parents that certain play materials are essential for a child's development. An advertisement in 1920 for a new-style rocking horse promoted this toy as 'a new era in nursery toys. Recommended by the Medical Profession, the "New" Riding Horse provides a permanent source of healthy, muscle-making, nerve-building, *instructive* [italics in the original] enjoyment' (reproduced in Ruth Bottomley's *Rocking Horses*, Shire Books, 1994).

The promotion of play materials as able to enhance every aspect of children's development, including learning to talk, is not therefore completely new. However, the extent of the marketing is significant, as is the implication that some play materials may perhaps do the job better than parents can.

TRY THIS!

Take a look around shops that sell children's toys and early learning resources.

- What kind of claims are made on the boxes and packaging?
- Do these look realistic to you? If you feel the claims are overblown, in what way?
- How do you think parents might react, especially if they are first-time parents concerned to do their very best?

Children's right to play?

In contemporary Europe, there has been an increasing emphasis on children's right to play. Forthright support for children's play did not start in the latter part of the twentieth century. In 1925, the British Prime Minister David Lloyd George stated that, 'The right to play is a child's first claim on the community. No community can infringe that right without doing deep and enduring harm to the minds and bodies of its citizens.' (Quoted in Gyles Brandreth, 1992.)

Yet all adults do not share this view of children's right to play and to have play spaces. There were some very negative comments on radio phone-ins during 1999 when the Children's Play Council was actively promoting the idea of home zones. These are residential areas in which peaceful zones would be created for adults as well as for children. Comments varied from enthusiastic support to snide disdain about children's so-called rights riding roughshod over those of adults.

Complaints about children's play and active attempts to restrict their play are not a recent phenomenon. Some grassy areas in residential areas still have signs demanding 'Keep off the grass', 'No ball games' or 'No skateboarding'. Yet, the back cover of Iona and Peter Opie's *Children's Games with Things* reproduces a public notice from Great Yarmouth in 1889. The wording was, 'Caution, notice is hereby given that all boys and others obstructing the public thoroughfares of the Town by spinning tops or playing at marbles and other games upon pavements or footpaths, will be summoned before the Magistrates and fined. By order Wm Brogden Chief Constable.' The original was laid out with many threatening capitals in the text.

The UN Convention

The importance of play has been recognised in the United Nations Convention on the Rights of the Child, an international agreement ratified by the UK in 1991. Article 31 of the Convention established that, 'States parties recognise the right of the child to rest and leisure, to engage in play and recreational activities appropriate to the age of the child and to participate freely in cultural life and the arts'. Related to this right are also children's rights to freedom of expression and association, established by articles 12, 13, 14, and 15.

Play today

Children live and learn within a time and place. To a great extent their childhood is shaped by the nature of the adult society and what it wishes boys and girls to become. Children who are growing up in the beginning of the twenty-first century have several broad influences on their childhood and therefore on their play. You could discuss some of these issues with colleagues or in your student group.

- Childhood has been extended in terms of statutory education to sixteen years and a range of legal restrictions that postpone full adulthood until eighteen or even twenty-one years of age for some issues.
- Children and teenagers are targeted as consumers of a wide range of products, with a deliberate attempt to create the belief that children are what they own, play with, eat and wear.
- There has been an expansion of out-of-home provision into the earlier years, compared with children growing up in the 1950s and 1960s. This development has many positive aspects. One possible negative is a growing belief that early learning needs experts rather than a partnership between parents and practitioners.
- Linked with the previous point, adult anxiety about later educational achievements has created pressure on children and sometimes threatened the early years tradition of relaxed learning through play.
- A serious concern about children's safety, if unsupervised outside the home, has led to significant restrictions of children's play outdoors with their friends, in comparison with previous generations.
- The shift to play contained within the home or approved early years and play settings has led to a situation in which children's play can be, although is not inevitably restricted.
- Related concerns have also been raised about children's health and physical skills if safety worries mean more sedentary leisure activities, including heavy use of television and computers.

✔ PROGRESS CHECK

1 Describe two ways in which children's opportunities to play might be shaped by adult concerns.

2 Children may be much the same as always but the society in which they play and learn has changed – suggest three main areas of change.

3 What is meant by the phrase 'children's right to play'?

Some play resources are very new

KEY TERMS

You need to know the meaning of the following words and phrases. Go back through the chapter to make sure you understand them:

reflective practitioner
social construction of childhood
socialisation
sociology of childhood

FURTHER READING

Brandreth, Gyles (1984) *Children's Games,* Chancellor Press
Descriptions of many games for children, some of which are of non-European origin.

Bruce, Tina (1994) 'Play, the universe and everything' in Janet Moyles (ed.) *The Excellence of Play*, Open University Press.
A thought-provoking discussion of play in the broader social context.

Curtis, Audrey (1994) 'Play in different cultures and childhoods' in Janet Moyles (op cit)
A helpful description of children's play in parts of Africa and in Sri Lanka.

Elliott, Clare (1992) *Childhood*, Channel 4 Publications
Discussion of play across time and place, with plenty of examples.

Fairman, Tony (1991) *Bury My Bones but Keep My Words: African Tales for Retelling*, Collins
A good source of stories from African countries but also with some explanation of children's play.

Hardyment, Christina (1995, revised second edition) *Perfect Parents: Babycare Advice Past and Present*, Oxford Paperbacks
A readable review by a social historian of how advice to parents has varied, the prevailing views about children and play in their lives.

Konner, Melvin (1991) *Childhood*, Little Brown and Company
A well-informed description of views of children and childhood in cultures around the world.

Mayall, Berry (ed.) (1994) *Children's Childhoods Observed and Experienced*, Falmer Press
An example of the sociological approach to childhood and children's experiences.

Opie, Iona and Opie, Peter (1997) *Children's Games with Things*, Oxford University Press
Since the 1950s Iona and Peter Opie have been enthusiastic collectors and recorders of children's games and playthings. Peter Opie died in 1982 and Iona Opie has continued to organise and write up the rich resources they valued so much. Earlier books record the language that supports children's play and their games. Their material is kept by the Bodleian Library in Oxford.

Perkins, Joan (1993) *Victorian Women*, John Murray
A social history of women that also covers aspects of family life and the experience of children.

Whiting, Beatrice Blyth and Edwards, Carolyn Pope (1988) *Children of Different Worlds – The Formation of Social Behaviour*, Harvard University Press
An insight into how children's experience is part of the fabric of their society and how adults believe children should be raised.

CHAPTER 2

Theories about children's play

PREVIEW

The key topics covered in this chapter are:

- Play and biological development
- Play as part of children's thinking
- Play as a therapeutic process
- Types of play.

Chapter 1 explored children's play across time and place. This chapter considers the ways in which adults have tried to explain play as well as describe it.

Theorists and researchers in child development have not all been interested in children's play for its own sake. Play has sometimes been of interest mainly as a way to illuminate how children think or as a window on emotional troubles. An interest in children's play has also arisen from study of play in the early lives of all young mammals. Commentators with a strong practical orientation have developed models of play and worked to define different types of play and their relative importance in childhood.

PLAY AND BIOLOGICAL DEVELOPMENT

Human beings are one species within the broader classification of mammals. Scientific observers of other mammals have suggested that the playful behaviour of the young of many mammals could be a positive aspect of early development that supports the continuation of the species. Play could have a survival function.

Play among young mammals

Young human children are certainly not the only mammals who enjoy behaviour that looks playful to an observer. Domesticated kittens and puppies rush around together, jumping, climbing and ambushing. They engage in play fighting that would be useful once they reached maturity, if they had to catch their own food. These animals also use props in playful activity: items to catch, drag and bat along a surface. Domesticated cats and dogs have to find only their food bowl. So they have time to spare as mature animals and may still engage in playful pursuits.

If you look in farm fields at springtime, young calves, lambs and goats all tend to show apparently spontaneous and playful behaviour with each other. The running and climbing does not get them anywhere in particular, except in relation to each other and seems to be pursued for pleasure. As the months pass, these animals cease to indulge in such activity and focus on eating, moving to other pasture and finally to reproduction. You may catch sight of non-domesticated mammals such as foxes, whose young also show playful physical exchanges and rough and tumble between siblings.

You can see gorillas, chimpanzees and other apes on television documentaries as well as in zoos. Biologically speaking, they seem to be our closest relatives. Within the years of immaturity, these young mammals can be seen enthusiastically using their physical skills but also imitating their older relatives. A number of these mammals have been observed to use tools like stones or long sticks in order to obtain food. Researchers have documented the growth of tool use over a period of time. One or two members of a troop make a fortuitous discovery and other mature animals start to copy the successful strategy. Soon youngsters copy what has become a common troop behaviour.

Biologists who observe ape and monkey troops over many years have gathered information on how younger ones learn. They watch their elders, try to copy their actions with the relevant tool and practise until they can cope. This imitation could be called play with an instructional purpose.

Why do mammals play?

Explanations of the function and biological purpose of play for young mammals include some of the categories that are used for children's play.

- Young mammals seem to be practising valuable physical skills and building strength, confidence in movement, balance and specific motor skills useful to the species.
- Playful exchanges seem to build social connections important for mammals who live in large extended family or tribal groups.
- Immature mammals copy the actions of their elders and these activities, once mastered, are usually important for later survival in terms of obtaining food and self care.
- One could argue about whether such direct imitation is actually play, but observation of young mammals shows that practical imitation often slips in and out of playful social behaviour.

So, observations of a wide range of mammals suggest that the immature members of the species engage in different kinds of playful behaviour. There

Human babies enjoy playing as much as other young mammals

is a strong suggestion that playful and exploratory behaviour might be pre-programmed. The play is not instinctive, that is to say the behaviour is not automatically triggered. Young mammals seem to be predisposed to play. It appears to come naturally to them when they live in a social group and play emerges, unless extreme circumstances prevent the development.

A kind of playful experimentation and sheer exuberance characterises young mammals' exchanges with each other and sometimes with the elders. This behaviour seems to support species-appropriate learning and development towards maturity. If you look back through Chapter 1, you will notice the evidence that human children have played over the centuries, in very different cultures and even under circumstances of severe stress. These observations all suggest that play is a form of behaviour likely to be followed by the young of the human species unless extreme social deprivation stops them.

TRY THIS!

Explore a simple observation project with children about whether and how animals play.

- Some children will have pets or know of families who have had kittens or puppies. Gather the observations or memories of the children about the playful behaviour they saw.
- Perhaps you may be lucky in local walks and see animals in playful exchanges.
- Watch out for any nature and animal documentary programmes on the television or illustrations in information books about mammals. Share these with the children and ask for their views.

✔ PROGRESS CHECK

1 Give two reasons that could explain why young mammals other than human children play.

2 What parallels can be made between the play of wild or domesticated mammals and children?

PLAY AS PART OF CHILDREN'S THINKING

One approach to children's play has been through an interest in their cognitive development, how children understand ideas and learn to think. The theory developed by Jean Piaget has been very influential for early years practice in the UK. However, other theorists and researchers have shown contrasting perspectives that can support adults in an effort to understand children's thinking and how it relates to their play.

The influence of Jean Piaget

Piaget developed his theories from the many observations made by Valentine Piaget (his wife and fellow-psychologist) on their three children. This resource was later extended to include the children of his researchers at Geneva from the 1920s and also through experimental studies. Piaget started from the observation that children seemed to share very similar sequences in their learning from babies through to adolescence. He noticed that children of an equivalent age made similar mistakes. They also appeared to develop very similar, although not identical, ideas about how the world worked. He was fascinated by how children's knowledge of the world could develop from their experience.

The child as active learner

Piaget proposed that children were active participants in their own learning. His image was that of the young scientist. In the 1920s, the prevailing belief was that children were empty vessels, who needed to be filled up with knowledge by adults. So, it was a completely new idea to claim that young children explored their environment, experimented with play materials and were capable of finding out ideas for themselves.

Piaget proposed that children's cognitive development (their powers of thought, handling ideas and understanding the world) progressed through a series of stages that unfolded in a definite sequence. His theory has a considerable amount of detail and only the main ideas directly relevant to children's play are covered here. Several references at the end of the chapter will be useful if you wish to explore Piaget's theory and research.

Competence or incompetence?

Piaget was interested in children's play activities as a way to support his theory about their language and thinking. He explored the abilities of young children under six years of age mainly in terms of what they could not yet do. Piaget was less focused on what children could manage, prior to those intellectual achievements that he most valued.

Piaget was very interested, for example, in the development of children's ideas in what he called 'conservation'. This term refers to how children steadily learn that the essential qualities of objects do not change just because they are made to look different. Piaget showed through experiments that children younger than five or six years tend to claim that a line of toy cars or teddy bears becomes 'more' when they are spread out rather than pushed close together. Piaget interpreted this mistake as proof that young children could not conserve number. The children had not yet grasped that number remains the same, unless actual items were added or taken away from the set.

Clearly younger children are wrestling intellectually with some complicated ideas, but other researchers have focused much more on the children's perspective. The work of Margaret Donaldson and her team in Edinburgh (and now spread around the UK) has been invaluable in showing how young children work hard to make sense of puzzling situations. When the children make mistakes from the conservation point of view, it seems very possible that they are talking about a different interpretation of 'more' (see also page 51).

Piaget's approach established a **top down** view of young children. They were defined in terms of what they could not do, in contrast with older children. This approach is also called a **deficit** or **incompetence model**. Piaget also claimed that young children could only see a situation from their own point of view and his descriptive terms have been translated into English as 'egocentric' or 'idiosyncratic'. Further research by Donaldson and her colleagues has challenged Piaget's claims. However, the label of 'egocentric' is still regularly applied to the behaviour and thinking of under-fives, with the risk that early years practitioners can be discouraged from looking through the eyes of young children.

DEFINITIONS

incompetence or **deficit model of early development** the approach of defining young children in terms of the skills they have not yet managed, rather than what they can do. Sometimes called a **top-down** approach, in contrast to a **bottom-up** perspective.

GOOD PRACTICE

- Watch out for taking the play and learning of older children more seriously than that of younger ones.
- Try to avoid a focus on what young children do not understand. Of course, it is important for you to home in on where their skills or understanding stop at the moment – so that you can help them learn further.
- Helpful adults focus on what babies or toddlers can do and how they show they do understand or nearly understand.
- Piaget did not mean the term 'egocentric' to be insulting to young children. However, it has unfortunate overtones of 'selfish' or 'self-centred'. Think about how under-twos start from their own position and move out. They are not fixed.

Are children 'lone scientists'?

Piaget was primarily interested in cognitive development. He did not focus on other aspects of children's development, such as communication, social interaction or emotional development. He persisted in viewing children as 'lone scientists' and was uninterested in the dynamics of play between children.

Piaget's theory that children constructed their own understanding led him to emphasise that adults should create environments in which children could discover for themselves. Self-discovery by children has sometimes been interpreted to mean that adults should scarcely intervene at all in children's play. Not everyone shares this view, but the problem of when intervention becomes interference continues to fuel discussion about an appropriate role for adults in early years and playwork settings (see also Chapter 8).

Young children explore through play

A focus on competence

A combination of circumstances will lead one theorist or researcher to have far greater impact on later thinking than others. It is important always to recall that the 'big' names like Jean Piaget take one possible approach out of many. Their ideas can be very useful, but they are not necessarily completely right. Nor did everyone agree with them at the time, let alone in later decades.

Susan Isaacs was also working and writing during the 1920s. She drew on many of the same theoretical sources as Piaget when she analysed children's thinking in her Malting House School. Yet, Isaacs took a **bottom-up** perspective, using positive descriptions of **cognitive competence** in young children: what they could do and how, rather than what they could not yet do. Isaacs has influenced early years philosophy and practice, but she is far less often mentioned than Piaget.

DEFINITIONS

cognitive competence a focus on what children can understand and how their thinking operates at a given time. Sometimes called a **bottom-up** perspective in contrast to a **top-down** approach.

TRY THIS!

Reflect on your own training and experience and perhaps gather some ideas in discussion with colleagues.

- To what extent do you feel you may be tempted to focus on what young children cannot do or have failed to understand?
- Perhaps experience, or the ideas of a colleague or tutor, have helped you to question the incompetence model. Why is it so important to challenge this view?
- In what ways have you, or your colleagues, used observations of real children to challenge a deficit model of play and learning?

Susan Isaacs also exerted an influence on nursery practice. During the 1930s she answered readers' questions on the problem page of *Nursery World*, under the name of Ursula Wise.

The contribution of Vygotsky

Lev Vygotsky worked in Russia through the 1920s and 1930s and was one of the first people to disagree with Piaget's views of children. Unlike Piaget, who had a very long academic career, Vygotsky died when only in his late thirties. His work was scarcely available outside Russia until English translations were published in 1962 and 1978. These books are a combination of ideas, informal experiments and practical suggestions about children's learning. Since the 1980s there has been considerable interest in Vygotsky's ideas and they have been developed further.

Social and cognitive development

Vygotsky placed greater emphasis than Piaget on the social context in which children explored and learned. Vygotsky also focused on language as a vital social tool and described learning within social interaction. He did not believe that children operated as the 'lone scientist' of Piaget's view. Vygotsky felt that early language, during the years when children speak out loud to themselves in play, was an important instrument of their thinking. He disagreed with Piaget's view that this stage was immature and egocentric. The whole feel of Vygotsky's approach is much more of a competence model, that young children already have skills and add to these through further experience.

The role of play

Vygotsky emphasised the ingenuity of children, as active participants in their own learning and creative users of play from whatever was available. He felt that play led children's development. In their play activity, children could step outside the restrictions of their real lives and explore meaning free from the constraints of what was possible as a child.

Vygotsky thought that all forms of play had some imaginary component and that play was rule bound within those imaginary elements. Vygotsky believed play was significant for learning, but did not see it as the only way that children learned. He warned against the risks if adults focused too much on the possible intellectual content of play and ignored the emotional content.

The zone of proximal development

Vygotsky was interested in how adults could best help children to learn, but he also believed that children could and did help each other through play.

Vygotsky used his concept of the **zone of proximal development** to explain how children's learning could be supported. The zone of proximal development is the area of possibilities that lies between what individual children can manage on their own — their level of actual development — and what they could achieve or understand with some appropriate help — their level of potential development. 'Proximal' is the English translation of a Russian word meaning 'nearby'.

Vygotsky believed that the focused help could come from either an alert adult or from another child whose understanding or skills was slightly more

DEFINITIONS

zone of proximal development the area of potential learning for an individual child at a given time

Vygotskian tutorial the helping approach offered by an adult to a child that is sensitive to that child's current zone of proximal development

mature. Vygotsky felt that play created a zone of proximal development, with this potential for learning. Some people use the phrase **Vygotskian tutorial** to describe the sensitive and appropriate help offered to a child within their individual zone of proximal development.

Looking ahead in learning

In contrast to Piaget, Vygotsky believed that the more valuable learning for children was that which was slightly in advance of their development. Using the zone of proximal development stretched the possibilities enough, but not too much, for each individual child. Vygotsky took the approach that children need to learn in order to be motivated — rather than being motivated to learn and this stretching gave them a boost.

TRY THIS!

Apply the ideas of the zone of proximal development to one individual child whom you know well.

- Perhaps focus on a single aspect of play, maybe pretend play. What does this child do at the moment? In what ways could you sensitively extend their play without imposing a completely adult perspective?
- Vygotsky also noted that children can help each other. Look out for examples, even brief exchanges, where one child helps another in play in such a way that the younger or less sure child learns something new.

Vygotsky's approach is a challenge to Piaget's view that children could not learn until they were ready in any area. Piaget warned of serious risks when an adult 'prematurely' taught children something that they could later have discovered for themselves. He believed that the children could not genuinely understand, because they had been prevented from inventing the idea for themselves.

Jerome Bruner and the spiral curriculum

DEFINITION

spiral curriculum the idea that children will revisit play materials and activities over the years, but then use them differently because their development has progressed

Bruner was influential in bringing some of Vygotsky's ideas to the English speaking world after the 1960s. Bruner further developed Vygotsky's ideas for the concept of the **spiral curriculum**. Bruner described how children learn through discovery, with the direct help of adults, and by returning again and again to the same materials or ideas. He proposed that children were able to extend their understanding over a period of years. Later learning could build on what they had learned previously and through sensitive help from adults.

Bruner felt that young children learn most easily through the medium of their play. Familiar play materials would remain of interest to children as the months and years passed, but older children used the same or similar materials in different ways. For instance, a rich array of building bricks is a creative source of learning for all children.

- Babies like bricks to hold, look at and drop.
- Toddlers relish bricks as a simple build up and knock down resource.
- Three- and four-year-olds use a good store of bricks as the construction material for buildings. But they also use bricks to create boundary lines

Adults can explain and help

essential for other games. They may make enclosures for toy animals or transport. Another use of bricks can be for stepping along or over and for delicate balancing games.

- Five- and six-year-olds and older children may still enjoy building with bricks but they may also use them as the raw materials for counting, weighing and exploring ideas of relative weight.

Bricks can be a valuable resource throughout childhood

TRY THIS!

You could use current and past observations of children you know. Build up a picture of how they have used the same or very similar play materials in different ways.

- You might explore the scarf and hats idea in the case study or the bricks examples given on pages 32–33. Or try observations of play with sand or recycled materials like egg boxes.
- If possible, combine your observations with those of colleagues who work with children of a different age or who knew these children when they were younger.

CASE STUDY

Scarves and hats

The team at Highwater Children's Centre became interested in how children of different ages used the same or very similar materials. Two parent helpers were equally fascinated and the adults worked together to track children's use of particular play materials.

One set of observations followed how children of different ages used scarves and hats.

- The under-twos liked their collection of soft scarves for playing 'Peek-a-boo', to put on each other's head and sometimes for wrapping up dolls or other toys. The very young children liked to put on hats sometimes, but were just as interested to use a hat as a container to carry around smaller objects.
- The three- and four-year-olds used hats and scarves most often as part of dressing up. So these items were chosen for whether they were suitable for pretend play. Long scarves were sometimes used as impromptu ropes for tying objects together and once for a washing line. Square scarves became flags in one game.
- Some of the children have attended the centre since they were babies. So it was possible to recall that older children had enjoyed scarf peek-a-boo and how one four-year-old had been very absorbed as a two-year-old in watching a fine scarf flutter in the breeze.

Some of the findings were made into a display with photographs and labels to explain. The children were just as interested in the display as their parents.

DEFINITION

schemas patterns of behaviour linked to a broad theme. A schema describes a child's way, often their favourite way, of exploring the world at a given time. Schemas include a combination of actions and ideas that shape a child's current approach to learning

Chris Athey and schemas

Jean Piaget proposed the idea of **schemas**, as patterns of behaviour that are linked through a theme and which form the basis of exploration and play for young children. Chris Athey developed this idea much further and applied it to observation of children's play. Her practical ideas can also guide how adults support play.

The play behaviour of one child may be described through a fascination with a schema of 'enveloping'. Perhaps this child explores many different ways of covering herself or objects, or investigates the possibilities through craft activities that include wrapping. From the 1970s, Athey explored the richness of young children's schemas and the possibilities of this approach to make sense of how they learned through play exploration. She applied the ideas to working with early years practitioners but also in partnership with parents.

The approach through schemas can help adults respect toddlers' play explorations and make sense of a child's play behaviour when it seems annoying or not 'proper playing' to adults. For instance, a child who is thoroughly absorbed in his 'transporting' schema may move objects from place to place. From an exclusively adult point of view, the child is 'messing up' the environment by putting toys and other objects where they do not belong. From the child-oriented perspective, he has a clear purpose and is learning.

✔ PROGRESS CHECK

1. In what ways were the ideas of Jean Piaget so different from how children had been viewed previously?
2. What are the drawbacks of a focus on cognitive incompetence?
3. Explain briefly Vygotsky's idea of the zone of proximal development.
4. In what ways can observation of schemas, as developed by Chris Athey, support work with toddlers?

PLAY AS A THERAPEUTIC PROCESS

Playing out distress and anxiety

Observers of children have long noticed that play can be a way for children to express and re-run experiences that were confusing, mildly upsetting or even very distressing. It is likely that play activities have always been used in this way by children – see the historical example on page 16 of children in the slave communities of the United States. Therapists work with children who have been traumatised by seriously distressing experiences. Sometimes the children have begun to play out the event before any adult intervention through therapy.

Daniel Goleman (1996) gives the example of children in Stockton, California who survived an attack by a gunman in 1989. Patrick Purdy sprayed bullets into the school playground, killing five children and wounding more, before shooting himself. The children showed many long-term effects of that terrifying morning. However, a game had developed called 'Purdy' which they ran in different ways. Some versions reflected the actual events, but in other versions the children played that they had the guns and had killed Purdy.

Children's play may be a means of coping with overwhelming feelings, but the play re-enactment does not necessarily resolve the distress. Goleman also describes the observation that a group of children who had been subjected to a frightening kidnap in California in 1973 were still playing out the event with dolls five years later.

Milder, less traumatic distress is sometimes worked out through play. Children may use play in preference to talking with parents or other carers. Alternatively, children may use play alongside talking about the incident or requesting that familiar adults talk around what happened. For instance, children who have been in car accidents sometimes replay the incident with their toy cars. Children who are coming to terms with a new sibling may play out some rough handling with their dolls or teddies. Some of the content of children's pretend play reflects their current concerns, as Vivian Paley has shown through observations of her nursery class (see page 58).

This therapeutic function of play for children appears to unfold relatively naturally. Sensitive adults can support children by commenting or becoming involved if the child allows. The possibilities have been used in a planned and

TRY THIS!

Look for examples of schemas in action as shown in the play of children in your setting. You are looking for themes that persist, rather than one-off interests. Children do not thread all their play through their current schema, but much of their exploration will revolve around the theme.

Possible examples to look for include the following.

- Rotation is shown through children's interest in things that turn like wheels and objects that can roll. Children may directly explore rotation with spinning around themselves or waving their arms in a circular motion.
- Orientation is explored when children are fascinated with how things or people may look from another angle. They may explore objects by turning the actual objects around or looking from an odd angle. Children may become intrigued by how the world looks if they twist or dangle upside down.
- Connection schemas are shown when children are curious about how things are, or could be, joined together. Children can explore connection within craft work or drawing and through play in which toys or other items are strung together or otherwise linked. The opposite schemas of separation and de-connection may be explored by children who have the physical skills to disassemble objects, but not put them back together again.

Make notes and compare your observations with colleagues.

deliberate way by adults who wish to help children. This organised use of play is known as **play therapy**.

DEFINITION

play therapy an approach to supporting children and helping them with concerns or problems through the medium of their play

THINK ABOUT IT

Do adults use play with a therapeutic purpose for themselves? First of all, you may want to think about the underlying question, 'Do adults play?' But think about, and discuss with colleagues, whether a therapeutic play process could be at work when adults:

- **play football, other team games or work energetically in an exercise class after a hard day or week at work**
- **pick up craft work like knitting or patchwork, perhaps as a contrast to paid work in which an adult feels she or he does not make anything**
- **cook up a batch of cakes or attack the weeds in the garden and say, 'I feel much better' afterwards.**

Psychodynamic play therapy

The psychodynamic or psychoanalytic tradition originated with the ideas of Sigmund Freud. The terms come from the Greek word *psyche*, for spirit or mind, and describe a focus on the workings of the human mind. This influential tradition is one approach to using the therapeutic value of play.

Childhood was of interest to Freud mainly because he believed the events of childhood were the source of later adult problems, for which lengthy therapy was the only solution. Freud believed that childhood included an inevitable crisis of jealousy between all children and their same sex parent and sexual feelings between children and their opposite sex parent. The impossible struggle to resolve this strain created anxiety and the motivation to defend oneself against distress by hiding or denying unacceptable feelings and thoughts. One application of Freud's ideas to children is that emotional turmoil, as well as a possible resolution of problems, is acted out through children's play.

Freud has been very influential, but his ideas have been challenged by many people, including those within the psychodynamic tradition. His claims about children's sexual feelings (the idea of infantile sexuality) are especially troubling, because the proposals were based on a small number of adult patients who recalled sexual episodes from childhood. It now seems a strong possibility that these adult patients were recalling actual sexual abuse. Freud, and colleagues whom he consulted at the time, were unable to accept this possibility. Freud dealt with the problem by explaining away what was said as a sexual fantasy and then applied his theory to all children.

Links to play in childhood

Melanie Klein and Anna Freud (Sigmund's daughter) applied his beliefs to work with children. Both Klein and Freud believed that the unconscious life of children was revealed through the themes and symbols of their play, especially the content of imaginary play. They disagreed, however, on many details of theory and therapeutic technique.

The traditional stance in **psychodynamic play therapy** is that the therapist deciphers and interprets the true meaning of a child's play. Ultimately this meaning is verbalised (spoken aloud) by the therapist to the

DEFINITION

psychodynamic play therapy using children's play to resolve conflicts that are believed to arise in childhood and to share the psychodynamic interpretation of play with the child

child or by the child him- or herself. Together the child and therapist come to understand that the child's play means something and the nature of that meaning. Children's play, much like adults' dreams, is believed to represent their inner conflicts. The role of the psychodynamic play therapist is to identify these meanings and share them with children.

GOOD PRACTICE

This section considers a specialist area of play. However, the wise caution about interpretation of children's activities applies more widely.

- Respect for children's play means you avoid swift judgements about what children are planning or the meaning of their play.
- Watch and listen and be ready to ask children to show you or help you to understand what they are doing and to what ends.
- The discussion on page 149 about children's pretend play takes up this theme of avoiding adult arrogance about play themes and quality.

Reservations about this tradition

Therapists and theorists within the psychodynamic tradition are interested in play as the vehicle through which children resolve disturbing experiences and crises of childhood. In this approach to children, much as in the traditional psychodynamic approach to adults, there is no clear vision of wellbeing. The aim of therapy is to identify and resolve the conflicts and emotional turmoil that are believed to be an inevitable part of childhood.

There are serious risks when adults have firm expectations about what is happening in children's play and what it all means. D.W. Winnicott expressed one area of concern with his comment, 'The psychoanalyst has been too busy using play content to look at the playing child and to write about playing as a thing in itself' (page 40, *Playing and Reality*, 1971, Tavistock). Elizabeth Newsom (1992) expressed even stronger reservations about play therapy undertaken by traditional psychodynamic therapists:

> (I) had become increasingly doubtful about some of what was going on behind these accounts. For a start, the stories seemed too neat and the children too articulate ... was I alone in being taken aback by Klein's certainty of interpretation, unswervingly shared with children of 7 and younger ... I wondered how she could assure the child that what he had chosen from the little toys was actually his father's penis with which he was trying to stir up the bad things in his mother's insides, without quailing at the thought, "But suppose I am *wrong*?" [italics in original] My overall conclusion was to be appalled at the opportunities for a prolonged ego trip at the expense of the child . . .' (Page 89.)

Non-directive play therapy

DEFINITION

non-directive play therapy using play to support and help children express their concerns or confusions but with an adult role that does not assume a particular theoretical underpinning to play behaviour

Play therapy has its roots in the psychodynamic approach, but by no means everyone follows this theoretical stance. It is important also to realise that the psychodynamic tradition continues to develop and evolve.

Non-directive play therapy developed partly from the client-centred approach of Carl Rogers to adult therapy and counselling from the 1950s onwards. This approach placed the emphasis on the development of self-concept and interpersonal relationships and not on unconscious conflicts.

The underlying idea of play therapy is that children will be able to express their feelings, doubts, concerns, hopes or fears through the medium of play and related craft activities. Spoken language has a part in the therapeutic process, but the aim is that children can express themselves through play at an age, or in an emotional state, when it will be hard to put their experience into words.

The rationale of play therapy is that play offers children a safe psychological distance to express their feelings. They may use a range of materials, creating a story in words or with figures or painting a picture.

Events can be re-run, characters re-organised and the child's own feelings filtered through a pretend play scenario or voiced by a character within their play.

Children have probably always replayed family live

Play therapy offers a guided version of what can happen in play with parents and familiar carers. Expression through pretend play or drawings can emerge in families or early years settings when a child's distress is less traumatic. Play therapists can support families, for instance after bereavement, if the adults feel themselves overwhelmed by their loss and unable to help their children.

Older children and teenagers may be able and willing to talk around and through their distress, but young children are less likely to have the words. Even older and articulate children often welcome a mix of play and talking therapy. With older children and teenagers, the blend may be with arts and crafts, music and expression through writing autobiographical stories and poetry.

TRY THIS!

- Through observation of children you know well, gather some examples of how individuals appear to use their play to express concerns and run through current issues in their lives.
- The children's concerns will not necessarily be highly distressing, but do be sensitive that they are personal.
- Take care that you do not over-interpret what you observe and make careful descriptive notes that you would be happy for the child's parent to read.

Different approaches to play therapy

Virginia Axline, working from the 1940s, developed a form of play therapy and guided conversation that stepped away from the psychodynamic approach and set a pattern for much of play therapy that has followed.

Axline's book *Play Therapy* was published in 1947 and set out the main ideas of her approach, but she is probably best known for *Dibs: In Search of Self* (Penguin 1964). This book is an account of her series of play therapy sessions with a five-year-old boy known as Dibs, whose behaviour was baffling to his private school and his family. Dibs emerged as a gifted child whose early family experiences had hurt him deeply and made him doubt his self-worth and abilities. The account gives an insight into how play can be used to bring out a child's feelings over time. Axline's account of Dibs is fascinating but does read as a tidied up version of the process, a reservation expressed also by Elizabeth Newsom (1992).

Other accounts of play therapy sometimes give a more accurate description of the likely pattern of play and conversation. Arietta Slade (1994) offers a refreshing description of how she learned as a therapist. She emphasises how the genuinely helpful play therapist needs to be a co-player with the child, resisting the adult temptation to direct and interpret. Slade provides believable examples to show that sometimes therapists also need to resist talking, because playing is doing the therapeutic job effectively. She quotes children who felt able to tell her, 'Shut up!', one who commented tartly, 'You want to know everything, don't you?' and another who directed her to be silent with, 'I'm working hard on this and I need quiet!'

Elizabeth Newsom (1992) describes the play therapy undertaken in her Nottingham unit. The team's approach is deliberately independent of a specific theoretical stance on how children develop. The unit has taken referrals of children who are seriously distressed, have sometimes experienced abuse or who are facing serious or terminal illness. The unit developed Margaret Lowenfeld's 'World' technique in which children create a world of their own choosing from a sand tray and a wide range of figures, vehicles, buildings and other items. Children are asked gentle, open-ended questions about their completed world and also have the opportunity to play in a well-equipped playroom. The Nottingham team has found that most children respond to the 'Make a World' game, even children with limited language and social development.

Play therapy has developed, with different strands of approach, to enable children to express what otherwise they find it hard to say out aloud. This therapeutic function is used to support children in hospital, facing unpleasant medical procedures and serious or terminal illnesses (see page 133).

TRY THIS!

In a low key way (you are not trying out play therapy), see what different children, or pairs working together, develop from the same basic play materials.

- You might have a dolls' house with figures or a low, wide tray with a range of animals or small creatures.
- Ask the children to tell you about what they have made. Show interest but do not ask probing questions

Play therapy and assessment

The approach to distressed and disturbed children through play includes, inevitably, a careful strand of assessment as well as the therapeutic goal. In some cases assessment is the main aim of adult involvement in the child's play. Sandra Hewitt (1999) describes the immense care that has to be taken if the play and words of young children are to form part of an assessment of possible sexual abuse. Professionals, who undertake such an assessment, need a thorough knowledge of the usual play patterns and bodily awareness of children of this age. The words and actions of a child who has been sexually abused can then make sense against the backdrop of children who have not experienced abuse.

Therapeutic playwork

Play has long been seen as a vital part of the childhood experience within the playwork tradition (see page 134). Play and appropriate adult support within play activities has been viewed as a responsible means to enable children to deal with stressful individual experiences. Guided playwork has also been explored as one way to approach deep-rooted problems within a community.

CASE STUDY

Marissa's play

The manager of Fairham day nursery is faced with an awkward problem after a long conversation with one parent. Mrs Butler had asked to speak in confidence and then explained her serious concerns about one of the practitioners responsible for the group attended by her daughter, Marissa.

The manager had already had reason to talk with this practitioner about her communication style with the children. Mrs Butler has now described how her daughter's anxieties about this practitioner have emerged through her play at home. Apparently, Marissa shouts at her dolls, using phrases like, 'You stupid little girl!' and 'Are you deaf!' She points her finger at the dolls, snarling, 'You stay there! You stay there until I say you can get up!' Mrs Butler is adamant that she does not talk to Marissa in this way and that she has overheard similar phrases from the practitioner. She wants Marissa moved into another group, unless the manager can guarantee to change this person's approach to the children.

1. How likely is it that Marissa's play with her dolls is an accurate reflection of her experience in the nursery group?
2. What should be the manager's next step?
3. If you judge the manager should talk to the practitioner, should Marissa and her mother be mentioned?

Bob Hughes (1998) developed the approach of Reflective Analytic Playwork in the context of working with the organisation PlayBoard in Northern Ireland. The aim has been to start with sensitive sessions with adult playworkers. Hughes describes how a first step has to be to enable adults themselves to admit that the violence of long-term community strife does affect children and can be seen in their play. The potential therapeutic impact of play for children cannot even start under these circumstances without prior attention to the needs and anxieties of the adults.

✔ PROGRESS CHECK

1. **How did Sigmund Freud see the significance of play in children's lives?**
2. **What are the broad aims of non-directive play therapy?**
3. **Suggest two ways that supported play might be a healing process for children who have experienced distress.**

TYPES OF PLAY

Some theorists and researchers have been specifically interested in play itself, rather than as part of broader developmental events. This approach involves a definition of different types of play and sometimes attempts to prove specific effects of play experience on children's development.

The word 'play' is an umbrella term that has encompassed many different activities, which undoubtedly have meaning for children. However, play also has meaning for adults who wish to define and categorise play. There is a wide range of terms and typologies of play. Neither academic researchers nor practitioners necessarily assign the same meaning to a similar or identical term describing play.

Jean Piaget and types of play

Piaget described what he believed to be the three main categories of children's play.

- ***Practice play*** was the play behaviour typical of very young children from birth to about two years of age. Piaget considered that babies from about six months onwards, engaged in exploratory play based on physical activities that led them to understand experiences within this stage of development.
- ***Symbolic play*** developed from two years onwards and became more varied up to six years of age. The essence of symbolic play was that children's ideas were visible through their play. There was evidence that children were thinking about their world and importing ideas into their play.
- ***Games with rules*** were deemed to develop from six or seven years of age and depended upon older children's grasp of abstract ideas, including the rule of a game shared with and understood by other children.

Children's play often does not fit neat categories

Piaget's three categories have been studied, challenged and extended in the subsequent years. A category of ***constructive play*** was added by later researchers, who had observed how much time children spent in play with building blocks and materials like collage or play dough. Within the Piagetian theoretical framework, this type of play was judged to enable children to create their own reality through the play materials.

Corrine Hutt and John Hutt

Corinne and John Hutt distinguished between two broad kinds of play.

- ***Epistemic play*** focused on acquiring knowledge and information, dealing in problem solving and exploration. They saw this kind of play as addressing the question, 'What does this object do?' The approach of this team seemed to be that epistemic play was the more productive kind of play because it was more likely to promote learning. Children are judged to be aware of what they are doing and so are likely to gain in competence.
- ***Ludic play*** is described as including symbolic and fantasy elements. This type of play is seen to be repetitive, involves children's preferences and is affected by mood states. Ludic play is judged to address the question 'what can I do with this object?'

The Hutts also distinguished a range of play activities within Piaget's main grouping of games with rules. They felt it worth breaking the group into finer categories of co-operative, competitive, games of skill or chance.

Sara Smilansky and socio-dramatic play

Smilansky explored and extended the idea of symbolic pretend play beyond Piaget's ideas. She proposed that this kind of play was far more than role play and that children's play behaviour was just as important as the thinking that supported the play. Smilansky further proposed that helping disadvantaged children to use socio-dramatic play was the best way to further their learning (see page 106).

Bob Hughes' typology of play

Playwork practice has a long history of valuing play as a vital part of childhood, as a means for children to express themselves and to learn in freedom. Bob Hughes' typology of play types is influential in the playwork field and an example of a detailed breakdown of play into different kinds. Hughes is aiming to reflect the richness of play, within a respect for children's purposes and to create a framework meaningful for adults.

Hughes (1996) makes the distinction between fifteen types of play in childhood.

- ***Symbolic play***: allows children to exercise control and explore without the risk of being out of their depth. A piece of wood may symbolise a person.
- ***Rough and tumble play***: close encounter play that is playful and obviously enjoyed by the children. Touching, tickling, chasing are all involved in chosen activities that are not genuine fighting.

- ***Socio-dramatic play***: when children re-enact actual or potential experiences of intense personal meaning to them. Scenarios may be domestic or exchanges between several people.
- ***Social play***: exchanges between children in which there are agreed rules or protocols, which can in turn be amended by agreement. Games, social interaction and conversation work as social play.
- ***Creative play***: this type of play activity allows children to make new connections as they transform existing information or awareness. Creativity with tools and a range of materials can be enjoyed for its own sake.
- ***Communication play***: playful activities using words and non-verbal communication. Examples include play acting and mime, jokes as well as singing, debate or poetry.
- ***Dramatic play***: a form of play in which children dramatise events in which they are not direct participants. Children may bring into their play a television programme, an event they observed on the street or festivals.
- ***Deep play***: activities that children use to experience risk and through which they can develop skills and deal with their fears. Possibilities include physically challenging activities such as balancing or climbing at a height.
- ***Exploratory play***: using physical skills and sensations to learn about materials and their properties, what they feel like and what can be done with them.
- ***Fantasy play***: when children rearrange the world in their own way, to create situations that will not occur in childhood and perhaps never. They may fantasise about flying an aeroplane or being incredibly rich.
- ***Imaginative play***: when children discard the conventional rules that govern the physical world and imagining they are a tree or petting an animal that is wholly pretend.
- ***Locomotor play***: activities that involve all kinds of physical movement for their own sake and enjoyment, not to achieve some other purpose.
- ***Mastery play***: engaging in play activities that exert an impact on the environment, for instance, creating change through digging holes, making dams in streams or building dens.
- ***Object play***: using physical skills and hand-eye co-ordination especially to create a novel use of an object.
- ***Role play***: ways of exploring daily activities and actions, for instance, brushing up, playing telephones or driving a bus.

TRY THIS!

If you work with children of four or five years and older, look for examples of some of the categories developed by Bob Hughes.

- Are some easier to observe than others?
- Do you feel that some categories merge with each other?
- Would you cut any?
- Talk over with your colleagues the range of categories and in what ways you find the list useful for identifying the richness of children's play.

Broad characteristics of play

Some commentators have been interested less in types of play and more in identifying the characteristics or qualities of play.

Catherine Garvey (1991) described play as a continuous moving back and forth among different activities, with different modes of action, interaction and communication. Garvey views play more as an attitude or orientation of children that shows itself to the adult observer through many different kinds of behaviour. The possibilities in play expand as children have

TRY THIS!

Watch and listen to children and gather examples that could support Catherine Garvey's view that children are aware of play and are able to step, by choice, in and out of the play scenario.

- For example, children may answer an adult criticism with the justification that 'we're only pretending'.
- Do children step outside their play to re-negotiate rules and roles in pretend play?
- Do they step outside the play to appeal for adult help: 'He won't play properly!'

new experiences and integrate them by choice into their play. Garvey pointed to children's sharp awareness and their ability to move in and out of play and non-play situations. Changes are based on children's understanding that some types of behaviour are permitted by adults in play and others are not, such as aggressive actions.

Tina Bruce has been especially interested in defining what she calls free flow play and identifying possible indicators for quality play – see page 147.

Limits to categories of play

Identifying broad categories in children's play has the advantage of bringing the value of play to the fore and of considering the range. Yet, the push to define clear categories also has a drawback. A rich range of play activities and children's interests can be absorbed under a basic heading. There is also the problem, similar to that raised in the context of play therapy, that adults may be over-keen to group and interpret play because of their own interests. Elizabeth Wood and Jane Attfield (1996) offer a wise warning:

> In the urge to explain and categorize play, we may be in danger of overlooking the fact that children define play themselves. They often establish mutual awareness of play and non-play situations. They create roles, use symbols, redefine objects and determine the action through negotiation and shared meanings. Often their enactments of play themes and stories or their creation of play scripts reveal far more subtleties than academic definitions can capture. (Page 4.)

THINK ABOUT IT

- What do you think are the main reasons why some writers about children's play feel it is so important to categorise play activity into different types?
- What might be gained by this adult mental and observational exercise?
- What could be the drawbacks or risks for a full understanding of play and what it means to children?

There is no definitive description of play that meets with everyone's agreement, but the following themes emerge through the substantial literature on children's play.

- Children seem to play regardless of cultural background, although play is not identical across cultures (see page 10).
- Circumstances can prevent or restrict play. Constraints may be placed by adults or the environment limits children's experience. Alternatively developmental problems, disability or illness can shape the possibilities for children.
- Children play for play's sake. The activity is an end in itself and is not undertaken for an end product, although children do sometimes make something in play.
- Play is an activity involving children's own choices. It is motivated by children's feelings and internal thoughts and it can be hard sometimes for adults to fathom these motives.
- Play is often episodic, with emerging and shifting goals developed by children themselves. However, children return to favourite play themes and activities over time.
- Play supports children's social understanding and play is in turn fed by their experiences. The roles and themes acted out during play both use and help children to understand social rules and conventions.
- There is a subtle interplay between communication, social interaction and imagination in play. These features often become clear when you observe children who have difficulty in play, such as autistic children (see page 182).

- Play stems from children's own perception of the world and how it works. So it is a very personal creative activity. Within children's understanding, their play is meaningful in its connection to the non-play reality.
- Children mirror each other in play and so they reinforce, highlight and develop their own views and experiences. Play is usually rule governed, even when it looks thoroughly disorganised to adults. The rules may be understood by children but not spoken out loud. Rules are voiced clearly by children if someone breaks them.
- Play provides a forum in which children can step back for a while, experiment and try out scenarios. Children can make their play represent reality in their own way, with an 'as if' or 'what if' quality.

Play is essentially a voluntary and pleasurable activity. It may be undertaken with great seriousness and attention and may give rise to significant learning. Children play because they want to and because it gives them enjoyment.

Children can be very absorbed in their play

✔ PROGRESS CHECK

1. Briefly describe three broad categories of play.
2. What could be the disadvantages of using categories in an attempt to understand children's play?
3. In what ways is pretend play different from other kinds of play?

KEY TERMS

You need to know the meaning of the following words and phrases. Go back through the chapter to make sure you understand them:

incompetence or **deficit model**
non-directive play therapy
play therapy
psychodynamic play therapy
schemas
spiral curriculum
Vygotskian tutorial
zone of proximal development

FURTHER READING

Garvey, Catherine (1991, second edition) *Play*, Fontana
A description of the kinds of children's play within their development.

Goleman, Daniel (1996) *Emotional Intelligence: Why it Can Matter More Than I.Q.*, Bloomsbury
A thought-provoking book that bridges the usual division made between intellect and emotions.

Hewitt, Sandra (1999) *Assessing Allegations of Sexual Abuse in Preschool Children*, Sage
A careful description of how play can be used by specialists in assessment of possible sexual abuse of young children.

Hughes, Bob (1996) *A Playworker's Taxonomy of Play Types*, Playlink
This description of types of children's play is also reproduced in Best Play Project Team (2000) *Best Play: What Play Provision Should Do For Children,* (National Playing Fields Association).

Hughes, Bob (1998) *Playwork in Extremis: The RAP Approach* (Seminar paper Childhood and Youth Studies Conference, Cambridge) and *Games Not Names: The Training Pack*, PlayBoard
Both these publications describe the careful use of therapeutic playwork under stressful conditions for adults as well as children

Jennings, Sue (1999) *Introduction to Developmental Playtherapy*, Jessica Kingsley
A flexible guide to different approaches to using play in a therapeutic context. Jennings stressed the importance of observation rather than imposing adult theories.

Lindon, Jennie (1998) *Understanding Child Development: Knowledge, Theory and Practice,* Thomson Learning
Source material on different theories of child development and their practical applications.

Newsom, Elizabeth 'The barefoot play therapist: adapting skills for a time of need' in Lane, David A. and Miller, Andrew (eds) (1992) *Child and Adolescent Therapy: A Handbook* Open University Press

Slade, Arietta and Wolf, Dennie Palmer (eds) (1994) *Children At Play: Clinical and Developmental Approaches to Meaning and Representation*, Oxford University Press
Different approaches to how adults seek meaning in children's play to fit theoretical or clinical perspectives.

Wood, Elizabeth and Attfield, Jane (1996) *Play, Learning and the Early Childhood Curriculum*, Paul Chapman
A thoughtful book that considers ideas about play and practical applications to children's learning.

CHAPTER 3

Ways to study children's play

PREVIEW

The key topics covered in this chapter are:

- Experimental methods
- Observation of children in chosen play
- Children's own views of play.

This chapter covers different methods used to study children's play and the possible meaning of play activities. Research is discussed in terms of experimental methods and observation of children in home or early years settings. Whatever the method, it is always important to consider whether adult interpretations of children's play make sense in terms of their overall development. Last, but certainly not least, consideration is given to what children think about play. Projects are described that have explored the perspective and views of children themselves.

DEFINITIONS

experimental method a planned approach, in this case to the study of children's play, when a situation is set up and questions asked of children in order to prove or disprove the researcher's hypothesis

hypothesis the detailed prediction made before an experiment. The hypothesis states what researchers expect to happen following particular events within the study. A hypothesis is developed from a theory; it is not the theory itself

EXPERIMENTAL METHODS

One way to study children's development is to design experiments that explore one aspect of children's abilities in detail. Many examples of the **experimental method** have implications for understanding children's play.

The advantage of the experimental method

The attraction of research through experiments has been a sense of control over the different features of play. Researchers decide on the play situation, the play materials and often the precise questions they will ask the children. The details are determined by the researchers' interests. They aim to test a **hypothesis**: a prediction that children will react in a certain way to materials and questions or requests.

> **DEFINITION**
>
> **objectivity** a presumed characteristic of the experimental method. An objective outlook is shown when researchers remain detached from personal preferences and assumptions about results and interpretations.

Experimental studies can highlight intriguing features of children's thinking and understanding. However, this method will not show children's self-chosen play, because the boundaries to any activities are determined by the research team. The experimental method is supposed to ensure **objectivity**: that the researchers' interests will not tempt them to shape the results or interpretation. However, researchers are people, and commitment to a particular theory sometimes closes the mind to other possible interpretations, including children's perspectives.

This section focuses on research that has explored children's thinking through play-based experiments and therefore links with the discussion about Jean Piaget in Chapter 2. However, research studies of children's play are not all controlled experiments. Some teams observe events unfolding naturally in a nursery or school and then make a more detailed exploration of possible interpretation of events. An example would be the studies of playfighting discussed on page 171. Some studies have sought to prove specific learning consequences from particular play experiences, for instance the exploration of socio-dramatic play discussed on page 106.

What are children thinking?

Piaget's ideas and studies have been very influential in shaping views about young children's thinking. Some of the ideas have also been applied to their play, specifically what children can or cannot learn through play when they are younger than five or six years old. The major problem for interpretation of Piaget's experiments is that his theoretical beliefs influenced what he believed was happening. He concluded that children under seven years of age were very restricted in their ability to think and reason because they gave 'wrong' answers to the particular questions asked in the experiments.

Margaret Donaldson (1978) approached the situation from the perspective of how the experiments might look to children. Her team (originally at Edinburgh and now at many different universities) worked from the refreshing perspective that what children said to researchers made sense to those children; it was not simply 'wrong'.

Can children take an alternative perspective?

Piaget claimed that children younger than six or seven years were unable to grasp the perspective of another person. He called young children 'egocentric', by which he meant they were self-centred in their thinking. (The word did not mean selfish in behaviour or emotions.)

Piaget used the 'three mountains' experiments as proof that young children were unable to imagine themselves into the position of someone else. In this experiment, children are presented with a model layout of three mountains, that are made different by a flag on one and a small house on another. The child remains sitting by the model and the researcher places a doll at different locations. Children are then asked about what the doll can see. If children do not have the words to explain clearly, they are asked to select a photo that shows the doll's view. Frequently children chose the photo that gave their own view of the mountains. Piaget claimed this evidence proved young children were still egocentric in their thinking.

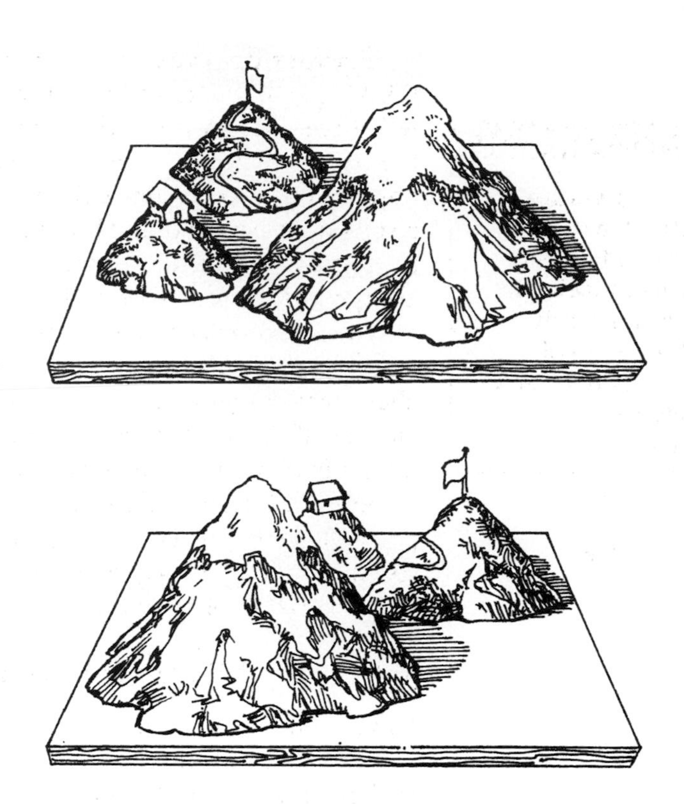

Different perspectives on Piaget's three mountains experiment

If Piaget was correct, then this egocentric outlook should be consistent even if the experimental scenario has different materials. Donaldson's team (1978) gave children, aged from three to five years of age, some experience of a layout in which a toy figure can see another figure from some positions, but not other locations. With a fuller understanding of the point of the experiment, most children could then identify correctly when the first figure could see the second figure and when the latter was hidden from view.

Donaldson (1992) reports that children made more sense of the blocked view experiments when the scenario was explained as 'hiding'. A naughty boy was said to be hiding from a policeman or a mouse from a cat. Given a recognisable context, the children were far more able to imagine themselves into the viewing position of one of the figures in the setting. Donaldson's approach helped children to understand the experimental situation, but the team did not train children in the 'right' answers. Four-, five- and even three-year-old children were more able to take up the perspective of another person than Piaget had claimed.

Children tolerate odd questions

It is striking that children try to answer some rather odd questions in an experimental situation.

What do children think adults mean?

Piaget was interested in how children understood the idea of categories of objects. One example is when and how do children work out that all cows are

CASE STUDY

New arrivals

Stoneway nursery school has recently admitted two children with learning and physical disabilities. Some team members had expressed doubts that the three- and four-year-olds would be able to make adjustments for disabled peers because, 'young children are so egocentric, aren't they?'

Before the new children started, the nursery teacher and nursery nurse gave simple explanations to the existing group. Matt (who had cerebral palsy) could not yet walk and Jane (who had Down's Syndrome) could not yet speak like the other children. Once Matt and Jane had started in nursery, the staff were ready to give practical guidance and to step in if any children were thoughtless or unkind. In fact, the children approached the new arrivals in a matter of fact way.

Two children who made friends with Matt had soon got into the habit of bringing the play materials to him, rather than expecting Matt to be mobile. The interest of playing with other children seemed to motivate Matt, who became much more interested to try to move independently. The children were not rude at all to Jane and several took pride in being able to interpret her expressive sounds and body language.

Comment

Many early years settings have an inclusive approach and adults make any necessary modifications for disabled children in the setting. The children are capable of adjustment as well. Observation of three-, four- and five-year-old children in nurseries and pre-schools shows that they can understand some of the implications of learning or physical disabilities in their peers. If children were the egocentric thinkers that Piaget claimed, they would unable to make such adjustments.

animals, but not all animals are cows, because 'animals' is a broader category that includes 'cows'. In Piaget's experimental situation children were asked a question like, 'There are three black cows and four cows. Are there more black cows or more cows?' Experimental results are usually tidied up for publication in academic journals. So, one can only speculate about the looks and comments that children made to such an odd question. Many adults' reaction to this strange query would be 'What?' or 'Come again?'

Children need questions to make sense

Researchers are more likely to understand children's thinking when they invite and listen to children's comments.

Martin Hughes (1986) reported that many three- and four-year-olds could manage 'What if?' questions related to number and counting, so long as the numbers were linked with a real situation of people or objects. However, four-year-olds were not yet ready to handle numbers with no reference point at all. Hughes reports a conversation with what sounds like an increasingly irritated four-year-old. Hughes' repeated question of 'What is three and one more?' is met by questions from the child of, 'Three and what?', 'One what?', 'One more what?' and finally, 'I don't know'.

THINK ABOUT IT

Once you reflect on the experiments of Piaget and others, it is sobering to realise that as adults we too easily decide that our perspective is the only or most sensible one. Piaget claimed that children were egocentric, but very often this term could be applied to the adults.

In an open-minded way, look at some of the play and other daily situations you face with children.

- To what extent do you, or other adults, persist in assuming that your perspective is going to be the same as that of the children?
- If children look confused, perhaps from their point of view the adult has asked odd questions that make no sense.
- Responsible practitioners are ready to consider how a situation looks and sounds from the child's side.
- We all need to consider what sort of answer a child is giving to a question, rather than simply deciding it is the wrong answer.

Children make sense of the situation

Martin Hughes and Robert Grieve (1990) demonstrated that children try hard to be co-operative. They asked children meaningless questions, such as 'Is red heavier than yellow?' The children offered replies that made as much sense as possible out of a nonsensical situation. For instance, some children proposed that red was the heavier because it was darker.

Children seemed to expect that adults ask questions for a reason and tend to want an answer. This finding is important to bear in mind if you are trying to make sense of children's play and conversation through asking many questions as an adult. (See also the discussion on page 169.)

Children like an adult sometimes to be a playmate

Children as active thinkers

The Edinburgh team varied the experiments used to explore children's conservation of number: when and how children grasped that the number of objects in a group stays the same, even if the group was made to look different. Donaldson (1978) reported that children were far more likely to say that two rows of the same number of toys were still the 'same' when a soft toy, 'naughty teddy', had pushed one row up tighter, than when the adult researcher had brought about the same change.

As Donaldson explains, the different results make sense when adults realise that young children are thinking about the experimental situation. They will use their experience so far and part of this insight will be their social expectations of adults. Children are confused when an adult makes a change in the toys, and then asks a question about whether 'it's still the same'. The children are misdirected into thinking that something must have happened. Otherwise why would an adult ask that kind of question? There is no such problem when 'naughty teddy' is involved, because he has messed up the toys. There is no genuine change to be explained and the toys themselves are still the 'same'.

Piaget's theory and research have been very influential in stimulating an understanding of how children think and many of the ideas have implications for understanding children's play. Subsequent research, especially that started by the Edinburgh team, has in many ways supported Piaget's view of children as powerful and active thinkers. He just seems to have underestimated how much the children were continuing to think during his own experiments.

✔ PROGRESS CHECK

1 What are the advantages of the experimental method?

2 In what ways may the experiments of Jean Piaget underestimate children's abilities?

3 Suggest two reasons why children might give apparently wrong answers when adults ask questions.

OBSERVATION OF CHILDREN IN CHOSEN PLAY

Over the decades of the twentieth century, there was a shift away from mainly undertaking experiments in specially organised settings. Research developed to use those settings where children usually played, such as home, nursery or school.

The observational method

In some studies, children have been observed in a setting that is familiar to them: their own home or an early years or school setting that they already attend. The researchers are less likely to direct the children's play, although they may be particularly interested in one kind of play or use of play materials. They may also have expectations or predictions they would like to check.

Researchers need to organise their observations, for instance by watching and listening in a structured pattern. Their observations are recorded in some way, minimally by note taking but sometimes by tape or video recording as well. Some observational research remains very informal. This approach can be informative so long as any report acknowledges that descriptions are of incidents that caught the observer's attention.

Observation of what naturally occurs in children's play and conversation has brought great richness to the understanding of play. It is still important to be wary about adult **values** and priorities in **interpretation**. Adult observers have expectations and hopes. So, objectivity can still be undermined by what adults want to see or how they wish to interpret what children are doing.

Play and interaction in family homes

Judy Dunn chose to watch and listen to children in their own home settings. She felt that too much information was lost when researchers tried for objective control through experimental settings or even within early years

DEFINITIONS

observational method an approach that focuses on watching and listening to children's chosen play. The ideal is that observers remain open-minded and allow the observations to shape the sense made of what children can do

values perspectives and priorities that adults hold as important, using them as a source of judgement and choice

interpretation the process of making sense of what is observed, finding meaning or explanation of reasons or motivations for actions. Adult values may also influence interpretations of play in terms of ideas of quality or acceptability

settings. Dunn also believed that misplaced assumptions, about the age at which children undertook certain types of play, arose because younger children were not observed in many studies.

From the 1980s, Dunn and her research colleagues observed children in their family home and often interviewed mothers for their views on their children. Dunn was interested in many aspects of family life, including sibling relationships. She was convinced, and her research demonstrated, that it was impossible to make sense of children's cognitive development when their thinking was treated as if it were separate from their emotional development.

Play between siblings

Dunn showed the subtleties of children's social and play behaviour when children of different ages were involved. Controlled experiments and even observation in age-banded early years provision have given the impression that play is the preserve of the over-threes and occurs within peer groups. In contrast, Dunn's observations highlighted the following.

- Within the family, children get to know one another's foibles in detail. Children early in the second year of life showed a clear grasp of how to annoy and comfort a sibling.
- Throughout the second year, young children show an increased understanding of the feelings of others and of the ground rules that operate in their family. They show learning of social skills needed in everyday interaction and play.
- In terms of ground rules, young children understand how matters should operate and when something is wrong. They also show ingenuity in getting around their parents or trying to make the rules work. They have a clear understanding that if a sibling is in the wrong, for instance hitting them in play, then they can appeal to their parents.

Siblings learn about each other in the day nursery as well as at home

Since siblings in families do not always get along, it can be easy to overlook their shared play sequences for the times when they need to be temporarily separated, for everyone's peace of mind. A strong belief has arisen that young children, especially those under two years, do not play together but only in parallel (alongside one another). This assumption seemed to be have been fuelled by observations of unrelated children who are very close in age. A wide range of play can be observed between siblings whose age difference means they are not peers. Dunn's observations offer a range of examples and others are given in the Case Study.

CASE STUDY

Diary extracts 1

I kept a detailed, although informal, diary of each of my children from birth to about five years of age. I have taken some examples of how Drew and Tanith played together from when she was mobile as a walker. Although two years younger, Tanith soon became an active participant in their play. They did not always play together and sometimes undertook activities side by side, but a noticeable amount of playtime was joint.

- Tanith, 13 months and Drew, 3:1: physical games of chasing have started. Drew started them initially, but now at 14 months, Tanith will initiate the game by hovering and looking until Drew chases her across the room or down the corridor.
- Tanith, 13 months and Drew, 3:1: shared constructional play has started. Drew builds brick towers for Tanith. He has a set phrase, 'What about this, Tanith?' and then it is understood that she knocks the tower down. They both laugh loudly and then he does it again. Within this same month, Tanith has started to bring Drew the brick box as an invitation to start the game.
- Tanith, 14 months and Drew, 3:2: they spend time together in the playhouse we made out of a huge cardboard box, playing 'Peep-bo' through the windows or just sitting together inside. Full body wrestling and physical rough and tumble has started. Tanith holds her own, partly because Drew is quite gentle with her, but also because she is not gentle with him.
- Tanith, 16 months, and Drew 3:4: Tanith had worked out how to provoke Drew into the chasing game by taking away his quilt or toy monkey. (Judy Dunn noted how younger children learned how to 'wind up' their older siblings.)
- Other forms of physical play through Tanith's second year include jumping together, bouncing on sofas or beds and Tanith pushing Drew around in her trolley.
- Tanith, 18 months, and Drew 3:6: they now share quiet activities, sitting together with their books or watching television.

1 Do you have any similar observations of children at play who differ in age by a matter of years?

2 How young are the youngest play participants?

Early pretend play

Dunn (1984) shows how even two-year-olds are drawn into pretend play, a form of activity that is often claimed to be beyond the understanding of this age group. She quotes the example of two-year-old Rose who enters into the imaginary play of her sister Nell, who is four years old, by insisting that she (Rose) is one of Nell's imaginary friends. One can imagine the kind of argument that probably followed this sequence. This example raises the possibility that many genuine play interactions involving siblings could be overlooked precisely because adults often need to intervene over conflicts. Another point is that the egocentric young child, as described by Piaget (page 48), could not possibly manage this mental leap.

Dunn's observational evidence shows how under-twos within the family are often brought into pretend play by older siblings keen to involve and instruct them. The dynamics seem to be as follows.

- Older siblings direct younger ones into pretend play, often from toddlerhood. The older sibling explains and often talks through the play, switching voices as appropriate.
- The younger children initially follow the lead and accept the role they are given.
- Once the older sibling has established the broad framework, younger siblings often add to it or insist on new versions, sometimes accepted but not always welcome to the older one.
- Two-year-olds and slightly younger children do not simply follow instructions and copy. They can be active participants, sometimes announcing a new identity within the given play fantasy.

By two and a half years, young siblings can be very active partners.

Dunn (1984) reported that about a quarter of two-year-olds, in their studies of families in Cambridge, joined their siblings in games that involved their taking on a pretend identity or being in a pretend place. The younger children took on the identities of parents or being the baby, but also of people outside the home such as car drivers or police officers.

Playful exchanges between toddlers

The observations between siblings have challenged the simplistic view that under-twos play only in parallel. Observations of young children in social interaction with each other extend the re-evaluation further.

Observational research shows that playful exchanges between older babies and toddlers may be shorter in duration than some play sequences for older children. However, there is a range of observational material, including video footage, to show how very young children make social contact and engage in what can only be called play.

Video material of Elinor Goldschmied

Playful contact and interactions between young children can be seen in the visual material collected by Elinor Goldschmied for her treasure basket (1986) and heuristic play videos (1992). The treasure basket is a container with a range of play materials that appeal to the senses and are not conventional toys. Heuristic play sessions for toddlers offer a wide range of materials

TRY THIS!

Seek a situation in which you can make your own observations where children of different ages come together, particularly toddlers and three- or four-year-olds.

If you work as a nanny or childminder, or have your own young children, then you may have a family situation available for observation over time. Alternatively, if you work in a day nursery, do consider ways of bringing together these age groups for some periods of play. (This variety in strict age-band organisation is a useful consideration for any nursery.)

- Over time, and not in just one session, look for how the toddlers are brought into the play of the older ones or manage to get accepted.
- What play activities and themes are involved where children of different ages come together?
- What role is assigned to the younger children?
- Do younger children take the initiative?
- Do the older ones seem sometimes to take pleasure in teaching and showing the little ones?

CASE STUDY

Diary extracts 2

The following excerpts from my diary of my own children highlight the ways in which they played together around imaginary themes once Tanith was an energetic and mobile toddler.

- Tanith, 15 months and Drew, 3:3: they play the chasing games and growl at each other. From Drew's words I understand they are monsters. Drew has created a rescue game. He lies down and calls out 'Tanith! Help, help!' Tanith comes up, gives her hand and they walk off. Tanith copies Drew's pretend actions such as going 'pow-pow' with a stick and offering pretend cups of tea.
- Tanith, 18 months and Drew, 3:6: Drew has invented more games for him and Tanith to play. Most revolve around chase and rescue: sharks, traps and a game in which they both chant, 'Hot, hot' and drag the pink bath towel around. (I did not understand this game until I asked Tanith as a teenager. She recalled it clearly and explained that they were escaping from volcanos). Tanith now copies Drew a great deal in her pretend play: how he handles the play dough and uses named Fisher Price™ figures in the dough, pretending to eat and drink with the tea set, counting like him and trying to jump as he does.
- Tanith, 2 and Drew, 4: Tanith is as likely now to initiate their pretend games together as Drew. They spend a lot of time in the playhouse and they jointly run a pretend cafe from behind the living room sofa.
- Tanith, 2:5 and Drew, 4:5: they play together a great deal and their shared pretend games are long fantasy sequences with assigned roles and scripts, mainly started by Drew but followed enthusiastically by Tanith.

and containers that children can explore however they wish. See page 77 for a further description of this practical research.

Children in these videos are sometimes absorbed in their own play, but even the babies of 9 —10 months show an interest in another baby's play choice, stare at one another and sometimes become involved in give and take of items.

The material collected by Elinor Goldschmied and Dorothy Selleck (1996) showed babies engaged in physical play, with the touch and whole body hugs that sometimes lead adults to intervene on the grounds that someone may be hurt. Some of this video footage is in children's own homes and some in nurseries.

Carol Eckerman's observations

Eckerman (1993) observed very young children in contact with each other. Since she was open to the possibility that even short exchanges were playful, her observations were able to highlight how shared play can start for older babies and toddlers. Eckerman noticed the following deliberate patterns of playful exchange.

These toddlers share an interest in shoes

TRY THIS!

With the parents' informed consent, collect some video footage of very young children at play.

- Watch how they make contact with each other and the games they create.
- Alternatively, video a treasure basket or heuristic play session and watch the tape later with parents.

Organise a meeting at which parents can watch the video and talk about their children's play and learning.

- Once babies are mobile and can exercise deliberate control over their hand movements, they create a joint focus of interest by making physical contact with an object that another young child (or adult) is handling. Eckerman noticed that the baby then imitates what the other child, or the adult is doing. This copying action seems to send a non-verbal message of 'I like this' or 'Let's do it together'. Sensitive adults pick up on the message but so, sometimes, do children.
- When toddlers are together, deliberate imitation seems to be a favoured opening move towards a playful exchange. Eckerman noticed that this imitation often happened swiftly after first contact between toddlers. The other toddler is encouraged to imitate in return and copying sequences then sometimes follow. Imitation seems to establish a connection between the two children through non-verbal means. See also the example in Think About It (page 58).
- Imitative games with deliberate turn taking are fairly common between toddlers and they do the same action, one at a time. Eckerman observed enjoyable jumping off the sofa games and versions of 'Follow my Leader' were also a common pattern.

Toddlers are selective in their imitation and do not copy everything. Sequences develop, especially if toddlers get to know each other over time. From two years onwards, young children increasingly use verbal as well as non-verbal messages to guide the play and extend it beyond the established sequences.

Anecdotal and informal observation by adults closely engaged with very young children produces many examples of games that are developed by the toddlers themselves. Sometimes, an adult or older child creates the game at the outset, but then the very young child takes an active role in initiating the game in the future or keeping the game going. Common examples include:

- communication games of sound making, giggling, blowing raspberries and nonsense talk
- babies and toddlers who lead a game with an adult, such as putting a hand on the page of a book to prevent it being turned and grinning to show that this is a physical and visual joke
- 'Hide and Seek' and 'Peek-a-boo' games with furniture or a cover like a tea towel or scarf
- the game of 'Now-you-see-me-now-you-don't' from behind or between curtains.

THINK ABOUT IT

Some of these playful sequences between toddlers are unwelcome to adults. Bouncing on a bed or joint posting of items into the video may be toddler favourites but one can understand that the play nature may be lost to adults in the wish to stop the actions. Looking through the eyes of a toddler, however, they are play. A positive and friendly adult approach to setting boundaries can co-exist with appreciation of the playful nature of some of children's actions.

TRY THIS!

Once you become interested, you will notice many playful imitative exchanges between toddlers. The play may occur in your day nursery or children's centre. You can also notice enjoyable sequences in everyday life.

- Collect examples of play between toddlers over the next few weeks. Perhaps you could start by looking out for the kind of examples given above.
- Watch out for the unhelpful adult filter that dismisses an exchange as 'not real play' or 'not long enough to count'. If very young children are behaving in a playful way, then it is play.

Observation in early years settings

Over the last few decades there have been many studies using observational techniques in early years settings or schools. The Oxford group led by Jerome Bruner in the 1980s was interested in play and learning in different types of settings and the actions of adults. Barbara Tizard and her team (see also page 151) explored how children might behave differently, and learn, in different settings and their own home. Some of the observational studies focus on children's play because it is deemed to be important for some other aspect of development. Some studies have sought to prove that certain kinds of play will support children's intellectual development (see page 146) or that adults with particular qualifications will better support play and learning. In this section, play is of interest from the perspective of the children's experience.

Vivian Paley's reflective observations

Vivian Paley (or Vivian Gussin Paley as is sometimes given on her books) was for many years a teacher of three- and four-year-olds in the United States. From the 1970s onwards, she has written up her experiences with the kindergarten class. Each book has revolved around a main theme and includes detailed descriptions of what children have done and said. Each book offers an intriguing insight into the particular children in the class each year, but also the dynamics between them and how their concerns are reflected in their play.

Paley tape-recorded at least part of the kindergarten day, so is able to give verbatim accounts of some of the play exchanges between children. Clearly, her

Adults can learn through watching children play

observations are organised around a theme, but the books nevertheless manage to avoid over-neatening children's play. The narrative shows the complexity, stop-start quality and recycling nature of children's play and their conversations. Themes emerge, disappear for a while during the kindergarten year and then re-emerge. Paley considers the possible meaning of pretend play for individual children and small groups of friends. She remains cautious about making firm interpretations and is well aware of being an adult observer.

In *Bad Guys Don't Have Birthdays: Fantasy Play At Four*, Vivian Paley notices how much Frederick, who has a new baby in the family, wants to be the baby in play throughout the kindergarten year. Some children are more tolerant of his emotional need than others. The following sequence highlights this four-year-old boy's feelings:

> When Frederick hears 'baby', he rushes into the block area. 'I'm the baby tiger.'
> 'You can be the daddy tiger,' Barney tells him.
> 'No, you said baby.'
> Christopher tries to help. 'Let him be the twin for the other baby, Barney. I'll be the dad.'
> 'No twins!' Frederick cries. 'I'm the only baby.'
> Barney shrugs his shoulders. 'Then who do I be?'
> 'You be the mommy for me,' Frederick says.
> 'No! I'm the baby tiger because I said it first. You be the mommy.'
> 'I hate you guys! I said I was the baby and you won't let me. I hate you! I'm hating you every day from now on.' (Page 53.)

TRY THIS!

Vivian Paley keeps records over a whole year, so she can track how play themes circle and return. In your own setting you will keep descriptive records of individual children. Try to keep some notes, perhaps helped by having a notebook always with you, of recurring themes in children's play.

- Watch out for examples of play in your setting where, over time, you realise that certain themes return in the play of one or more children.
- What do you think is going on? Obviously, be cautious about leaping to conclusions.

Different themes for reflection on observations

Paley's books are full of detailed description of the children's play. Equally valuable for early years practitioners, each book is also an account of how she reflected on the year and learned from the children.

- Within one year, Paley documented how she worked hard to tune genuinely into the experience of a black child in a predominantly white kindergarten. (*White Teacher,* 1979, Harvard University Press.)
- Another year, the predominant play themes made Paley want to stand back as a female teacher and approach the different play of boys and girls, acknowledging the importance to the boys of their pretend play choices. (*Boys And Girls: Superheroes In The Doll Corner*, 1984, University of Chicago Press.)
- During yet another nursery year, Paley focused on the power of story telling for all the children. Yet she also highlighted the changes for Jason, an isolated child, who used his pretend play focused on a helicopter as a way to cope. (*The Boy Who Would Be A Helicopter: The Uses Of Story Telling In The Classroom,* 1990, Harvard University Press).
- Another time, Paley's main theme was the struggle for children to cope when they felt left out of play. She tracked the possibilities of a new kindergarten ground rule for handling the ways in which young children shut each other out of play or created no-go areas. (*You Can't Say You Can't Play*, 1992, Harvard University Press.)

✔ PROGRESS CHECK

1. **What are the possible advantages of an observational method in understanding children's play?**
2. **Describe three kinds of games that toddlers may play and initiate.**
3. **How may careful observation support you as a reflective practitioner?**

CHILDREN'S OWN VIEWS OF PLAY

There are many books on the library and bookshop shelves that have the word 'play' in their title, but most of them scarcely acknowledge how children may view play. The absence of children's perspective is a serious oversight and brings risks when adults are very sure of the role of play and what it will deliver, whether in a therapeutic or educational context.

Steadily, this imbalance is being corrected by observers who are really interested in the children's perspective. Researchers and practitioners recognise that ambitious adult goals are unlikely to be achieved if the children's view is overlooked. Interest in genuine involvement of children in decisions and consultation with them has also led to creative work bringing in the views of children as young as two and three years old.

Jacqui Cousins' observations

Jacqui Cousins (1999) has gathered observational material from nurseries and playgroups. She draws on her years of research, but also from her experience as an OFSTED inspector, when she became increasingly concerned about what was happening to children's play.

Jacqui Cousins illustrates that children have opinions about play, about what works and what does not, what is interesting and boring, what is scary and what is worrying. By four years of age, children have preferences and views and they are willing to explain them to an adult who shows genuine interest.

- Children were keen to show Cousins their favourite parts of a nursery or playgroup and to describe their most favourite activities. They enthused with, 'Come and look at our beautiful books!' and told how they liked stories but often disliked group story time because of 'being squashed all together ... everyone wriggling and all that'.
- The outdoors was greatly appreciated by those children who had easy access and time to play in the garden. They liked chasing and hiding, the bikes, climbing and other physical activities that clearly stretched them, like 'climbing high up and jumping off ... Wheeee, that's *really* scary!'
- Children liked dressing up and pretend play, real cooking, friendly and conversational mealtimes and exciting equipment like scientific apparatus. However, they also stressed the importance of being with their friends, to play and as one girl said, 'We enjoys a good natter in the sun'.

Young children like a good chat

- Yet, these four-year-olds had already taken on board the anxieties and the pressures felt by the adults. Cousins noticed that the children would imitate the adults and sometimes interrupt each other, one child saying to Cousins about another, 'He's big now ... got to get on with his proper work'.

- Children had a clear idea of the pressures, especially the time pressures in their setting. One boy explained how much he liked a miniature world model-making kit, but that he did not use it, because there was never enough time to make a proper model.

The Mosaic method

Alison Clark and Valerie Wignall of the Thomas Coram Research Unit in London have developed inventive methods to gain an understanding of children's perspective on their everyday lives. The value of talking with children is not overlooked, but it is recognised that other techniques help to build a more accurate view when consulting with under-eights. The variety in the approach also helps to avoid adult bias and enables children to communicate about what they feel is significant.

The techniques

The Mosaic approach used five broad techniques to gain the ideas of children in the Thomas Coram Early Childhood Centre.

- ***Careful observation by adults*** allowed the gathering of 'nursery stories' that were considered in an open-ended way.
- ***Child conferencing*** combined more formal and informal interviews. A short interview schedule covered children's views on why they come to nursery, their favourite people and play activities. However, this method was flexible and the interview continued on the move when three-and four-year-olds wished to show the interviewer parts of the nursery.

  The Coram team repeated the conferencing process with children who were still attending the centre five months later. They found that children were interested in what they had said earlier and that the recordings stimulated further discussion.
- ***Cameras*** were used as a way for children to share their views. They were given a camera, short training in how to use it and asked to take photos of things that were important to them in the nursery. The word 'important' was deliberately used, rather than 'favourite', since the team believed that asking for importance would encourage children to give their priorities.

  The researchers found that issues of importance to the children emerged both at the time they took their photos and afterwards when the developed shots were used for discussion. Some children took a large number of photos, some very few, but it was their own choice.
- ***Child-led tours*** occurred when children took the adults on a tour of the nursery. The children took photos, produced drawings and notes and made audio tapes as the tour progressed. Information was communicated to adults during the tour and children were enabled to be the experts.
- ***Mapping:*** a visual and very personal mapping of the nursery was supported by all the material gathered by the children.

The children's views

The range of methods and time spent attending to children's priorities raised issues of relevance to individual children and the nursery as a whole. The

Mosaic method aims to give a sense of fitting together the different parts of a pattern into the whole. It is very important that children and adults gather documentation together. Then the children and adults engage in a process of dialogue, reflection and interpretation to make sense of the material.

This process showed that children placed a high value on the outdoor space, including areas of the garden that the practitioners had regarded as 'empty space'. Areas by the shed and beside the fence in this nursery were used by the children in their play. The spaces were significant exactly as they were and the children certainly did not want them tidied up or made into a more 'useful' area as defined by adults. Children also defined the important areas, such a curved bench where the 'monsters' lived.

Children placed great emphasis on the importance of friends in the nursery: that you had a friend to play with, and looking forward to that part of the day when you would be with your friends. This focus on the social side to the nursery supports Jacqui Cousins' findings from spontaneous comments made to her by children (see page 61).

Children are only too pleased to tell you about activities they enjoy

Children's views of school grounds

Learning Through Landscapes (LTL) is an organisation that works to transform school grounds, so that they are designed and can be used better by the children. LTL promotes genuine consultation with children and highlights that even the younger primary school children have clear views about the playground and other school grounds. Wendy Titman (1994) explored

TRY THIS!

The use of a camera has become more common in nurseries to produce photos as evidence of early learning goals. The camera can be equally important as a visual resource for children to encourage reminiscence about activities and outings. Photos can also be a means to communicate with parents about what the setting does and why.

Consider sharing the use of a camera with three- and four-year-olds in your setting. Explain to them carefully how it works and that you trust them to take care. Cameras can be carried in a little shoulder bag (the method used by the Coram team).

- See what range of photos the children want to take. You can give them an open brief or perhaps encourage some of them to make a record of the important things in nursery or their favourites.
- Allow plenty of time for them to show you their photos and talk you through what is important about the image.
- Discuss how you will display or keep the photos carefully. You need to discuss security with very great care if you use a digital camera and store the images on a computer.

CASE STUDY

The camera

Drummond Road After School Club bought a camera several years ago but the equipment was initially used only by the adults. They have now bought a digital camera and decided to share its use with the children.

The staff are learning alongside the children about how to work with the technology. The children are careful with the camera, they understand that it is an expensive item and are pleased to be trusted. Groups of children take turns and are interested to record different aspects of play. One group of enthusiastic builders has been keen to use the camera to make a record of a large work in progress. The children created a photographic record of each stage of their substantial enterprise. Other children have wanted to record local outings and then to make a display board of interesting trips.

1. More nurseries and after-school facilities now consider letting children use the camera. What do you think will be important in how children are introduced to the technology? How can they be helped to learn?
2. What are the main issues of security that need to be considered when there are photos of children?

children's views in her project for LTL. Some findings are discussed in this chapter, but you will find further discussion from page 176, about insights for the role of a helpful adult in play.

Messages from the environment

Titman took an approach developed from semiotics, a philosophy and technique that has been used in gathering adults' opinions in market research. The semiotic approach proposes that a researcher cannot understand the perspectives of other people, unless she or he unravels the shared cultural meanings in the design of a setting. Titman explains how:

> ... school grounds give out coded messages to the children who use them about their identity as part of a group of 'users'. Are they expected to be 'carers', 'big tough sports players', 'hiders and seekers', 'horticulturalists', 'confident occupiers of space', 'involved with the elements', 'a young animal', a 'socialised proto-adult' or what?' (Page 16.)

Children's evaluations

The report draws on children's views, supported by photos and sketches. The richness of the material shows clearly that children have opinions about the advantages and disadvantages of their own playground.

- Children were clear about liking trees and flowers, but much less enthusiastic when school rules were mainly about not touching or climbing.
- They liked shady places, seating areas where they could sit and chat, small places to play, making a den and climbing. Some of their frustrations were that useful areas might be out of bounds. Even very climbable trees were not usually permitted for this activity.

Children nowadays still like 'dens'

- Bushes and dens were highly valued but, 'In the majority of the schools visited, concern that supervisors should be able to see the children at all times precluded their having dens. Where bushes existed, these were often used as dens, albeit "illegally".' (Page 45.)

Being valued or dismissed

Children took meaning from how the grounds were maintained. They noticed changes that did not involve their views and rules about use of the playground. Titman noted, 'Where children believed that the grass could not be used because it would get damaged, they read this as meaning that the grass was more important to the school than they were, particularly where playtime on tarmac was unpleasant, uncomfortable, boring and in their view dangerous.' (Page 35.) When the school grounds were poorly maintained, with rubbish or damaged items, the children expressed the view that people did not care about them, the children.

Children had good ideas about making changes and liked to be asked. Yet, they were quick to recognise and dismiss tokenistic forms of consultation, when adults just pretended that children's views would make a difference to the final decision.

Children were enthusiastic and energetic participants in those schools who mobilised their skills, for example as gardeners. On the other hand, children were disdainful of pretence. One child commented, 'A lot of money was spent on a painting on a wall but the little children take no notice of it. The only people who respect it are the parents as they think their children learnt the ABC from it but it's just a waste of time. This artist came and tried to make it look like we did it – even I could have done better than that – what a waste of money.' (Page 83.)

Children's views as part of adult self-appraisal

The Effective Early Learning (EEL) project, led by Christine Pascal and Tony Bertram, offers a structured approach enabling early years settings to appraise their current practice and improve it. Each setting undertakes in-house research at the start of their involvement. Part of this information gathering is to talk informally with the children. The project material suggests that conversations are conducted in small groups of three or four children. Photos of activities and people in the setting can help the ideas to flow and the EEL interview schedule offers open-ended questions.

Pascal and Bertram (1997) report case studies from the project highlighting children's views. Children seemed most to like those activities where the organisation of the setting allowed for initiative on their part. They liked a range of play and craft materials and also shared the pleasure of playing outside and just talking with the adults. The dislikes that were reported in brief were times when children had to wait or sit down quietly, as one child commented, 'listening when it's not a story'. Children did not like noisy times or quarrels and, in one nursery class, a lotto game that was used by adults to offer structured language practice.

Local consultation with children

TRY THIS!

- Contact your local EYDCP and ask how to obtain their annual report. It should not be difficult, since the report is a public document.
- Look in the report and see to what extent children and young people have been asked for their views about play and leisure facilities for them. What ideas have emerged?

The increase in genuine consultation exercises that involve children has been partly stimulated by the focus on children's rights and children as young citizens. Another strand has been that the childcare audits carried out by each Early Years Development and Childcare Partnership (EYDCP) are supposed to include consultation with children, as well as local parents.

Daycare Trust (1998) reported a project in which the opinions were gathered of three- and four-year-olds in three North London day nurseries. The objective was to understand what the children liked and thought was important in their day nursery. This information was used for the information leaflet to guide parents on what to look for in choosing a childcare setting. The methods of the research highlight creative ways of encouraging children to express their views.

- Children were invited to join the researchers, who had become familiar in the nursery, and chat in an open-ended way.
- A teddy was used as a prop and children invited to suggest how they would ensure that Teddy enjoyed going to nursery.
- Children were given paper and pens to draw if they wished.
- A Polaroid camera was available and some children took photos

Key themes emerged from children's recommendations for Teddy and their comments about what they liked about their own nursery.

- The children emphasised that the chance to play with other children at nursery was really enjoyable. They all named friends and chatted about the games they played.

- Play and the chance to play mattered very much to the children and they gave vivid descriptions of what they did in play.
- Pretend play, involving dressing up, was important to many children.
- Playing outside in the garden was top of the list of 'best things' at nursery for most of the children. The freedom to go outside whenever they wanted was valued. The garden was liked for its equipment, its use as a venue for some pretend games and the chance to look after the garden itself.
- Making things through play was valued by children. They often wanted to show the researchers what they had made or a corner to which they had all contributed.

It is also useful to note, although not an issue usually regarded as relevant to play, that the children were very forthcoming about food and meals. Food was a social time in these nurseries and much appreciated by the children. Eating was an activity shared with friends and special meals such as picnics were the source of happy reminiscences.

Adult reminiscence

Another option in exploring play is to ask adults to recall their own enjoyable play activities. Adults may have a selective memory, but an open-ended discussion can be productive, so long as it steps aside from any sense of 'children today and how they can't play!' A number of books about play include contemporary reminiscence or the evidence of social history (see Chapter 1).

Paul Bonel (1993) highlights the nature of memorable play. His ideas, and those of other writers, raise the following themes about what made 'good games'.

- Adults recall the delight of making camps, hideaways and dens. It was important to have special places that the children had found or created and that they felt were secret in some way. Some locations, like the local allotments, were that much more attractive because they were out of bounds.
- Pretend play of many different themes emerges on a regular basis, including dressing up, complex scenarios to which a group of children return and clear cut roles and rules.
- Many play activities are recalled with rueful laughter as 'we shouldn't have been doing that really', 'it was risky and we knew it; that was the point'. Upright citizens will recall climbing forbidden trees, putting coins or wood on the railway tracks, adventurous bike riding or simply winding up cantankerous neighbours.
- Adults describe happy childhood activities that probably looked like 'messing about' to the adults of the time. The current generation of adults can, with encouragement, clearly recall their childhood purposes.

TRY THIS!

Think back to your own childhood and involve colleagues or friends in this recollection.

- What stands out in your mind as memorable games or play experiences?
- What did you do, with whom and what made it so enjoyable?
- Discuss some of the ideas and themes you have gathered.
- If you have clear memories from early childhood, compare your play reminiscences with the play experiences of children now in your setting.

✔ PROGRESS CHECK

1. **Describe two ways to invite the views of young children on the play environment and activities.**
2. **Add two more ways that would be possible with school-age children.**
3. **What are the advantages of consulting with children about play?**

KEY TERMS

You need to know the meaning of the following words and phrases. Go back through the chapter to make sure you understand them:

experimental method
hypothesis
interpretation
objectivity
observational method
values

FURTHER READING

Bonel, Paul (1993) *Playing for Real*, National Children's Play and Recreation Unit
A discussion of the nature of play in childhood.

Clark, Alison and Moss, Peter (2001) *Listening to Young Children: The Mosaic Approach*, National Children's Bureau
A report of the methods and findings of the Mosaic approach to exploring children's views and perspectives.

Cousins, Jacqui (1999) *Listening to Four-Year-Olds: How They Can Help Us Plan Their Education and Care*, National Early Years Network
Rich observational material from children in nurseries and pre-schools that illustrates the perspective of children and offers practical advice to adults who want to support their learning through play.

Daycare Trust (1998) *Listening to Children — Young Children's Views on Childcare: A Guide for Parents*
A report from DCT of the consultation they undertook in three London nurseries.

Donaldson, Margaret (1978) *Children's Minds*, Fontana
A ground-breaking book that approached children's thinking from what they did understand and the children's perspective.

Donaldson, Margaret (1992) *Human Minds: An Exploration*, Penguin
Further discussion of the research on children's thinking with some practical application to how children are helped to learn.

Dunn, Judy (1984) *Sisters and Brothers*, Fontana
Detailed reports of Dunn's observational research in families, especially on the arrival of a second child.

Dunn, Judy (1993) *Young Children's Close Relationships Beyond Attachment*, Sage
Dunn shows through observational research how children's social development links with their communication and their play.

Eckerman, Carol 'Imitation and toddlers' achievement of co-ordinated actions with others' in Jacqueline Nadel and Luigia Camaioni (eds) (1993) *New Perspectives In Early Communicative Development*, Routledge
Detailed observational research describing the earliest communication and relationship skills.

Goldschmied, Elinor (1986) *Infants At Work: Babies of 6—9 Months Exploring Everyday Objects*, with Anita Hughes (1992) *Heuristic Play With Objects: Children of 12—20 Months Exploring Everyday Objects* and with Dorothy Selleck (1996) *Communication Between Babies in Their First Year* (all these videos available from the National Children's Bureau.)

Grieve, Robert and Hughes, Martin (eds) (1990) *Understanding Children: Essays in Honour of Margaret Donaldson*, Basil Blackwell
A detailed collection of studies that look at how children think, often by approaching experiments from the children's possible perspective.

Hughes, Martin (1986) *Children and Number*, Blackwell
An exploration of the development of children's understanding of number.

Pascal, Christine and Bertram, Tony (1997) (eds) *Effective Early Learning: Case Studies in Improvement*, Hodder and Stoughton

Reports from early years settings that have been involved in the EEL project. Some case studies describe children's views.

Titman, Wendy (1994) *Special Places, Special People: The Hidden Curriculum of School Grounds*, WWF/Learning Through Landscapes

A detailed study of how children see their play opportunities within the grounds of the primary school.

CHAPTER 4

Playing throughout childhood

PREVIEW

The key topics covered in this chapter are:

- Play in early childhood
- Play in school
- Children's leisure activities
- The play of girls and boys.

Important questions about what and how children play swiftly raise possible disagreements between adults about what is, and what is not really, play. This chapter covers some of the issues that relate to how play and playfulness unfolds with children's development and to what extent the nature of children's play changes as they get older. Consideration of how disabled children play highlights unspoken adult assumptions about the boundaries to play. There are also useful insights into the ways in which play skills are linked with children's social skills. Finally, consideration of how the play of boys and girls may differ raises important issues about social learning.

PLAY IN EARLY CHILDHOOD

The main features of what is usually regarded as play can be seen even with very young children. A play activity starts, persists and is repeated apparently because it gives pleasure to a child or baby. Babies become interested in objects within their first year. Some of these may fall within the category of 'baby toys', but their play certainly is not limited to conventional playthings. Babies play, explore and learn using their own fingers and toes, or with the support of an adult or older child.

Playfulness in early communication

The very first play object that babies enjoy is likely to be their mother or father. Their very early playful exchanges are part of the building blocks of communication. Babies' behaviour includes imitation of facial expressions, communicative gestures, sounds and touch.

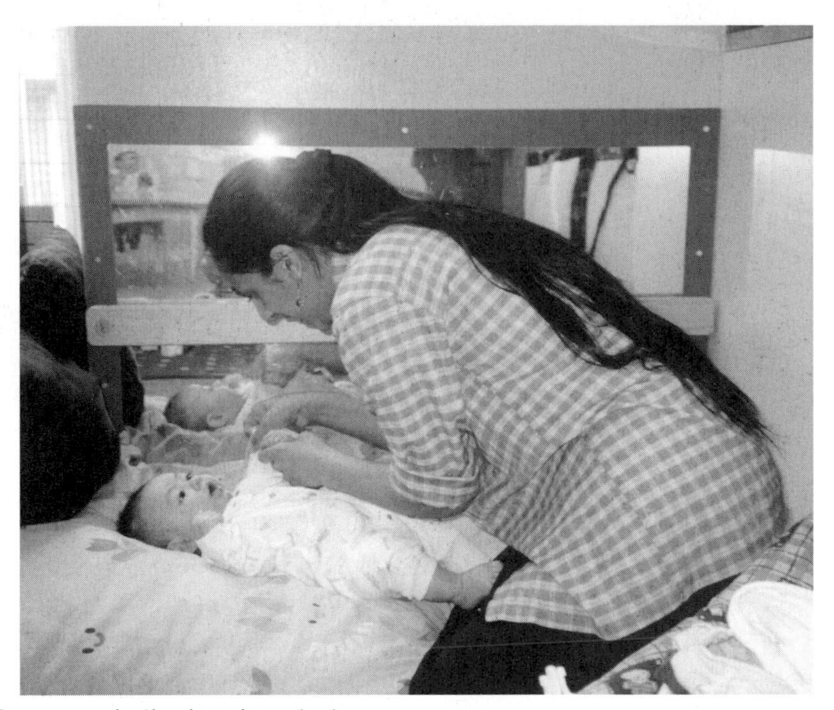

Early communication is so important

These first elements of play are linked with the subtleties of happy communication when a caring adult, or older sibling, is tuned into the baby. Exchanges can develop with sensitive timing, give and take between partners and mutual enjoyment. Babies of even a few months of age show their active involvement and try to start a playful exchange by smiling and gestures. They promote the continuation of playful communication by grins, mouth movements, hand waving and squeals of delight.

The abilities of most babies to initiate and take part in their playful exchanges is highlighted when parents or carers become aware of the low level of responsiveness of some babies. Sometimes, it emerges later that the baby has disabilities within the autistic continuum (see also page 182).

THINK ABOUT IT

- **Do you sometimes hear comments about babies and very young children that show adult assumptions about play?**
- **Why might some adults, including early years practitioners, assume that babies and toddlers do not yet play? Why may some carers not count these playful exchanges as 'real play'?**

Exploratory play

The play of babies within the first year of life is closely linked to their increasing control over their own bodies, including hands and fingers and the co-ordination of holding and grasping with what they see. Babies tend to use their current skills on whatever objects catch their attention. Of course they have no sense of danger, nor of what are 'official' toys and somebody else's prize possessions. So, it is possible, especially in a family home, that recognition of early play may be distracted occasionally by concern for redirecting a baby's grasp. If you watch babies, you will notice that their exploratory play with objects tends to be guided by their preferred physical method of the moment.

There is not a firm developmental pattern but the following themes tend to emerge over the months in terms of how babies approach single objects.

- ***Holding***: very young babies have to put all their energy into combining vision and stretch to get hold of an interesting object or part of a person. Initially they cannot easily open their grasp to let go again. So, if they have got hold of your ear or their elder sibling's hair, you often have to undo their grasp.
- ***Mouthing***: babies explore by putting objects to their mouths and continue to use this method into the second year of life. The nerve endings of a baby's lips, mouth and tongue are the most sensitive in their body. So, they are using the most effective means to play and learn.
- ***Inspecting***: once babies can hold and look, they often stare at an object of interest. They may look at what appear to be very minor details, but everything is new to them. Continued experience is needed before objects and people become familiar.
- ***Hitting***: babies now have greater physical control and can follow through by looking. So they can connect with an object or substance with more energy. They may tap at a teddy or pat down on a wet surface on their highchair.
- ***Shaking***: the ability to hold tight and then make movement allows babies to move an object from side to side. Perhaps it makes a noise, like a rattle or material cubes with bells inside. Then the pleasure of making something happen encourages babies to repeat the action. There are limits to their visual field and control and these become clear when babies manage to hit themselves on the head with a vigorously shaken rattle.
- ***Examining***: once babies become able to use both hands and to shift their grip, they can examine in detail. Babies become interested in moving an object around and taking a close look, and perhaps a poke, from different angles.
- ***Combining several actions***: babies who have achieved control over a number of ways to manipulate objects no longer restrict themselves to one movement. They may try several different approaches to the same item of interest.
- ***Tearing***: babies who manage to explore paper objects may discover the delights of tearing. This action provides a mixture of sound and interesting cause and effect. Of course, they do not know the difference between magazines that are ready for the recycling bin and an older sibling's artwork.
- ***Rubbing***: babies become interested in texture and may move a soft toy or piece of material against their cheek of mouth.
- ***Dropping***: babies' ability to grasp, let go and track with their eyes adds the intriguing possibility of dropping objects. This action is even more interesting to do from a height as that adds a noise as the object hits the

TRY THIS!

- Make observations of two or three babies within their first year.
- Look for their favourite method of exploration of the time and perhaps observe closely again a few weeks later for any changes.
- In what ways are you, or their carer if it is someone else, helping the baby to learn some boundaries about what can dropped or thrown, without spoiling the playful learning?

ground. Dropping often becomes combined with sounds and gestures from the baby to indicate that somebody should retrieve the object, so the dropping play can be repeated.

- ***Throwing***: babies' physical skills continue to develop until they can manage the complex sequence of holding something and then combining the throwing and letting go actions.

Games babies play

Once babies have a repertoire of physical action, they become ever more creative in what they do with objects. Until they are about nine months old, they tend to use their current skills on objects without attention to their usual purpose. Increasingly, however, you will see older babies and certainly toddlers, playing with objects with more obvious awareness of the function and purpose of this particular item. Toddlers are still very flexible and may bring items into their play without apparent awareness of the usual function, especially of non-play items in the home. A further development of their awareness of objects is that they begin knowingly to use an item differently from its original function and this shift marks the very beginnings of pretend play (see from page 96).

TRY THIS!

Observe any games that toddlers play with adults. Perhaps you will see the games of:

- 'I give you this and then I take it back again'
- 'I drop this, look at you and you put it back so I can drop it again'
- 'I point my arm and finger and you look'.

Make some notes of what you observe, including how the toddler communicates that she or he wants a particular game. Share your observations with colleagues and the toddler's parent.

EXAMPLE

The development of pretend with a household object

Beyer and Gammelhoft (2000) give an illuminating example of how a very young child changed over the months in his approach to the television remote control. They are especially interested in how autistic children develop and the difficulties they experience in the skills and understanding needed to play. They describe their observations of Lukas, who is not autistic, as a contrast.

- At five months of age Lukas liked to play with the television remote control. He would put it in his mouth. He also liked to knock it to the floor and then would squeal in delight at the effect he had created.
- By eight months of age Lukas would sit with the remote control and point it at everybody and everything. He did not seem to be aware of its function in controlling the television, but did seem to have grasped that this was a valuable object. He had watched his older siblings regularly squabble over the right to use it.
- Yet within just a further month, nine-month-old Lukas was able to find and press the red button as he pointed the remote control towards the television and switched it off in the middle of his older sister's favourite programme. He squealed happily at his achievement and the effect.
- By twenty-two months, Lukas had understood what the remote control usually does and is choosing to pretend that it is something else. He runs around the home with it, sometimes holds it to his ear and says 'loh'. He is pretending to speak on a mobile telephone.

TRY THIS!

If possible, make regular observations of a baby and toddler that, rather like the example with Lukas, enable you to track how the same very young child handles and plays with a common object that is not a toy.

- For instance, you could follow a baby and then the toddler's use of a telephone (either getting hold of the real one or a set that is made available for play). Other alternatives might be a good-sized cardboard box or a collection of hats.
- How does her or his use of the item visibly change over the months and what can you suggest this implies about the child's learning?

Physical play

Once they are independently mobile, older babies and toddlers engage in a great deal of physical play. They use their current skills in creative ways, sometimes in order to attain a related play goal, but often it would appear for the sheer joy of movement.

Playing with scarves can be absorbing

- Once babies are confident crawlers they sometimes crawl towards an object they want and their calls and chortles show how pleased they are to be able to reach a part of the room or somebody they want to greet.
- Adept crawlers appear sometimes simply to find joy in the movement. Toddlers who can walk often still enjoy crawling-chasing games with older children and adults.
- Children gain competence in the physical skills of walking, running and jumping and they often use these abilities as the main part of a playful activity.

CASE STUDY

Under-twos

The team at Highwater Children's Centre have been keen to highlight how the younger children play and the importance of their play for learning. They decide to observe regular physical games that are started by the under-twos themselves, as well as those more organised by the staff. They take photos over a period of several weeks and create a display to show positively that under-twos really do play together. Some of the featured games include the following.

- There is delight for the toddlers in playing with the canvas tunnel. The staff realise that this is also a favoured activity of the older children who ask for a go too.
- Several toddlers like to practise jumping off a step or another low height. They also like to walk along the low garden wall or other walls with a hand held when they are out on a local trip.
- Several toddiers started a game where they experiment with 'funny walks'. Their lively movements raise a laugh and are then repeated many times and with variations.
- Other toddlers are especially keen on run, chase and hide games when the staff have to pretend not to see the children.

1. You could make similar observations in your own setting, whether group care or a family home. Keep some descriptive notes.
2. Look for links to other kinds of play and suggest what young children can be learning through exuberant use of their physical skills.

The great value of physical play

There is increased interest in the value of physical play for young children. One source is the concern that older children seem to be getting less physical exercise (see also page 86). Study into the development of the brain has also highlighted how much babies and toddlers need to have physical experience and play in order for those vital connections to be made. Sally Goddard Blythe (2000) described how much very young children learn when they are enabled to enjoy physical play. She points out that, 'Attention, balance and co-ordination are the primary ABC on which all later learning depends'.

DEFINITION

proprioception the skills and bodily awareness that enable a child to recognise what it feels like to be in balance or about to lose their balance. They are learning to interpret the messages of sensation sent from the body into the brain

Creeping and crawling by older babies and toddlers help them directly to synchronise their sense of balance, what they see and the skills of **proprioception**. These skills enable a child to recognise what it feels like to be, for instance, in balance or about to lose their balance. They are learning to interpret the messages of sensation sent from the body into the brain. The co-ordination of moving hands and vision in crawling is also undertaken at the same distance that children will use some years later in reading and writing. So, apart from being enjoyable now, crawling games are a support for the future.

Goddard Blythe also makes the vital observation that, 'The most advanced level of movement is the ability to stay totally still'. Young children need to move in order to gain plenty of practice in what all the different physical skills feel like and to gain in confidence. However, balance is hard without movement.

GOOD PRACTICE

- Young children need enough space and a comfortable floor surface to move around in their preferred mode for the time being.
- Although they may like to sit up for some activities, toddlers should not be made to sit still for long periods.
- They can learn and concentrate on the move and will only be distressed and distracted if they are made to restrict their movements.
- Adults need to get on the floor with children or use comfortable large cushions and low adult seats.
- Babies and toddlers need plenty of happy practice in crawling, walking and clambering. They will be thrilled to have adults either join them or show genuine pleasure at the toddlers' activity.
- Young children need a wide range of interesting materials to explore safely through their preferred method of the moment.

THINK ABOUT IT

We need to remind ourselves how much physical play is needed so that children can learn the skills of movement and later of staying still.

- Watch young children who are starting to walk, or pushing along wheeled trolleys. As soon as they slow, they start to wobble. Beginner walkers tend to plump down to sitting and then get up and try again.
- What will happen if we try to make children sit still too soon and for too long?

Very young children playing together

There is a persistent myth that very young children do not and cannot play with other children. The proposition is that they only play alongside other children in what is called parallel play. This belief seems largely to have arisen from research that showed how older children spent relatively more time in co-operative play and less in parallel or solitary play than the younger ones. Observation of young children soon shows that they do play together but not necessarily in the same way as older children.

Young children like to join together in a game

Researchers interested in the development of early communication patterns have sometimes highlighted how toddlers become involved in playful exchanges with one another. Look back at the description on page 57 of Carol Eckerman's observations of very young children and the deliberate patterns she identified in their play together:

Elinor Goldschmied and heuristic play

Goldschmied made many observations of the exploratory play of under-twos in their own homes and during consultancy work in English and Italian day nurseries. She recognised the continued fascination for young children of ordinary objects: the pleasure of playing with saucepans and a wooden spoon.

Goldschmied was concerned about the loss of such natural materials and of meaning for children. She believed parents and practitioners felt obliged to narrow their view of children's learning to the use of bought toys and play equipment. Goldschmied has stressed the importance of materials that support all of children's five senses. However, she has also identified the importance of what she called the '**sixth sense**': children's sensitivity to their own bodily movement and recognition of what physical skills feel like to the child. This idea is very similar to that of proprioception (see page 75).

Elinor Goldschmied developed two kinds of play resource to promote the relaxed exploratory play for under-twos that she called **heuristic play**. The phrase is developed from the Greek word eurisko, meaning 'serves to discover' or 'gain an understanding of'.

- The treasure basket is intended for babies who can sit comfortably with support. The resource includes a range of materials, including safe household items that vary in feel and texture and are presented in a low, open basket for babies to explore however they wish. There is no required list of items. They could include a wooden spoon, safe little containers, a woollen ball, a lemon or other item with scent or a pine cone. Goldschmied intends that adults should sit close and watch, but should not join in or comment on the play.
- Goldschmied further developed her ideas into special play sessions that she introduced into day nurseries. There is a similar emphasis as with the treasure basket on a wide range of natural materials, no commercially made toys and scope for toddlers to play as they wish. Materials can include cardboard and transparent tubes, small and larger containers, large wooden clothes pegs, lengths of metal chain and other safe recycled materials. There should be enough materials that turn taking does not become an issue. As with the treasure basket, the idea is that adults are available, if toddlers want to share their interest. The adults do not direct the play by action or words.

Observation of babies and very young children at play with the treasure basket and heuristic play materials has shown that they can be very absorbed. Watching them in their play puts to rest any myths that young children are unable to concentrate. Peaceful exploration, experimentation and watching are common. Toddlers are absorbed as they place clothes pegs all around a container. They explore putting materials into and out of containers, working out what will fit and how. Sometimes children play at handing each other

THINK ABOUT IT

How may it arise that parents and early years practitioners may overlook or somehow do not count the play of young children, especially under-twos? Is it because:

- the exchanges may be short and 'real play' is supposed to be more sustained.
- toddlers' games sometimes end in minor conflict or actual tears that adults need to manage? Surely a playful exchange does not become 'not play' just because something temporarily went wrong.
- a sense is gained from adult comments that toddlers are not playing 'properly', so it does not count?
- some of the playful exchanges at home such as bouncing on sofas or beds use objects as play equipment when adults would rather they were not?

DEFINITIONS

sixth sense Goldschmied's focus on children's awareness of bodily movement and use of physical skills – similar to proprioception

heuristic play a form of exploratory or discovery play, with suggested materials developed by Elinor Goldschmied

items, often in a repeating sequence. Minor conflict over the materials is rare because there is always plenty from which children can choose.

Different ways of playing

Children's play does not evolve through simple and fixed stages of development. You may still encounter the claim that young children can only move from one kind of play to another as they get older. However, children's development and learning is more subtle than this picture suggests. It is certainly possible to consider broad kinds of involvement in play such as:

- ***solitary play*** in which children are occupied in their own play, without the involvement of others
- ***spectator play*** in which children are on the sidelines, onlookers upon the play of others. Sometimes spectators may be trying to join the play but some children just seem to enjoy watching
- ***parallel play*** when children play side by side, often with similar materials to each other, but with little apparent social participation
- ***co-operative social play*** in which children share toys, talk and play together with complementary role taking.

The simple description of play sometimes promoted is that babies engage in solitary play, toddlers play in parallel or may look on and children of three or more years play co-operatively. Observation of children, as well as a range of studies, confirms that children do not evolve from one stage to another, leaving earlier play behaviour behind.

Two painters have fun together

TRY THIS!

- Watch the play of children older than three years.
- Track an individual child over several hours of a session or day.
- Approximately how much time is spent playing alone, watching others, playing alongside, hovering on the edge of a group and being part of a group?

Babies and toddlers are often more socially involved than a simple stage theory predicts. Three- and four-year-olds do not spend all or even most of their time in co-operative play, and spectator or onlooker play is still a large part of their activity. Some children, of course, will raise your concerns because they seem so rarely to become involved. Yet, if you observe children in a group, you will notice that all of them spend some time watching, often with apparent interest and sometimes as a precursor to finding their way into an ongoing play activity.

Similarly, over-threes can spend as much time in absorbed solitary or parallel play as in co-operative activities. Children often want to play in their own way with materials, perhaps to plan and construct their own building. A helpful adult often needs to enable children in a group to have the space and peace to see through their own play plans.

Other sections of this book discuss different kinds of play through childhood: types of play (page 40), pretend play (Chapter 5) and outdoor play (page 127). The following section considers play and disabled children.

Do disabled children play?

DEFINITIONS

medical model of disability an approach, now largely discredited, that treated disabled children as medical cases. Children's individuality and their play and social needs in childhood risked being lost in specialist treatment of their condition

inclusion the approach that disabled children should, as far as possible and with careful consideration of their disability, be enabled to attend mainstream early years and school provision

Attitudes and practice towards disabled and very sick children has changed dramatically over the last few decades. The previously dominant **medical model of disability** has been challenged by practitioners. Disabled adults have added expert voices to the debate by recalling a childhood in which their choices to be children were restricted. The approach now is of **inclusion** and programmes to support a child's special educational or health needs are far more likely to be required now to fit a model of learning through play.

Micheline Mason is one of a number of disabled adults writing about children or early years practice with the additional perspective of her own childhood memories. She points out:

> The important thing is to get the proportion right. Some children do need physiotherapy, or speech therapy, or carefully designed learning programmes, especially if it will lead to more scope for self-direction later on, but this is nothing to do with the inner drive which directs real play, and should never be allowed to take its place. (Page 5.)

The shift has been resolutely towards a stance that, of course, disabled children play. Furthermore, children who are temporarily sick or have a long-term health condition need to be able to play as well. (See page 130 about play in hospitals.) The challenge to adults is to make the necessary adjustments to play materials and equipment. Any setting needs to ensure that children can easily reach and use play materials (the issue of accessibility).

An important initiative for play was started in the 1970s at the Hester Adrian Centre in the University of Manchester. The researchers subsequently spread around other academic locations. The team's work evolved from their conviction that disabled children could play and that play activities would support their development. Working with parents was an equally valued strand in the research. The team valued close partnership with parents to

GOOD PRACTICE

Children with disabilities or continuing health conditions share all the social, play and learning needs of any other children.

- Of course you need to pay attention to the child's disability or health condition. What changes or adjustments does this require? Talk with the child's parent and continue to be observant when the child has started at your setting.
- Otherwise, you need to ask what do disabled children need as children? In your setting, how can you best enable them to have access to play materials? Do you need to offer support to encourage social contact for children to make their own friends?
- You may need to look at easier access to the setting and corners in your environment. Disabled children will get bored if they cannot reach play materials or make their own choices. Looking at mobility and accessibility for a few children can sometimes create a better play environment for everyone.
- Children with severe learning disabilities will need play materials suitable for a child of younger years. However, they will still get bored if the same range is brought out each day.
- You may need to buy some specialist equipment but many 'special needs' play materials are truly inclusive. Large foam wedges and ball pools have proved to be immense fun for all children.

enable them to become involved and confident in the lives of their disabled sons and daughters. It is important to note that in the 1970s, partnership with parents was not a usual feature of work with children, disabled or not.

Dorothy Jeffree and Roy McConkey (1993) promoted ideas for play that could be undertaken by parents at home and that were grounded in starting with the child's current learning and abilities. The wide range of ideas for play with young disabled children were developed within a philosophy that stressed success and 'can do' rather than 'can't'. Other practitioners have continued in the vein. Roma Lear (1996) has written a number of practical books that focus on the need to play and how to adjust play materials or activities for learning or physical disabilities.

Dorothy Jeffree and Sally Cheseldine (1984) raised the profile of older disabled children. They pointed out that ideas for play and leisure were often overlooked once early childhood was past. Older disabled children were sometimes given nothing to do or only unstimulating activities that would irritate any older child or teenager. Jeffree and Cheseldine made the point that some of the so-called behaviour problems of older disabled children arose from sheer boredom. They described case studies to highlight that disabled young people needed play, enjoyable leisure activities and hobbies that they found interesting.

There are a number of organisations focused on promoting play opportunities for disabled children. Kidsactive has focused on adventure play in particular and has been central in developing adventure playgrounds suitable for disabled children. The Kidsactive team have addressed issues of concern about the balance between appropriate caution and over-protection and their facilities aim to be inclusive, for instance that siblings attend with their disabled brother or sister.

✔ PROGRESS CHECK

1. **Describe three physical ways that a child under one year might explore interesting objects.**
2. **Give two reasons why physical play is so important for children's later development.**
3. **Suggest three reasons why the importance of play for disabled children might be overlooked?**

PLAY IN SCHOOL

There has proportionately been far more researched and written about the play of young children, especially those in the years before statutory school. The reasons for this imbalance seem to be that learning through play is a perspective of early childhood education in Europe and the United States. Most energy has been applied to document evidence for this framework to the learning of young children. Once formal education starts, the focus on learning switches to different methods and outcomes. Of course, children do not stop playing once they enter statutory education. However, the study of their play then tends to focus on:

- breaktimes within the school day and play, therefore, that is restricted to the school grounds
- study of the leisure activities of older children or organised sporting activities
- time spent in after-school care in clubs and playschemes run by play-workers.

Play within school breaktimes

Several research teams have studied children's play within the boundaries of primary school. This research is described in this chapter in terms of the way it illuminates children's play. The studies are also discussed in Chapter 7, because of the implications for a positive adult role in the play of school-age children.

The range of play

Researchers like Peter Blatchford, Sonia Sharp, David Brown and Wendy Titman have built a detailed picture of how children spend their time in school grounds during breaktimes. Observation of what children actually do, and tell researchers they do in play, has shown the great variety around the country. Common games in primary school seem to be:

- football, although this is more a boys' occupation than that of girls
- ball games in general
- chasing, hiding, tag and variations around this basic game
- pretending and fantasy games that may last over days, as children return to them
- dares, including going places in the playground that children are not supposed to go and encouraging activities (climbing trees, walking along the edge of flower beds) that are banned or at least subject to adult disapproval
- games using the playground markings when they exist and playground equipment when it is made available
- conversation and just enjoyably hanging out together with friends.

There seem to be both regional and seasonal differences in how children spend their time in the primary school playground. There are also gender differences in the games of girls and boys and their use of space (see page 92).

Children of school age become more able to understand and follow the rules of active physical games like football or to enjoy simple board games and cards. Many physical games also need a certain level of dexterity, balance and hand-eye co-ordination that is too difficult for younger children. However, slightly older children, who are helped to learn and practise these play skills, then use them in activities with their friends that do not need adult involvement.

The breaktime researchers have not included after-school club activities. However, informal and anecdotal information would suggest that freely

Boys, and girls, need space for ball games

chosen play outside in clubs and playschemes is relatively similar to play in school grounds at breaktime. Clubs and playschemes also offer games organised by adults, as well as a range of indoor activities including table-top and craft activities.

Have 'traditional games' disappeared?

It seems to be an open question whether so-called traditional children's games have disappeared. Adults quite often pronounce on how 'children don't play anymore' or indulge in bouts of nostalgia for some version of the 'good old days'. The same adults are sometimes busy stopping the games that children obviously do want to play in school grounds.

David Brown (1994) points out that adult commentators have been claiming a decline in the range and quality of children's play for close to 100 years. He quotes a leader in *The Times* newspaper written in 1909 and suggests that, 'Such views are frequently based upon the contrast between adults' idealized memories of the games of their childhood and upon the often limited understanding of the games which children are currently playing' (Page 51.)

Games that last and games that evolve

Children still play games with a long history like tag or games with associated chants such as skipping rhymes. However, the restrictions on children of playing out may well have blocked some of the easier handing on between children that happened in earlier generations. Observation of children, combined with what they are willing to tell adults, suggests that invented games with rules are created within friendship groups and sometimes run in school breaktimes or out-of-school play. Some games that are revisited many times can be the older versions of pretend play, with negotiated rules, roles and scripts.

Peter and Iona Opie documented (see also page 7) a very wide range of children's games and associated songs and chants. They carefully recorded the presence of such playful occupations and the fact that 'traditional' games had not only failed to disappear, but have also evolved over time into new versions. However, the Opies were not trying to quantify how often such games were played or to detail the geographical spread of such activities. Research does not exist that could enable one to say authoritatively that 'these kinds of games are played this often in these locations'. Available research gives a useful survey of the range of play.

Peter Blatchford (1989) points out that nostalgia about traditional games and rhymes overlooks the fact they many of these had aggressive or ribald content, as do some modern versions. He describes the game of 'AIDS' that was explained to him by children. This was a chasing game in which the person who was 'it' tried to catch the other players and the only way to escape was to say 'condom'. Whatever you may think of this game, or others that develop in the primary school playground, the way to support children in their play is unlikely to be censoring anything we, now the adults, do not like.

What play means for children

David Brown (1994) describes his research in the late 1980s in two Leicestershire primary schools. The following are the main themes emerging from his study.

- Children identified over 100 different games and activities that they enjoyed in the playground. There was a wide range, although many fell in the broad category of games with shared and understood rules.
- Some of the activities important to the children would not necessarily be classified as games by adults. Older children, like younger ones (see page 61), greatly value just being with and talking with their friends.
- Some games, as defined by children, might have been viewed as reprehensible by adults. One activity, enjoyable for some children who spoke with Brown, depended on interfering with an on-going skipping game of other children.
- Playful activities moved in and out of 'adult' play categories. For instance, a narrative game in which children acted out a story might easily move into rough and tumble, and sometimes into real fighting.
- Preparing for play was just as important to children as the actual play. Choosing the activity and the participants was a significant stage, sometimes with agreed chants or 'dips' and clarifying the rules.
- An important, and delicate, part of football games is the choosing of the teams and the importance for children that they are not left until last.
- An equally important part of play was the search for an appropriate and free space to settle and get on with the game.

The importance of play space(s)

Brown points out that adults can misunderstand children's actions. Children are sometimes on an active search for a play space, when watching adults describe the children as wandering about aimlessly in the playground. Brown's research confirms what children will often say, that spaces and places are important in the school playground (or any other play space).

Brown noticed that children often played a particular game in one location in the playground, the 'right' place for this game. In one primary school, Brown spoke with the parents and grandparents of the current school population. He established that the game 'Round and Round the Stew Pot' had taken place in the same area of this school playground for three generations.

Conflict can also erupt over play space. Large open spaces can actually give rise to more conflict, because the boundaries to different games overlap and so territory becomes an issue. Play is supported, and avoidable conflict reduced when playgrounds have some protected areas. Boundaries can create quiet areas in which social activity and conversation can proceed undisturbed. Corners and seating areas also allow children to gather and to talk. Narrative games often need a corner as the base from which play can begin and small sheltered spaces tend to be preferred for clapping games and individual skipping.

> **TRY THIS!**
>
> - Explore the meaning of play spaces in your setting through being guided by the children. You can try this activity in an early years setting with four-year-olds as well as in a primary school or after-school club.
> - Use one or two methods from the Mosaic approach (see page 62). For example, asking children to take photos of the 'important places' in your setting. Then invite them to walk you round, guided by the photos.
>
> What have you learned from the children?
> - Are there perhaps spaces that could be improved, but from the children's point of view?
> - Are there some spaces that should just be left alone, because they are fine as they are for the children?
> - If there are some spaces that provoke conflict, try a problem-solving approach with the children's full involvement.
> - What is the problem as the children see it? What are the possible solutions and what, over all, seems to be the best solution to which everyone will commit? What will happen now and when will you all review the situation?

Children need space for discussion and planning

The rules of play

Children understand what is going on in most games and can explain to an interested adult, detailing any rules and interpreting the action. Children seem to gain status in the society of the playground when they understand the rules of a game, can interpret to others and correct play behaviour. Temporary status can be gained by bringing in the necessary equipment for a game, but the enhanced status does not seem to last beyond the game itself.

TRY THIS!

Turn to your memories of your own primary school experience.

- How did you and your friends spend your time in the playground?
- What other activities went on that you can remember, but that did not involve you?
- Were there some games or ways of playing that you and your friends liked, but were curtailed by the adults in the playground?
- Were there any activities – play or otherwise – that caused you trouble from other children?
- Did the adults help and in what way? If not, what would you have liked the adults to do for you and your friends?

If possible, share these memories with colleagues or fellow students. What picture emerges and how much variety? Of course, you are dealing with your own selective childhood memories. But what insights does this offer for your approach to children now?

Children usually resolve their own conflicts within a game. Adults who listen and observe see that monitoring the behaviour of the group by the children themselves is an important part of play. It is important to children that everyone 'plays properly' in the context of the game. Some individual children may be regarded as good mediators in play and are appealed to by others to arbitrate in disagreement. Social skills are an issue in the school grounds as much as in early years settings (see page 179).

✔ PROGRESS CHECK

1. **Explain why study of children's play in school may not be the complete picture of their play as older children.**
2. **Suggest three ways in which play is likely to be different for older children in contrast with under-fives.**
3. **Describe two activities that could be important to children but that adults would not call play.**

CHILDREN'S LEISURE ACTIVITIES

Study of the play of children younger than five years of age, or six in the United States, tends to be undertaken in early years settings. Adults are involved in one way or another in determining the environment and creating some boundaries to play. It is likely that young children play differently within their own home than within an early years setting. The home routine is likely to be different, perhaps significantly so, from a nursery or pre-school. The adults are in a different ongoing relationship with the children and have varied adult responsibilities and agendas.

Play with peers

There is limited research information about how children play with their peers, but without adult direction of even observation. There are several practical issues involved.

- It is much easier to plan and run a study in a school, after school or organised leisure setting. Useful insights have been gained from the breaktime studies (see page 81), but we need to recall that this is only part of children's play.
- Furthermore, the very presence of adults watching and listening will change the nature of freely chosen peer play.
- Adults (parent or researchers) can ask children what they do with their friends, but this conversation will probably elicit only part of the story.

TRY THIS!

Compare notes with some friends or colleagues.

- What do you remember doing in your childhood that was really absorbing?
- To what extent was your play risky: low, medium or high risk?
- What enjoyable play activities did you get up to and your parents remained ignorant of what you were doing?

If you think back to your own childhood, some very enjoyable activities probably had an element of risk or of something you were not supposed to be doing. So, you would not have admitted those facts to an adult. It also seems that much of happy peer interaction involves hanging out together, talking and a motley array of activities that are described as 'doing nothing much in particular' to adults.

Less free play nowadays?

Traditionally, children of school age have also been of an age when they spend proportionately more time with their peers out of the sight and control of adults. There is some suggestion within the UK that adult fears for children's safety have restricted this amount of free time. It is claimed that children do not play out as much as they used to do and that peer play has consequently been reduced. There is concern about an increase in more passive and less energetic activities, like watching television and videos or joint computer use.

Anecdotal evidence suggests that such a change has occurred at least to some extent, but objective data are hard to obtain. We probably have to conclude that changes have most likely occurred, but resist firm conclusions as to exactly what they are and how extensive are the changes.

Games organised by adults

Older children have a greater understanding of rules and working together to a shared aim. So, they can become involved in team games such as football, simple cricket and rounders. The advantage of such play for children can be sheer enjoyment, although often tempered with some level of conflict and disagreement and the issues of winning and losing.

Adult approval of team games tends to include an expectation that it will foster co-operation, an ability to work together and some sense of 'team spirit'. An honest appraisal of team games leads to a conclusion that such positive developments are by no means inevitable. Problems arise when adults become over-involved in the success of their team or overlook the subtle skills for children of team playing.

During the 1970s in the UK, team games fell out of favour, because they were judged to be activities that promoted disruptive competitiveness rather than co-operation between children. The pendulum has to an extent swung back with an understanding of the importance of physical exercise for children. There is also more creativity about the kind of games that can be taught.

The issue of skill

A key point is that enjoyable physical activity is much broader than team games. Even if they are taught with sensitivity, competitive team games do not seem to hold the attention of the less-skilled players beyond the time when children or young people have no choice but to be involved at school.

Taught without care, team games can be a depressing experience for some children. They can emerge with their confidence dented and convinced of their own lack of any physical dexterity. Children's health is supported by a longer-term interest in some active physical pursuits. However, some children are encouraged by activities that focus on improvement against their own skills, rather than daunting comparisons with more adept or motivated peers. Sports like yoga or karate can help children and young people to identify their own progress. Skills such as swimming do not have to be taught in a competitive, win-lose team framework. Advanced karate involves structured fights, but neither boys nor girls have to take their skills to that level unless they wish.

TRY THIS!

Undertake an informal survey among friends and colleagues.

- Ask people to share their childhood experiences of team games. What did they play? Was it at school or organised by their family?
- How did they feel about the games: satisfied, keen, daunted, miserable?
- What do they feel they learned from the games experience? In the broadest sense what did they take away with them from those months or years?

Consider the range of experiences you hear.

- To what extent were the aims and expectations of the organising adults met within the actual experience of the children or teenagers?
- What practical implications can you draw for your work with children now?

A balanced approach to team games

There are cultural variations in the approach to team games and sports. Child development texts written for the United States usually include some discussion of Little League Baseball. This national pastime occupies boys from about nine to twelve years of age, and increasingly girls.

Much like competitive team games in the UK, Little League has been promoted as a way to develop co-operative team working, healthy competition and a sense of community. Studies and anecdotal evidence of the Little League activities suggest that some of these positive consequences may result for children who wish to become and stay involved. On the other hand, there are potentially negative consequences for children who are less keen. Their spontaneous enjoyment is reduced by the obligation to practise and to win. The risks are exacerbated when adults' sense of self-esteem, as a team coach or supporting parent, becomes unduly linked to the success of their team. Anecdotal evidence suggests that this risk exists for any competitive sport in which children play and adults are closely involved.

Learning through team games

Team games can be a positive experience for children if adults address their own responsibilities. They have to approach the organisation and running of such activities with an explicit focus on children's learning needs and a decent level of sensitivity to children's self-esteem.

Age-appropriate expectations

Adults – teachers, parents and amateur team coaches – must hold realistic expectations of the physical skills and co-ordination of young children. Boys and girls of under about ten years need to learn and practise the skills and get in tune with their own body and its co-ordination pattern.

Unless they have striking aptitude, six- and seven-year-olds will look 'clumsy' in how they handle a bat, kick or throw a ball. They will become more co-ordinated and find pleasure in their skills if adults create a learning environment in which getting personally better is the genuine focus. Children are daunted when adults approach the task as one of finding out who is 'good' or 'useless' now.

Essential coaching

Children need observant adults who encourage them for their existing skills and home-in on the cutting edge of their learning to improve. They can do this best in fun games when winning and losing is kept in its place. A good environment for learning means proper coaching for skill, masses of encouragement and lively games with plenty of movement.

Is children's play different without adults?

The adult perspective on children's play can be limited, especially when the professional status of the adult tempts them to be non-reflective and strict about what is, or is not, defined as play. Many adults' childhood memories will remind them that children do play differently when out of the sight and hearing of the current generation of responsible adults. The play is not necessarily dangerous or reprehensible, although sometimes it is.

GOOD PRACTICE

These points about support and skills training are broader than just physical games.

- You often need to support children's learning step by step and be ready to tune into what the children have not yet understood.
- Older children can be ready to learn card games, draughts, Monopoly or any game where some understanding of rules and skill is needed. Make sure you are clear about the rules, so you can explain them in simple language.
- Be patient because children will not always understand first time around.
- Be ready to watch and listen. How can you make their task easier when they are struggling?
- Many enjoyable games involve winners and losers. Discuss in your team, how you can all help children to handle disappointment.

CASE STUDY

Supporting physical skills

Drummond Road after-school club runs a regular session from the end of the school day and also organises holiday playschemes. After one half-term playscheme the team discuss how they run games with the children.

Some children had become very disheartened and did not seem to be enjoying the games.

One member of staff shared a useful insight from a recent workshop on coaching children. He explains that, in competitive games with teenagers and adults, the objective is to kick a football or lob a tennis ball in such a way as to make it difficult to kick or hit. The whole point is to make life hard for the other players. However, in games with children, you need to do the precise opposite: kick or throw so that the child has the best chance to connect. The whole point of good coaching is that you support children's confidence and make their task easier, while they need to practise.

This perspective makes sense to the after-school team and they start to explore the whole idea of coaching physical skills. Their aim is not to turn themselves into 'team coaches' but to tap into how children learn. They begin to apply these ideas to games with the after-school club. Staff find that their alertness to what children can currently manage helps the adults to be encouraging about children's growing skills.

1. Look for ways to apply these ideas in your own time with children.
2. You will find some applications, even if you work with children younger than those who go to after-school clubs.

The idea that children's unsupervised play is anarchic, even violent, seems to arise from examples where the play action or themes have truly set adults' hair on end. Research studies and fiction have sometimes fed the myth that children are, by nature, cruel and uncivilised.

Uncontrolled children?

One research study sometimes quoted is the 'Robbers' Cave' experiment run several times by psychologist Muzafer Sherif in America in the 1960s. Sherif was more interested in conflict between groups than children's play. He took eleven-year-olds of very similar social background and put them into different groups. The adults then ran activities designed to make the groups feel intense competition with each other. The children descended fairly quickly into verbal and physical aggression along the artificial group lines. One version of the experiment had a stage in which the adults created a crisis about the water supply. This shared problem brought the warring groups together at least to an extent for the welfare of the whole group. Without this artificial intervention, the competing groups simply became more hostile.

A parallel is sometimes drawn between the Robbers' Cave experiment and the novel *Lord of the Flies* by William Golding, in which a group of shipwrecked children slip into mayhem and murder. There are several problems with this line of argument about the supposed uncivilised nature of children's play when left to their own devices.

The Robbers' Cave groups were manipulated by researchers in order to study conflict and competitive group identity. A sense of shock about what they had provoked even seeps a little through the articles that report the work. Furthermore, it was generally known in academic circles that one unreported study in the series was halted prematurely. The inter-group hostility had become so extreme that the research team was frightened of what they had unleashed. William Golding wrote his novel as a reaction to what he felt was a sentimental and idyllic image of shipwrecked children promoted in *Coral Island* by R.M.Ballantyne. Neither the book nor the Robbers' Cave studies are objective observation of children.

Additionally, as some readers may already be aware, there were no girls in either the research study or the novel. The reaction of a number of young females to whom I have explained the Robbers' Cave experiment and of teenage girls who studied *Lord of the Flies* for GCSE, could well be summed up as, 'Huh, boys!' The point is not of course that female groups do not get involved in conflict; females can become extremely unpleasant, even violent. The key issue is that it is unacceptable to generalise from research that involved only one sex as if both were fully involved.

A further point is that the image of boys as uncaring, semi-savages does not hold up when real life extreme situations are studied. Melvin Konner (1991) described what is known about street children in parts of South America and Africa. Observation of a group of 'los abandonados' (the abandoned ones) on the streets of Guatemala City showed a tough life on the edge of survival. Yet, there was genuine support within the group, with practical organisation and effective protection of the younger boys by the older ones.

✔ PROGRESS CHECK

1. **Suggest two reasons why older children might be less than honest about their play activities out of sight of adults.**
2. **Identify two key points that are essential if children are to learn through organised team games.**
3. **Why should we be sceptical that unsupervised children will get out of control in their play?**

THE PLAY OF BOYS AND GIRLS

There are many similarities between the play of young boys and girls and many differences that can be explained by a child's individual temperament. Yet some broad average differences remain that follow the sex difference between boys and girls. It can be hard to unravel how much of the difference is explained by the biological sex difference and how much by the social role of **gender**.

DEFINITION

gender a word used to describe the social role taken by boys and girls, men and women. Gender differences are shaped by children's learning and cannot all be explained by the biological sex difference of being male or female

Early social learning

Very young children, 18—24 months, can show **gender-stereotyped** preferences over play materials, for instance girls playing more with dolls and boys with trucks. It is difficult, probably impossible, to decipher how much of any average sex difference observed in children's play is biologically determined. The problem arises because many adults treat boys and girls noticeably differently from birth. This differentiation is present in most observed cultures.

DEFINITION

gender-stereotyped
behaviour that follows social expectations about how males and females should behave. Children learn ideas about how boys and girls should play as well as their own expectations about what older children and adults can do

Young children play with whatever resources are available

Adult expectations

In Western society, many adults still choose to dress babies in colours deemed appropriate to their sex. Adults often ask about a baby's sex as the first question. They are often unsettled if asked, in experiments, to relate to a baby or unisex-looking toddler and not told the sex. Young boys and girls seem to be touched differently. The expectation grows in Western culture that boys will want to retreat from the closer affectionate touches and hugs. Some boys may create more distance, but it is hard to distinguish a genuine choice from the message given to many boys that 'big boys' should not want to be mollycoddled.

Parents and relatives often buy toys by gender, even for very young children and will probably step over the gender divide more for a girl than a boy. In early and middle childhood, girls seem to be given more latitude to be 'boyish' than the reverse. Even very early behaviour is judged differently, depending on whether the baby is a boy or girl. Crying girl babies are more likely to be soothed and rocked whereas crying boy babies are more likely to be judged in need of a bounce and physical play.

Adult expectations can shape how children are guided and how their behaviour is received. An older sister's kindness towards a new baby may be seen as evidence of girls' natural motherliness. On the other hand, an older brother's gentleness is interpreted as a sign that he stands out as a 'sensitive' or 'caring' little boy.

CASE STUDY

Gender stereotyping

The reception and nursery team of Croft primary school have become interested in the subtle influences on children about how they should behave as a boy or a girl. The team wish to open children's possibilities, but without pushing them towards interests that do not enthuse the children. Anecdotes collected over a period of weeks help the team to recognise how much pressure is placed on some children.

- Even brief actions by some children are interpreted by adults as gender-appropriate. One three-year-old boy is brought by his grandmother, who seems very concerned that her grandson plays appropriately. Whenever the boy lightly touches a train or moves towards the garage set, his grandmother announces approvingly, 'Now, that's what I like to see. He's a real boy'.
- A mother has spoken in confidence with the staff. Her son asked for a tea set for his birthday and his mother was happy to buy it. She anticipates snide comments from some relatives and wants some ideas on how to counter the criticism.
- The nursery has a well-equipped dressing-up box for pretend play. The team has realised over the years that it is more usual to face parents, especially fathers, who are concerned about their sons in dresses and feather boas. There has rarely been any concern about 'cross dressing' for girls.
- The team has also tried to become more aware of their own behaviour. In sensitive discussion, practitioners have reflected that it is too easy to express mild surprise that a girl is enthusiastic about a lorry or that a boy has the patience to sit and complete a jigsaw.

1 How do you think the nursery and reception team could best use the ideas they have collected?
2 You could listen and watch in your own setting.

TRY THIS!

Look around some large toy stores and consider how play materials and sets are promoted. Toys are less rigidly gender-stereotyped than they used to be, but messages about the likely child player still abound. Who is featured on the box or packaging of the following:

- dolls, dolls' equipment and dolls' houses
- garages, cars and transport
- construction sets of different kinds
- soldiers, soldier dolls and fighting equipment
- astronauts and space play items
- domestic equipment such as cookers, cleaners or tea sets?

What messages do you think that the images give to children who look at and choose the toys and to the adults who pay?

Children watch too

As well as direct and indirect guidance, young children often observe that adults have gender-specific roles in daily life. Society is not as sharply divided as it was several generations ago, but domestic chores still appear to be relatively gender-stereotyped. Children import their observations into their pretend play. So, it is hardly surprising that socio-dramatic play in the home corner tends to have some fairly clear-cut gender roles. Even children whose parents have worked very hard to cross gender roles can find that more rigid roles are absorbed from outside the home and into the children's play.

Whatever the exact sources for the behaviour, boys observed in early years settings are often, but not always, the noisier ones. Boys, given the choice, tend to develop more energetic physical play including rough and tumble. Their pretend play themes are more likely to include conflict and lively physical exchanges. This important issue for practice is further discussed from page 172 in terms of a positive adult role.

Gender differences from middle childhood

Children in primary school tend to play with their own sex and such divisions can be seen in nursery as well. It is not only that boys and girls often play different kinds of games. Older children who cross the gender lines are likely to be teased by their own and the other sex.

Play observed within boundaries such as school grounds tends to show the following characteristics.

- Girls tend to play in smaller groups than boys and to spend less time in the more competitive team games.
- It is the boys who usually play football in school playgrounds, although girls do get involved sometimes. When adults organise other team games such as cricket or netball, the gender split seems to be less stark.
- Girls play games with rules, such as skipping games and there is a competitive feel. However, girls tend to be competing against other children's scores, for instance, a count of how many skips, rather than the direct game-centred competition of football.
- Girls more than boys tend to talk more with each other as part of interaction, or as the central point of a social group.
- Boys do talk together; they are certainly not all 'strong silent types'. Boys negotiate the rules of play and organise teams. They also talk about shared interests, but school-age boys seem to have taken on the social learning that males do not talk about feelings.

Play among children is not utterly segregated and you will see mixed groups in school playgrounds, parks and in family homes.

Do girls and boys stop playing?

George Bernard Shaw said, 'We do not stop playing because we grow old, we grow old because we stop playing.' It is an open question whether some grown-up children ever stop playing. Perhaps it depends on your definition of play.

- Some adults are highly enthusiastic about collecting and playing with dolls' houses, model railway layouts and small scale cars or aeroplanes that can be radio-controlled.
- Are sporting activities still play? What about exercise classes and similar leisure and recreation?
- Some parents show every sign of enjoyably playing with their children in the park or on the beach and building sandcastles.

- Amateur dramatics are a natural development from 'let's pretend'.
- Some groups enjoy re-enacting historical battles and this activity also involves dressing up and shared fantasy.
- The fun of the dressing-up box continues with some social groups for whom a striking fashion style flags up a shared identity.

CASE STUDY

Adult play

Certainly, it does not seem too late in adulthood to start playing. Stoneway nursery school has worked to offer support to isolated parents and to make them welcome in the nursery. It has emerged that some of the parents had a relatively deprived childhood. They are very keen that their children do not lose out in the same way.

The nursery team tried a few sessions in which parents joined in with their children in construction and craft activities. Some parents found it hard to focus on their own children and seemed in many ways to be making up for lost time from their own childhood. On several occasions adults were almost in competition with the children for resources and the nursery team's attention.

The nursery team discussed this experience and decided that adult play and craft workshops would be appropriate. Several sessions have now been run. Parents gain the opportunity to explore and play themselves and to make links to how play can support their children.

1. What do you think will be important to make 'adult play workshops' positive?
2. What will be important in making them effective?

✔ PROGRESS CHECK

1. **Describe why it is so difficult to explain differences in the play of boys and girls just through biological differences.**
2. **Describe three broad ways in which the play of boys can be different from that of girls.**
3. **Suggest three ways in which adults may continue to play.**

KEY TERMS

You need to know the meaning of the following words and phrases. Go back through the chapter to make sure you understand them:

gender
gender-stereotyped
heuristic play
inclusion
medical model of disability
proprioception
sixth sense

FURTHER READING

Blatchford, Peter (1989) *Playtime in The Primary School: Problems and Improvements*, Routledge

Blatchford, Peter and Sharp, Sonia (eds) (1994) *Breaktime and the School: Understanding and Changing Playground Behaviour*, Routledge

Both of these books offer a useful insight into children's play and adult perceptions of the play in school time.

Brown, David (1994) 'Play, the playground and the culture of childhood' in Moyles, Janet (ed) (1994) *The Excellence of Play*, Open University Press

A collection of valuable chapters taking a different perspective on children's play in a range of social and cultural settings.

Goddard Blythe, Sally (2000) 'Mind and body' in *Nursery World*, 15 June 2000)

This article describes the importance of physical skills in overall development.

Jeffree, Dorothy and Cheseldine, Sally (1984) *Let's Join In*, Souvenir Press

Ideas for the play and leisure needs of older disabled children.

Jeffree, Dorothy and McConkey, Roy (1993 second edition) *Let Me Play*, Souvenir Press

Practical ideas for play at home with disabled children.

Lear, Roma (1996 fourth edition) *Play Helps: Toys and Activities for Children with Special Needs*, Butterworth Heinemann

One of several books by Lear that offer practical ideas for play with disabled children.

Mason, Micheline (1993) *Inclusion, the Way Forward*, National Early Years Network

Practical suggestions about play for disabled children that recognises their needs as children as well as any special needs.

Petrie, Pat (1987) *Baby Play: Activities for Discovery and Development During the First Year of Life*, Century Hutchinson

A practical book for parents and carers mainly in a home setting. The ideas and illustrations demonstrate that babies do play.

CHAPTER 5

Let's pretend

PREVIEW

The key topics covered in this chapter are:

- Young children and pretend play
- Complex pretend play
- Pretend play and children's thinking
- Adult concerns about pretend play.

Children play in many different ways and with a range of interests, themes and equipment. You will find descriptions of different kinds of play throughout this book. This chapter is focused on **pretend play,** because this particular kind of children's play has sometimes been seen as more important than other types. Pretend play has also been presented as especially vital for the development of children's thinking.

> **DEFINITION**
>
> **pretend play** the play of children from very young characterised by the presence of imagination and that children act as if something or someone is other than is the case in reality

This chapter considers the development of pretend play from very early childhood and the links with other aspects of children's development. Complex pretend play is explored in terms of the nature of children's play and the possible involvement of adults in that play. The chapter finally considers the dilemmas when adults are concerned about play themes.

YOUNG CHILDREN AND PRETEND PLAY

On balance, probably more research and discussion has been dedicated to trying to explain the development of pretend play than, say, physical play. There is increasing interest now in physical play and learning outdoors (see page 125). The imbalance has probably arisen from Jean Piaget's great interest in play as symbolic of children's thinking (see page 28).

Terminology

A number of phrases are used when talking about pretend play.

- ***Pretend or imaginative play*** is usually used to cover the wide range of play themes and action that are dependent on the premise of 'Let's pretend' or 'I'm pretending'. Pretend play always has a quality of 'as if', because children transform what is in front of them.
- ***Symbolic play*** is used as a term to highlight that children in their play are deliberately making one object stand in for, or symbolise, another.
- The term ***socio-dramatic play*** is used more for the pretend play of children older than toddlers who develop make-believe games in which several involved children take on agreed roles.
- ***Fantasy play*** is sometimes used to distinguish between pretend that draws on re-enactments of everyday life that children observe and the play that is based on non-real characters experienced from stories or television.

Different terms are less important than observation and description of what children do, although it is useful for you to be alert to the different phrases you may encounter in discussion. In this chapter the general term 'pretend play' will be used, because those words sum up what is happening. Other terms will be used when the section refers to specific terms used by named researchers.

The beginnings of pretend play

Once young children are clear about how an object usually fits into everyday life, they become able to manipulate their world through ideas. They can pretend that one object is temporarily something else. This development in play seems to be linked with children's growing language skills. Such skills in turn represent impressive shifts in young children's ability to think about their world and their own part in it.

Observation of babies and toddlers has highlighted links between how they play and their early use of communication and spoken language.

TRY THIS!

If possible, make observations of the same babies or toddlers over a matter of months. Every few weeks, make some detailed notes about the children's communication and their play in line with the ideas given earlier.

- What patterns do you observe as you watch and listen to a baby or a toddler? Note that the ages given are within a range and individual children will vary.
- Gather examples that are individual to these children in terms of their words and their play interests.
- If you observe a toddler whose language is a little later than average, does he or she follow a similar route for play, although also a little later?

When children play by:	They will probably:	At about this age:
exploring objects and people close at hand	communicate with gestures and sounds	0–10 months
relating one object with another in play	produce many patterns of sound	9–15 months
simple pretend actions applied only to them	say first words	11–18 months
simple pretend actions that involve other people and toys	say two-word combinations or short phrases	12–30 months
sequences of pretend play and other play involving other people and play materials	say three-, four- or five-word sentences	19–36 months

The early development of pretend play

Young children develop pretend play in different ways. They obviously also have different interests, depending on their individuality as well as the play materials that are made available for them. You will observe different kinds of pretending by very young children under two years.

The first pretend play actions are usually fleeting and you can miss them easily. A toddler will use a toy spoon to pretend to feed himself or a brush and pretend to brush his hair, not touching his head.

A young baby watches closely

Pretend play is at first directed by toddlers at themselves, but soon they pretend with someone or something else. Qualities are projected onto an object and the pretend play depends on this representation. An example would be that Teddy is treated as alive, with emotions and needs similar to the young child. Teddy may be fed, cared for and sung to sleep. Some young children use a teddy or some other toy to speak on their behalf and to express feelings or anxieties.

First of all, toddlers make a direct replacement of one object by a pretend representation. For instance, a child pretends that a brick is a car and shows this shift by moving the brick around and making car noises. Then they start to experiment with completely pretend actions with no object replacement at all. An example would be when toddlers pretend to drink but have nothing in their hands, the cup is imaginary. Or they may brush their hair with a non-existent brush. Perhaps they look at their parent or carer and grin. This play now depends on an understanding between the child and others that could be summed up as, 'You know that I know that you know that this is all just pretend'.

Toddlers become able to direct the pretend actions through another object. So perhaps one doll is made to feed or comfort another one, with the toddler determining and stage directing all the actions, probably accompanied by appropriate sounds and words.

When children are two years or more, you will observe some complex imagination. Some pretence involves imagining the existence of something or someone else. Pretend play may require pretending that there are monsters in the garden. Some children have an imaginary friend, often lasting months or years. Of course, some young children imagine creatures that frighten them. You are unlikely to be sure that this development has happened until children put their ideas or concerns into words.

EXAMPLE

Diary extracts 3

Here are some highlights from the diary I kept of my son. These examples show that by two and a half years of age, Drew was engaging in a range of pretend play.

- He played imaginatively with dolls, teddies and a doll-sized bed.
- He used the Fisher Price™ dolls' house with its small scale people, to some of whom he gave names. The fire truck and its fire officers came to tea at the house.
- He built with his set of wooden bricks. A line of bricks became 'a high wall', of significance to him as a keen climber. Another line became 'a train with a man'.
- He played with water at the sink and his words and actions explained that he was 'cooking'.
- He used his store of home-made play dough to do pretend cooking. But also the piles of dough became a source of danger for the Fisher Price™ figures. The one he called 'Daisy' came to grief in the dough and had to be rescued, but she was sometimes the rescuer.
- He used toy pots, pans and a cardboard box cooker, cooking with a store of conkers and wooden bricks.
- Several large wall cushions became at different times a wall, a castle or train tracks. His pink quilt usually acted as the water.

1. Build up some of your own examples from young children you know well.
2. Observe how the pretend play of young children is varied, depending on their interests and experience.

✔ PROGRESS CHECK

1. Give two examples of what could be very early pretend actions by a young child.
2. In what way is 'fantasy' play usually different from simple pretend play?
3. Suggest two ways in which the pretend play of a 2–3 year old might be completely in the imagination.

Toddlers are often busy pretending

COMPLEX PRETEND PLAY

There are no firm age boundaries and the development of pretend play follows different patterns with individuals. However, the shift around three years or so is towards pretend play in interaction with other children. This play takes on the characteristics of what is usually meant by the term **socio-dramatic** play. Younger children may join in the play (see page 106).

The nature of socio-dramatic play

Children can have complex pretend play sequences, complete with roles and negotiated scripts, to which they return over the days and weeks, often with the same group of friends.

Pretend play can incorporate roles and activities that children have observed and understood, or partly understood from the adult world. Themes may be taken from family domestic routines such as cooking, cleaning and baby care. Children also build in work roles that may be relevant to their parents, such as being a nurse or an office worker and having meetings. However, some play will draw on wider sources of jobs that may be observed on the street like police or fire officers. Children's experience may be broadened through visits such as to health clinics or drawn from the illustrations of books.

Children may create settings from recycled material such as cardboard boxes. An indoor corner or outdoor covered area may change from one

Small world pretend play with dinosaurs is fun

DEFINITIONS

socio-dramatic play the pretend play of children older than 3—4 years in which they develop make-believe games with agreed roles and plans for actions and words

small world play the term sometimes used to describe pretend play with miniature people, animals and settings that are made to scale with the figures

fantasy play the term often used to describe pretend play in which the characters are drawn from fiction, television or video stories

setting to another over time. Some settings will be full child size, like running a café or a car breakdown service. Other settings will be smaller scale, using miniature figures in a dolls' house, farm or garage in what is sometimes called **small world play**.

Children draw on wide source material. Their own observations are important and adults can be surprised, even embarrassed, at the subtle detail of what children see and hear, then build into their play. Children may imitate words and a tone of voice. Yet, their verbal and non-verbal exchanges are creative and certainly not limited to straight copies of the adult world. Children are able to step in and out of role, in order to guide, negotiate and sometimes argue about how the scene should unfold.

Children's language and cognitive skills, as shown in socio-dramatic play, are impressive. They discuss, consider possibilities, negotiate who will play what role, including a rough script. They draw from previous experience in a 'what if?' sense and reshape ideas according to the interests of the group of children. Themes are recalled and the action often started another day from the point at which the scenario finished.

Children also draw from favourite books, television programmes, films and videos. This type of pretend play is sometimes called **fantasy play**, since the source material is removed from ordinary life. Over the years, some of the fantasy play sources have concerned adults. Staff in nurseries and pre-schools have judged that the material is more aggressive than energetic, or includes themes contrary to the value that the adults wish to promote, often related to gender stereotyping. The areas and forms of play that concern adults (mainly female) are far more often those enthusiastically promoted by the boys. The issues of play and gender, including questions of good practice are discussed from page 110.

TRY THIS!

Over a period of weeks, gather observations about the pretend play themes of three- or four-year olds that you know well.

- What is(are) the main theme(s)? Observe carefully until you understand.
- What roles do the children take and how much do they exchange roles?
- Is the play limited to a small defined group of children, or do individuals come and go?
- What equipment, if any, do the children use?
- Do they have a preferred area in your setting for this play? How much space do they need? Is it indoors, outdoors or either?
- Are adults welcome in the play? If so, in what kind of roles?

CASE STUDY

Television viewing

In Fairham day nursery, the children have an agreed amount of television viewing within the day. Watching a morning or afternoon programme suitable for children is part of the day's activities and often forms a peaceful, sit down time. Children are also allowed to bring in a video of their choice and on some days a video is watched. Every child has their choice over the weeks.

The team who work with the 3—5 year olds have listened with interest as a programme or video has led to deep discussions between children about how they will play at being these characters. Conversations range about who will be which character and how the story they have just watched will be developed for their play. The staff join in as appropriate and when invited.

1. Television and video can be a good source of ideas for children. The disadvantages of this media develop from long hours of unselective viewing. How do you handle television as a medium in your setting?
2. Some children may need to take a more active approach to television if it is to support their play. In what ways do you use television as a source of conversation with children?

Toddlers' involvement in complex pretend play

Younger children tend not to initiate complex pretend play, but they can be happily involved when playing in mixed age groups. Most of the research on pretend play has been undertaken in settings like nurseries or pre-schools, that are organised with a narrow age band. Observation within family and friendships networks confirms that mobile toddlers are often involved, once they can be given a play role and accept instructions from older siblings or friends.

THINK ABOUT IT

- **The impression that complex pretend play only ever involves children older then three years has arisen from the limitations of research studies.**
- **It is a timely reminder that our knowledge can sometimes by constrained by adult boundaries. In this case, much of the research has been undertaken in nursery education settings and in narrow age-banded groups, rather than family home settings.**
- **Think about whether you or your colleagues may be making assumptions about what and how children play, just because you keep the age groups fairly separate in your setting.**

Children's awareness of pretend

Pretend play is judged to be so valuable for children, because they can weave in their past experience and that of other children. They are able to reflect on and handle a great deal of information. By three and four years of age, children show a high level of awareness of what they are doing in pretend. Wood and Attfield (1996) point out:

> ... play is not just about fantasy. It doesn't have a life of its own which is divorced from reality. Children continuously weave in and out of their play their knowledge, skills and understanding learned in the other areas of their lives. (Page 4.)

Vivian Paley (1988) explains that she has recorded children's fantasy play:

> ... because it is the main repository for secret messages, the intuitive language with which children express their imagery and logic, their pleasure and curiosity, their ominous feelings and fears. (Page vii.)

In her observational research of the nursery year documented in *Bad Guys Don't Have Birthdays*, Paley shows through verbatim descriptions of play how the children direct the action. They step in and out of role, deal with fears and rework them, sometimes bringing them under control within the play. Paley describes how she gives the children's fantasy themes space for development within their own stories told and developed out loud. Paley provided a time each day when children could dictate stories for the record. Early years practitioners are sometimes resistant to commercial figures and pretend play arising from them (see also page 149). So, it is striking that Paley accepted how the children wove the favourite cartoon and book figures of that time into their play

Paley offers examples of children's active direction of their play, how they negotiate, re-negotiate and create rules and roles. An example follows from *Bad Guys Don't Have Birthdays*, but there are many similar descriptions in Paley's other books:

> 'A lion's going to eat you Carrie,' Margaret says.
> 'Why?'
> 'Because you're not under the blanket.'
> Emily responds immediately to the new storyline, 'Put your feet in, sister. A lion is coming.'
> 'The lion will eat you up,' Mollie says, 'and then you'll be a brand new baby again. Just close your eyes, Carrie.'
> 'Pretend that lion already ate me up. Pretend I'm a new baby right now'. (Page 49.)

Jane Hislam (1994) also emphasises the deliberate quality of children's pretend play, that they are very aware of what they are doing. She makes the valid point that:

> Young children are often said to blur fantasy and reality but it is the adults who tend to confuse the two. Adults are apt to take too literally what is actually a far more flexible and non-literal process ... 'Now you have a broken leg and I'll make it better', my daughter exhorted her friend as they repeatedly reworked the scenario in the wake of a real broken leg event. (Page 44.)

TRY THIS!

- Watch and listen to the children in your setting.
- Gather examples that you observe to show how the children move in and out of the pretend play themes.
- Make some descriptive notes of what they say and how you feel this shows their ability to work with the pretend element.

EXAMPLE

Choosing to pretend

Young children show they have understood the essence of pretending. In my diary notes of my daughter, by 2:1 Tanith would say something she knew to be untrue, such as somebody's name, would laugh and say, 'Just pretend' or 'Just teasing'.

Older children can step in and out of pretend play, sometimes to guide their playmates but sometimes adults. I recall learning early in my career about appropriate adult behaviour from a kindly four-year-old. I was going somewhat over the top joining in with her cake making in the sand tray. She looked at me with slight concern and said, 'It is pretend, you know'. Her expression suggested that she feared this over-enthusiastic adult beside her might just eat the 'cake'.

- Why not gather examples from your own experience of how children show through their words that they make an active choice to pretend.

Do children pretend in all cultures?

Almost all of the research on pretend play has been undertaken in industrialised countries and in organised settings prior to statutory school. The few

Generations of children have played at dressing up

studies of this kind of play in non-industrialised countries have tended to find that pretend play usually draws closely on the adult models of daily life. Figures of pure fantasy are less likely if children do not have access to television, video, film or books with such characters. The absence of such flights of total imagination does not make the children's play any less rich, although some commentators seem to imply this difference.

Clare Elliott (1992) notes:

> Dressing up as pirates and dragons, and building whole make-believe worlds is very common with children in Western culture. However, in many other societies make-believe is almost never seen. In rural Indian villages there is a great deal of chasing, teasing and galumphing around amongst children, but rarely elaborate fantasy play. Children carefully copy adult behaviour. Caring for a doll or stalking lizards with a bow and arrow is preparation for work, as they watch what their parents do all day in the fields and forest. (Page 35.)

Elliott seems to be drawing a line between complete fantasy and pretend play that imitates observed actions in daily life. The wilder fantasies in play need some sources and children in the Western world draw on books, along with the visual media of cartoons, television and video. However, Elliott draws a contrast between make-believe and imitative play when the skills are those that a child will use in later childhood or adulthood. From a child's perspective, these may be points on a continuum rather than separate categories. The child caring for a doll or making play lorries (see page 13) is engaging in pretend play.

Melvin Konner (1991) describes the play he observed in Kung children, whose society is a hunter-gatherer community:

> One group of three-, four- and five-year-olds I observed among the Kung were using clumps of earth to represent hyenas. The 'hyenas' surrounded a hapless goat, represented in turn by a root. 'Pudi zaha ki' they shouted gleefully over and over – 'The goat's already dead'. Thus they acted out the drama of competition, hunting, killing and survival around which they knew their lives turned. (Page 176.)

THINK ABOUT IT

Adults – researchers, writers, practitioners – have become very engaged in children's pretend play and what it means for their more general learning. The risk then arises that adults may judge different kinds and sources of pretend play in an evaluative way. They may judge that some play is richer or more 'proper' pretend play, or that flights of imagination reflected in play have to draw on material acceptable to the adults.

Children in traveller families

The outlook of families within traditional traveller communities can show that distinct views of children's learning and the place of play can exist within one society. Traveller families vary of course and some families are relatively new to the travelling way of life. The more traditional approach regards childhood as an apprenticeship for adulthood, not as a stage separate from the rest of life. In this way some traveller families have much in common with families from cultural backgrounds where learning through play is not a familiar or necessarily admired concept.

Traveller children may be adept at life skills that their peers from settled families only explore through pretend play and toys. Children are likely to learn the real care of younger siblings and not solely from doll play. They start to take responsibility for looking after animals or stripping down scrap material. Some travellers divide family work along clear cut gender lines. So, you may find that girls learn childcare and other domestic tasks and the boys learn about dealing with scrap metal and working with the horses. Such division can sit uncomfortably with early years and playwork values about blurring rather than accentuating gender lines.

The play of traveller children reflects their particular experience. In the limited area of even a large caravan, children have to learn a careful use of space and avoid wastage of water. Different ways of cooking and storage will be reflected in their play in a home corner if they attend nursery or playgroup and, like any children, they re-create their home.

Do children stop pretending?

Jean Piaget saw play as central to the egocentric (self-centred) thinking of children younger than six or seven years (see page 28). He linked play very closely to his view of intellectual development. Consequently, Piaget assumed that pretend play should give way in middle childhood to the rule-bound play integral to board games and organised sport. The complex pretend play, that can be observed in young children and younger primary-school-age children, does seem to disappear to an extent. However, there are some indications that it is probably just less obvious to adults — see the discussion of play of school-age children on page 81.

Children certainly do not stop pretending, but they do seem to take on board that other forms of play are socially more acceptable to adults. Lively, role-based games still develop in welcoming school grounds and in children's own homes. Pretending also has a form of expression in written work and more formal drama. Teenagers, and adults too, exercise the sense of 'let's pretend' through direct involvement in amateur dramatics and the fun of dressing up for themed parties. Pretending is also necessary for the suspension of disbelief involved in watching drama on television, film or the theatre.

✔ PROGRESS CHECK

1. **Suggest three sources for the themes of children's complex play.**
2. **Describe two ways in which children could demonstrate their ability to move in and out of pretend play.**
3. **Explain possible risks when adults want to evaluate and judge the themes and content of children's pretend play.**

PRETEND PLAY AND CHILDREN'S THINKING

Three- to five-year-olds can show sophisticated thinking through the window of their pretend play.

Thinking power and pretend

Two areas are especially stressed by observers interested in how children handle information and ideas. As adults, you may need to think carefully to appreciate what children are managing.

DEFINITIONS

metamemory means the deliberate transfer of strategies and skills between different tasks and problems. It is a skill of active use of ideas and ways of thinking already stored in the memory

metacognition means children's aware and conscious work on problem solving and their use of existing ideas and knowledge

Metamemory

Children are deliberately using the contents of their memory. The term **metamemory** means the deliberate transfer of strategies and skills between different tasks and problems. If you watch and listen to children, they will show and say how they recall other times and play themes. They are consciously bringing the previous ideas to bear on the current situation.

Metacognition

Children use their knowledge and ideas in a conscious way in play. **Metacognition** describes how children are able to participate in problem solving and draw on their previous experience and learning. In pretend play, and other forms of play, you will see children predict the consequences of an action or event. They check the results of an action (Did it work?), monitor on-going activity (How am I doing?), engage in reality testing (Does this make sense?) and they co-ordinate and control their deliberate attempts to solve problems.

Of course, children's impressive thinking and memory skills do not always result in the solving of a problem, nor in complete agreement over pretend play scripts and roles.

Socio-dramatic play and thinking

Sara Smilansky explored what she called socio-dramatic play as a direct challenge to Piaget's approach to children in the framework of cognitive incompetence (see page 28). Smilansky especially opposed Piaget's conviction that children younger than six or seven years of age could not handle

Children bring what they know to their pretend play

abstract ideas. She claimed, and supported her views through observation of play, that children played with meanings and ideas from a young age. She stressed that sophisticated levels of thinking could be observed in socio-dramatic play.

Smilansky identified six elements that she felt were characteristic of socio-dramatic play and that demonstrated the sophistication of children's thinking.

- ***Role play through the process of imitation***: children undertook make-believe roles that were expressed both through action and words.
- ***Make-believe in regard to objects***: children used physical movements or verbal declarations to substitute for the real objects.
- ***Make-believe in regard to actions and situations***: verbal descriptions could be made to substitute for the action that was identified in words.
- ***Persistence in the role play***: that genuine socio-dramatic play (as defined by Smilansky) produced episodes of at least ten minutes duration.
- ***Interaction in the play***: the episode involved at least two players.
- ***Verbal communication***: there was interaction in words related to the play episode.

Smilansky worked in Israel and the United States during the 1960s and 1970s. She observed that children from disadvantaged homes were far less likely to engage in socio-dramatic play. The problem seemed to be that children had not received sufficient adult attention and personal communication. The children did not have the experience and skills to start complex pretend play.

Smilansky judged that this lack put the children at further disadvantage when they entered the school system, because they lacked the skills that their peers had been able to develop through play. Smilansky considered that socio-dramatic play promoted:

- creativity in children as they drew on their past experience and reworked it within the boundaries of a play scenario
- intellectual growth through experience of thinking about ideas and handling knowledge, beyond what was just in front of children
- social skills within the give and take of socio-dramatic play, with the development of tolerance and consideration.

THINK ABOUT IT

Sara Smilansky made significant claims for the importance of socio-dramatic play in supporting children's development. To what extent do her claims make sense on the basis of your experience with children?

Socio-dramatic play and play tutoring

Smilansky extended her exploration of socio-dramatic play to claim that children's intellectual competence could be enhanced through this type of play, especially when the children came from socially disadvantaged backgrounds.

The next step taken by Smilansky was to propose that this form of play should be taught to disadvantaged children by adults to avoid the loss of such experience. She developed a method called **play tutoring** in which adults initiated role play with small groups of children. They then helped them to sustain and develop the play themes over time. Four variations were used within the play tutoring format.

DEFINITION

play tutoring an intervention programme designed by Sara Smilansky in which adults helped children to learn the skills necessary for socio-dramatic play

- ***Modelling***: an adult joined in and acted out a role in pretend play, for instance that of a doctor. The advantage was anticipated to be in enhancement of the play and in sharing knowledge about what a real doctor does.

- ***Verbal guidance***: the adult did not actually join in the play but made comments and suggestions from the sidelines.
- ***Thematic fantasy training***: children were helped to act out familiar story dramas, for which the plot was usually known in advance.
- ***Imaginative play training***: children were trained by an adult in the skills to support fantasy play, such as using finger puppets or how to pretend it is a rainy day.

In a series of studies by Smilansky and her colleagues, the play tutoring approach did increase the extent to which children explored socio-dramatic play, especially when their level of such play was low at the outset. The increased socio-dramatic play was maintained after the play tutoring stopped. Children in the play tutoring group, in comparison with a control group, also showed an improvement in their social and intellectual skills. Smilansky presented the findings as an endorsement of the power of play tutoring and the essential nature of socio-dramatic play for children's learning.

THINK ABOUT IT

Peter Smith's research highlights a practical point for anyone in early years or school settings. Children appreciate attention and the support that comes from adults who stay close and become closely engaged, as appropriate, in children's activities. The activities themselves are relevant, but adult behaviour supportive for children's learning appears to have a broader impact than the particular activities of the time.

Lessons from the play tutoring studies

The picture was not quite that straightforward however. Peter Smith (1994) described other research, including those studies undertaken in the 1980s by his own research team. His main points are as follows.

- Smilansky had overlooked the possible impact of increased adult attention. She had assumed the whole effect was caused by the socio-dramatic play that she believed to be so crucial.
- In Smilansky's research, the children in the play tutoring groups must have received a great deal of adult conversation and encouragement.
- In contrast, the reports of Smilansky's studies present the adult role in the control groups (no play tutoring) as fairly passive.
- So, it was not genuinely possible to know how much of the effect was caused by play tutoring itself and how much was the impact of interested adult attention for children.

Peter Smith undertook a number of studies designed to check this uncertainty and he reviewed other research. In one study by Smith's team, children in nursery classes were given a full term of either play tutoring or skills training. Observation was undertaken to check that the adults' level of contact and verbal communication was equivalent in each group. Children showed improvements in the play tutoring groups, but the skills training groups showed similar improvements on measures of intellectual and language development. Several other studies, that allowed for the amount of adult attention, also found that close involvement with children was important, rather than a specific effect of play tutoring.

The careful research of Peter Smith and others challenged Smilansky's claims for the exclusive impact of play tutoring, but the results are far from negative. The studies confirm the importance of involved and attentive adults and the value of supporting children's learning through play. There is no sense of discouraging either socio-dramatic play or play tutoring as such. The research points out the need for a sober approach to claims about the essential role of one kind of play and one type of adult involvement.

TRY THIS!

Consider and discuss with your colleagues the practical lessons you could take from the discussion about socio-dramatic play in this section. You might discuss possible changes in your daily practice. Or you could highlight your current good practice in close attention to children in their play.

Pretending may support problem solving

The ability to engage in 'let's pretend' seems to help children to make sense of some logical problem-solving situations, such as those posed in the exploration of Piaget's ideas.

M.G. Dias and Paul Harris offered two versions of a logical problem to children between four and six years of age.

- In each exchange the problem was the same: 'All fishes live in trees. Tot is a fish. Does Tot live in the water?'
- In one version the adult presented the problem to children in a matter-of-fact tone of voice.
- In the second version, the adult started by saying, 'Let's pretend I'm from another planet' and continued to present the problem in the kind of dramatic voice that is used for story telling.

There were striking differences between the two groups. Those in the 'matter-of-fact' group made many errors of logic, holding to their knowledge that fishes lived in water. However, the children who were in the 'let's pretend' group stepped outside their knowledge and were far more successful in reasoning their way to the point that Tot did not live in the water. The children made comments like, 'We're pretending that fishes live in trees'.

Dias and Harris seemed to have found an effective way, through the pretend-play scenario, to enable young children to solve a logical, yet nonsensical, problem at an age when Piaget argued they were not intellectually able. This research is reported in academic journals but a more accessible source can be found on page 369 in Cole, Michael and Cole, Sheila (1996) *The Development of Children*, W.H. Freeman.

✔ PROGRESS CHECK

1. **Explain three ways in which complex pretend play could support other areas of children's development.**
2. **Describe briefly how Smilansky overlooked the importance of close adult involvement with children in the apparent impact of play tutoring.**
3. **Suggest how 'let's pretend' might enable a child to step back in thoughts and words from a problem of logic.**

ADULT CONCERNS ABOUT PRETEND PLAY

Adult enthusiasm for the value of pretend play has some boundaries. For some time, early years practitioners have had serious doubts about the value of some kinds of play content and roles. Children are often not given free choice in using their powers of thinking and memory in application to pretend play themes.

Gender and pretend play

Jane Hislam (1994) described some of the dilemmas arising from a home corner, if early years practitioners who are usually female do not observe and reflect on what is happening. Hislam suggests that despite the renaming of the 'Wendy corner' as the 'home corner', this area can still be seen and treated as girls' territory. Girls sometimes chase boys out of the home corner and those who stay have to fit into the domestic play that predominates in this space. Some boys' involvement in the home corner can seem inappropriate to sensitive adults. Perhaps the boys sit about being waited on, but this behaviour will reflect what some children see at home.

These children take tea together in the home corner

Subjective adult evaluations?

Practitioners sometimes judge that boys are less involved in socio-dramatic play, just on the basis that they do not enjoy the home corner. Alternatively some boys' games may focus on actively disrupting the home corner scenarios. Hislam and other commentators have pointed out that such an adult outlook is very restrictive. Furthermore, the creation of other socio-dramatic possibilities or a change of scenario in the home corner can bring about significant changes in the boys' play behaviour.

War play or just pretend?

Guns and weapons play give rise to strong emotions in early years settings. Teams often have deeply held reservations about aggressive forms of play and socio-dramatic themes. The prevailing policy in early years and schools for some time has been to ban toy guns and discourage aggressive or war play to the point of stopping it within the setting. Furthermore, this ban on war and weapons play has frequently been extended to any kind of superhero play, on

CASE STUDY

Role-play areas

The team of Highwater Children's Centre has recently looked closely at how they organise the different areas of the centre. They had tried to be flexible with the home corner, but decided that other areas needed to be developed to support more varied pretend play. Two new role-play areas were organised:

- an office setting with phones, three (non-working) computers with keyboards and generous amounts of stationery
- a garage and repair shop with tools, overalls and a large cardboard box van, made with the children's enthusiastic involvement.

The new role-play areas are a swift success, for girls and boys. Children run different activities in the office area, talking animatedly on the telephone and making notes about the conversation. One child, whose mother works as a travel agent, brings in old catalogues but the office is not only a travel agency.

The repair shop is very busy and other games involving transport regularly link with the repairs. One child has visited the garage with his father in order to pick up the family car. He comes in with the idea of making a board just like the one he saw, with the day's instructions fixed to the board.

At the same time as developing the new role-play areas, the centre team had been looking at how to spread activities like writing throughout the learning environment. The children's wish to extend play in the new areas has made this development possible through their choices.

- There is no reason why pretend play has to revolve mainly or only around the home corner. What other areas could you develop in your setting?

the grounds that it is just a stylised cartoon form of war play. The whole topic has been opened up within recent years, with an awareness of the possible injustice done to boys' play when their lively, noisy and physical socio-dramatic play is curtailed as 'aggressive'.

Adult guidance or intolerance?

Penny Holland (1999) undertook research in a North London nursery centre to track the experimental removal of the ban on what adults judged to be war and weapons play. Like many such settings, the ban effectively covered many of the pretend play themes that thrilled children, especially boys, and were inspired by some television programmes. Superhero play and favourite cartoons such as Power Rangers were discouraged as soon as they appeared in play.

The change in policy was led by reflection and serious team discussion based on observation in the setting. Holland summed up the centre's dilemma as follows.

- The ban was not working: 'Despite our most vigilant efforts, weapons were being made and superhero games were being played'.

- The boys were pushed into a position of protecting their preferred play themes with remarks to deflect the adults, like, 'It's not a gun, it's an aeroplane/hosepipe/thingy/de-doo dong/broom' or 'we're not fighting, we're just pretending' and 'it's not really a batmobile, it's a fire engine'.
- Holland sums up the team's concern with, 'we had got to the point where we felt that all we were doing was teaching a small group of young males to lie creatively.'
- The boys were experiencing persistent negative adult reactions to their enthusiasm and chosen imaginative themes. Adult were concerned that the ban could be the beginning of the disaffection that some older boys feel about school and study.
- It was hard for young boys to interpret the nursery ban as anything other than personal rejection of their interests and play preferences.

The centre discussed a trial removal of the ban and sent an explanatory letter to parents. No special announcement was made to the children. There was trepidation among the centre practitioners, but Holland reports that the result was not mayhem and violence. For a limited period of time, there was an increase in children's playing the previously forbidden games, especially involving weaponry.

With their parents' permission, Holland shadowed and videoed three boys who had shown a consistent interest in weapon, war or superhero play. Analysis of the video material and interviews with practitioners at the centre showed positive developments in the play.

- The boys moved on from bouts of gun play to complex imaginative games, involving dressing up. This development seemed to be possible because the boys' play no longer had to be keep a secret from the adults.
- Once the boys could continue and extend their play, the adults observed that it was rich and flowed potentially into other areas of learning. The superhero play was, after all, pretend play, with all the positives that can result. A Power Rangers game lasted nearly 50 minutes and involved visits to many locations in the boys' imagination, including one child's family homeland thousands of miles away.
- Once the ban was withdrawn, the boys also extended the imaginary games into other forms of expression. They used art materials, once it was no longer banned to draw weapons and related scenes.
- Despite the team's fears, girls' play was not marginalised by the lifting of the ban. On the contrary, they become more involved in the active group play and the presence of practitioners (all female) seemed to encourage this participation.
- Once the adults lifted the ban, it became possible for them to enter the play. They could introduce a greater variety of action, themes and language, but without undermining the children's chosen pretend play themes.
- The boys were happy for an adult (Holland herself) to be part of some of the play. She gives examples of how she suggested, but not imposed, extensions to the play such as hunting 'flat monsters' in the Batmobile and the character of the Sheriff of Nottingham into a Robin Hood game.

Sometimes children need superheroes

Similar developments have been tracked in other centres where an equivalent ban has been lifted. Staff no longer move in swiftly to stop certain types of play, but observe with an open mind the themes and actions in pretend play, often of the boys. Teams can and do remain concerned that genuine aggressive acts towards other children need to be handled and that the television diet of some children is unsuitable. These are, however, issues to manage separately and are not solved by banning children's pretend play. A related issue to consider is that girls may be dissuaded from joining more physically active pretend games when they observe that the play gets boys into trouble. So, equal opportunities for girls may be unintentionally blocked by a ban that mainly affects the boys.

TRY THIS!

Penny Holland raises legitimate concerns about boys and their play.

- To what extent can you observe these themes with the boys in your setting?
- Do you operate a war and weapons ban in your setting? Do you effectively extend it to a wide range of superhero and good guy—bad guy play?
- What are the genuine consequences of the ban?
- In the light of Holland's project with the London centre, what would you like to consider for your setting?

Research on 'war' toys

There are genuine concerns about children's exposure to violence and the possible development of aggressive play. Jeffrey Goldstein (1992) reviewed studies of war toys and play. He summarised the findings as follows.

- There is no evidence of long-lasting effects of play with war toys on children's level of aggression, delinquency or violence.
- A genuine problem arises within studies and in any comparisons that adults cannot agree on what exactly is a 'war toy' and what are the consistent characteristics of 'aggressive play'.
- Linking with the research into play fighting (see page 172), Goldstein makes the point that children are well able to explain, and largely to agree

on, how to tell real from play fighting. Play fighting involves running, jumping and chasing and is accompanied by laughter and smiling. On the other hand, real fighting has grimaces, clenched teeth and fixed gazes. Play fighting lasts longer than real and children stay together once it is complete.

- Making war toys available seems to stimulate the fantasy play and play fighting among boys. This play is often imaginative and has a co-operative quality. Sometimes exposure to war toys affected the level of aggression in boys' play immediately after exposure. However, the increase is not usually striking, even though some experimental methods have tried very hard to provoke such a change.
- The same effects are not observed with girls, so it cannot be a simple and powerful effect of the toys themselves. Social messages about play are also relevant and the social learning experienced by boys.
- The gender difference is also noted regularly between adult males and females. Women are far more likely than men to classify an incident as aggressive, when it contains any weapon or fighting element. Childhood experience of toy guns seems to make some difference. In one study reviewed by Goldstein, women who had played with toy guns as a child judged significantly fewer incidents as aggression rather than play in comparison with women who had not such personal play experience.

GOOD PRACTICE

A ban on pretend weaponry and any game judged by adults (usually female) to be aggressive has become accepted wisdom in early years practice. Good practice has to evolve and this requires reflection on what adults do, including the unintended consequences for children – in this case the high risk of negative experiences for the boys.

The practice issues to consider are as follows.

- Adults do not help children to deal with and consider peace and violence by arbitrary bans – and they do seem arbitrary to children.
- Lifting a ban on weapons and opening up adult understanding of superhero play is not the same as opening the door to violence.
- How do adults justify broad-based bans that remove any kind of imaginary weapon, struggles between good and evil, bad guy—good guy play, superheroes and killing monsters?
- Not all physically lively play by boys, or the livelier girls, is necessarily aggressive. This cannot be treated as a foregone conclusion.
- The development and self-esteem of boys is not supported in a learning environment where their favourite games and socio-dramatic source material are judged as unacceptable and negative by adults.

Discuss these issues within the practice of your own setting.

Eli Newberger (1999) argues that toy guns are not a major moral issue for all children. They are overwhelmingly a 'boy issue', but are not necessarily linked with aggressive play for all boys. Newberger makes several practical suggestions.

- He stresses that all children, but again probably more the boys given the social pressures on them, need experiences and plenty of play opportunities to promote a sense of achievement and competence that is non-violent.
- They need ways of dealing with conflict that use words and negotiation rather than hitting out. Such support needs active adult involvement and will not be achieved by extensive bans.
- The serious concern is for boys who have developed a habit for violence at a young age. Violence and exposure to violence at home, or through television and video, can bring serious aggression even into the play of two- and three-year-olds. However, this is a problem to be faced and managed with some children, certainly not all.

Like other authors writing in the United States, Newberger also builds in a very serious undertone about guns. Children in the US are far more likely than those in the UK to have a real weapon somewhere in their home. He feels strongly that toy guns should look like toys and not replicas. There are undoubtedly some areas in the UK where the children who attend your setting are likely to see, or hear, real violence with weapons.

THINK ABOUT IT

When children, very often girls, play families and babies in the home corner, adults do not judge this to be 'sex play' and therefore as something to be stopped and discouraged. The babies are regarded as pretend. The fact that real babies in the real world are produced through sexual relations is not raised as a source of concern. (Unless children's play suggests a developmentally inappropriate knowledge of actual adult sexual behaviour.)

The situation of children, usually boys, and weapon play is treated very differently. The children's view that 'it's just pretend' is not allowed to justify and explain the play. Adults immediately make the link to what the use of real weapons would mean with real people.

- Why do you think this divergence has developed? Is it reasonable? Is it respectful of children's play?

✔ PROGRESS CHECK

1. Explain why early years settings have usually banned or seriously discouraged pretend guns and superhero play.
2. What are the potential risks of this approach?
3. What are the possible advantages of lifting a ban and increasing adult involvement?

KEY TERMS

You need to know the meaning of the following words and phrases. Go back through the chapter to make sure you understand them:

fantasy play
metacognition
metamemory
play tutoring
pretend play
small world play
socio-dramatic play

FURTHER READING

Carlsson-Paige Nancy and Levin Diane (1990) *Who's Calling the Shots? How to Respond Effectively to Children's Fascination with War Play and War Toys*, New Society Publishers
A balanced book that asks difficult questions and makes some practical suggestions.

Elliott, Clare (1992) *Childhood*, Channel 4 Publications
Discussion of play across time and place, with plenty of examples.

Goldstein, Jeffrey (1992) *'War' toys: A Review of Empirical Research*, The British Toy and Hobby Association
A detailed review of research studies and reviews to explore the impact of war toys and fighting themes in children's play.

Hislam, Jane (1994) 'Sex differentiated play experiences and children's choices' in Moyles, Janet (ed) *The Excellence of Play*, Open University Press
A useful chapter that raises some of the dilemmas in responding well to boys and girls, especially in mainly female early years teams.

Holland, Penny (1999) 'Is "Zero Tolerance" Intolerance? An Under-fives Centre Takes a Fresh Look at Their Policy on War/Weapons/Superhero Play', *Early Childhood Practice* Vol. 1, no. 1
Thoughtful and practical research that looked at the real effects of a broad ban on 'aggressive' play and what happened when such a band was lifted.

Konner, Melvin (1991) *Childhood*, Little Brown and Company
A well-informed description of views of children and childhood in cultures around the world.

Newberger, Eli (1999) *The Men They Will Become: The Nature and Nurture of Male Character*, Bloomsbury
A practical book that considers broad issues of how boys are raised.

Paley, Vivian (1988) *Bad Guys Don't Have Birthdays: Fantasy Play at Four*, Chicago University Press
One of a series of books written by Paley to describe and reflect upon children's play in her nursery class. See page 60 for other titles.

Smith Peter (1994) 'Play and the uses of play' in Moyles (op cit).
A thought-provoking chapter about how play has been regarded and the care needed in apparently objective research.

CHAPTER 6

Approaches to play and early learning

PREVIEW

- The key topics covered in this chapter are:
- Traditions of learning through play
- Outdoor play in early years
- Development of play in hospitals
- The playwork tradition.

The perspective that children learn through play is a very strong strand informing practice for practitioners in early years and playwork. This chapter considers the origins of this approach, including some of the innovators within early childhood education. Outdoor play in particular has a long history and a renewed focus has developed on the value of the outdoors. The development of play within hospitals has a separate tradition, although with links to other areas of practice. Finally the playwork tradition has been largely separate from that of early years. Events towards the end of the twentieth century have built more links.

TRADITIONS OF LEARNING THROUGH PLAY

Play as a way to encourage children to learn ideas, outlooks and skills is not a new idea. This approach was in place long before the educational innovators of the eighteenth and nineteenth centuries (see page 120).

Play and learning at home

Over the centuries, prosperous families have bought their children play materials or had them made. Parents' aim has been that specific toys and forms of play would encourage learning appropriate to later adult life. Toys were deliberately used as miniature versions of the adult world to enable children to learn and practise relevant skills.

Horses and riding

Push along horses and hobbyhorses were seen as an appropriate toy because they trained children, especially boys, towards riding skills. Illustrations from the eighteenth century show rocking horses equipped with saddles and stirrups. The lowered head of the horse and steep rocking action were deliberate features of this play item. The rocking horse would throw a child who was not sitting correctly.

Soldiers and forts

Boys were given sets of soldiers and forts, as a form of play experience that was supposed to provoke an interest in military pursuits. A future career in the military, or at the very least a respect for that profession, was judged an important focus for many boys.

Domestic play

Girls on the other hand, again in homes that were financially well off, were given dolls' houses, tea services or miniature kitchen equipment. The aim was that girls gained suitable practice in home-based skills necessary for their adult role in a family.

In prosperous households of previous centuries, the lady of the house would not of course undertake the domestic work personally. The play and learning objective for girls was that they should understand what needed to be done and that they would later supervise. With the loss of domestic staff in the twentieth century, the objective became more to learn skills that girls

Good nurseries blend real and pretend domestic play

would directly use when they grew into women. Sewing and craft sets served a similar purpose.

Constructional skills

Constructional toys were mainly, although not exclusively, aimed at boys. The Meccano™ set was designed by Frank Hornby at the end of the nineteenth century to encourage his sons towards an interest in mechanical engineering. Most illustrations on boxed constructional sets reflect the view that physical dexterity was the preserve of boys. However, one illustration reproduced in Basil Harley, *Constructional Toys* (page 12, 1990, Shire Publications) does show girls involved in the building play.

Puzzles

The first jigsaw puzzle dates from the late sixteenth century and they were first called 'dissected puzzles'. John Spilsbury is credited with being the originator of the idea when he dissected a map to provide a learning aid to support the teaching of geography to children.

Board games

From the nineteenth century, board games were developed for children with an explicit learning objective. 'Snakes and Ladders' started as a means to communicate a Christian moral lesson. The virtues shown in the board illustrations (the ladders) led to acceptance into heaven and the vices (the snakes) created setbacks in this progress. 'Lotto', at first a game for adults, was developed into various versions for children to serve an educational purpose. Different versions followed varied themes and the topics were supported by pictures, letters or historical dates.

The idea that children can learn important ideas and skills through play materials is not exclusive to Western culture. See, for example, the discussion on page 11 about the use of dolls to help children learn cultural and spiritual traditions.

Changes in early childhood education

The tradition of play and learning within middle and upper class families in the UK was related to learning in the home and was separate from education. The educational form of learning was delivered by a home tutor or governess or through formal schooling. Play appears to have had no part in schooling until educational innovators took a radical approach to the learning of children younger than school age. The new ideas were that play would be an improvement over the highly formal and structured approaches that dominated schools at the time.

Changing views of children

During the eighteenth and nineteenth centuries childhood was mainly seen as a kind of immature form of adulthood. The childhood years of some children were short and came to a swift end when they entered the workforce, either in factories or as a necessary part of family work to survive.

The prevailing view of children was strongly influenced by the Christian idea of original sin: the belief that children had a natural tendency towards wrong-doing. Moral ideas and good habits had to be forced into children, with generous amounts of physical punishment within the family or formal schooling. Not all families followed such harsh beliefs, but the social attitudes were not kindly to children of any social background.

A French philosopher-educator, Jean-Jacques Rousseau (1712—78) promoted a dramatic change in views of children and childhood. He challenged social beliefs that children were born evil and had to be directed towards goodness. He proposed an equally strong view that children were naturally good and their positive nature could be harnessed through nurture, care and the educational process.

Rousseau's image of children was occasionally as extreme as the perspective that he challenged, although in the opposite direction. He offered a romantic and very idealised view of children and their inclinations. His philosophy was linked into concerns for social justice and a more egalitarian society.

Rousseau's child-friendly philosophy proposed letting children indulge their natural playfulness in safe havens away from the harsh realities of adult life. The ideas were applied to the work of tutors in family homes and to schools. Rousseau and his followers were convinced that early educational establishments should be fitted to the learning needs of children and that rigid, rote learning methods were inappropriate.

Innovators in early childhood education

Several educational innovators exerted a long-term impact on the development of early childhood education across Europe. Their exact ideas and practice differed, but they shared a commitment to what would now be called a more child-centred approach.

Friedrich Froebel (1782—1852)

Froebel worked in Germany within the first half of the nineteenth century and built on the ideas and work of the Swiss educational reformer Johann Pestalozzi (1746—1827). Strongly influenced by Rousseau, Pestalozzi had stressed that instruction of children should start with the familiar and move on to new ideas. His educational practice was radical for the time. He believed that any programme should be paced to follow the gradual unfolding of a child's development. Pestalozzi also promoted the use of activities on which children worked together. The idea was that children would move from observation to understanding and so form ideas.

Developing Pestalozzi's ideas, Froebel pioneered schools for children younger than formal school age and he called this setting a 'kindergarten' (literally 'the children's garden'). Froebel believed that teachers should encourage children's self-expression through individual and group play. Children were to learn through freely chosen activity within a guiding framework of what he called **occupations** and with the support of learning materials called **gifts**.

Froebel described sixteen occupations that were intended to occupy and interest children and help them to be useful and productive. Many of the occupations were art activities (drawing, painting, stencilling) or craft (paper folding, plaiting or weaving, pricking and sewing). Some activities required attention and physical dexterity (stick plaiting, ring laying with metal rings of varied sizes, table laying to make designs from pieces of polished wood).

DEFINITIONS

occupations the sixteen activities that Friedrich Froebel designed to interest children and support their learning

gifts the term used by Froebel to describe learning materials designed to support children in exploring the structured nature of the world

Play with wooden blocks is still popular

The gifts were a precisely made series of wooden blocks that used familiar basic shapes such as cube, ball, cylinder, square and rectangle. The objective was to teach young children that everything around them was structured. The gifts were made and sold in sets. Some were small blocks in a box and others hung from a stand.

Froebel's practice may not seem extraordinary now, but his ideas aroused great resistance at the time. Eventually the authorities in Prussia (an area in what we now know as Germany) accused Froebel of being subversive, an atheist and a socialist (these were all highly negative criticisms) and closed all the kindergarten.

The original Froebelian approach was more structured than what would now be called 'learning through play'. It was not until the 1930s that the philosophy developed towards allowing children more free expression in their art and craft work. Yet, the daily practice in the original kindergarten contrasted sharply with the educational approach in Europe at that time. Schools favoured repetitive drills and teacher-led routines. Froebel's ideas became dominant throughout Europe and the methods for early childhood education in many countries were significantly shaped by his approach.

Maria Montessori (1870—1952)

Montessori was based in Italy and initially worked with children with learning disabilities and those from very impoverished backgrounds. It was later that she and her supporters extended the approach to young children in general. Montessori, rather like Froebel, was not a pioneer of learning through play in the way the term came to be applied from the late 1960s. Montessori believed that children preferred to work while at play and that this focus of activity was more challenging than frivolous pastimes.

Montessori developed the educational equipment first designed by the French medical physiologist Edouard Seguin (1812—80) for children with learning difficulties. Seguin promoted the idea that children's bodies and minds were linked, not separate. He developed an educational method for work with children with disabilities. He started with the training of the children's muscular system through exercises and activities. Then, Seguin led children from education of their senses to development of thinking and ideas.

Montessori extended Seguin's innovatory play materials into her system of **didactic apparatus**. The aim was to stimulate and develop children's physical and sensory abilities, through their own efforts and use of equipment designed with a purpose. Montessorri believed it was possible to enlist children's spontaneous interest appropriately at their varied stages of development. Button and fastening equipment was to help children learn how to dress themselves. Shape sorting apparatus was to train the eye. Design and geometric equipment assisted children to develop stronger hand co-ordination. Sandpaper letters and numbers were to help them learn through touch.

DEFINITION

didactic apparatus the set of learning materials developed by Maria Montessori to support children's physical and sensory abilities

Montessori opened the first *casa dei bambini* (children's house) in 1907. There was a clear focus on enabling children to manage basic skills of life through self-education and exploration. She did not promote learning through play in any way that would fit the views of the later twentieth century. Her learning materials were designed to encourage individual rather than co-operative effort. However, group working was actively promoted with shared domestic responsibilities.

Froebel and Montessori in the context of play

These innovators did not value children's play in itself; they wished to use the potential of play for educational purposes. Both Froebel and Montessori are sometimes misleadingly presented by late-twentieth- and early-twenty-first-century commentators as the people who elevated play into the prime vehicle for children to learn.

Neither of these educational pioneers developed their materials, and the supporting educational philosophy, to promote play in itself. They aimed to support sense training, self-discipline, orderliness and good habits. The materials were supposed to be used in a particular sequence and in a carefully structured educational environment. The new element of their approach was that children were believed to learn best through self-directed activity, supported by intrinsic motivation. Both innovators broke away from the view that children needed to be driven by adult instructions and rote learning.

Maria Montessori did not believe that children needed to play and did not value play as a creative force in itself. She developed the design of the special child-sized equipment and modified environment in order to promote and train practical independence and autonomy in children. Despite assumptions that arise in modern practitioners upon seeing her materials, Montessori was not at all interested in stimulating imaginative role play. Her aim was to get children, especially social deprived and disabled children, closer to real life and to enable them to practise important skills of self-reliance through exploration.

Froebel's approach and philosophy was less formal than that of Montessori, but his structured approach still brought a more formal learning environment than is often assumed. Froebel believed strongly in the value of children's spontaneous play as an integrating mechanism that would stimulate language, reveal their feelings, thoughts and actions.

Margaret McMillan (1860—1931)

McMillan pioneered the idea of a nursery environment in which the outdoors was as important, if not more so, than indoor learning. McMillan was concerned about the wellbeing of children who lived in poverty. Her contribution to nursery education was part of her broader social and political work to address extreme social inequalities. Like Montessori, McMillan was also influenced by the ideas of Edouard Seguin.

McMillan made a direct link from the home-based learning of privileged children to the details of a positive nursery environment for the less privileged children. She was very concerned about the diet, lack of fresh air and lively physical exercise that blighted the chances of poor children. Having been a governess in well-to-do families, McMillan said that:

> The ideal of such buildings (nurseries) should be home life, not school life as we know it; that is what is required for the children of wealth. It is needed for the children of all classes. (Quoted in Marjorie Ouvry, 2000, page 5.)

Her sister, Rachel McMillan (1858—1917) had extensive experience in what we would now call a health visitor role, working in rural areas. In 1911, both Margaret and Rachel were instrumental in setting up an outdoor camp to improve the health of girls aged six to fourteen years from slum areas in Deptford, South London. The experience with this age group convinced Margaret McMillan that the experiment should be extended to younger children. In 1914 she set up the Open Air Nursery School in Deptford and later named it after her sister to be known as the Rachel McMillan Nursery School. This revolutionary open-air nursery allowed children to move freely between inside and the extensive garden, set on many levels, in which children played and worked, equipped with real tools.

The aim was that children were enabled to learn in the outdoor environment, benefiting from air and physical activity. There were buildings, if children and adults needed shelter, but the majority of time was spent in the open air. All possible activities, including meals happened outside. The children were expected to choose their own activities. As well as the gardening projects, there were also nursery animals, scientific equipment and dressing- up clothes.

The husband and wife team of Paul Abbott and Marjorie Abbott used the prototype of the apparatus designed by Margaret McMillan to develop their own line of sturdy learning toys that were sold in their child-friendly shop in Wimpole Street, London from 1936. The Abbotts believed there was a correct toy for each separate stage of development and marketed their play equipment according to these learning objectives.

Susan Isaacs (1885—1948)

Isaacs was part of a different tradition from the other figures described in this section. She was very influenced by Anna Freud and Melanie Klein, both of whom where practising psychoanalysts (see page 36). Isaacs moved on from this perspective to become involved in education. She was clear in her objectives for the Malting House School that teachers should not try to act as analysts for the children.

THINK ABOUT IT

Perhaps inevitably, the original ideas of educational innovators are blurred, as later enthusiasts shape them for another decade. It can be interesting and useful sometimes to understand key figures within their own time and social setting.

Margaret McMillan has been influential in the nursery education tradition of the UK, but in her lifetime was most concerned about children who lived in poverty. She was also significantly involved in political movements.

Some nurseries have remained enthusiastic about outdoor play

Isaacs valued children's play because she believed it was important for creating imaginative meaning and had intellectual value. Imaginative and manipulative play were seen as the starting points for children's journeys of discovery, reasoning and thought. She accepted some of the psychoanalytic perspective that symbolic and fantasy play was a release for children's feelings. She accepted that play might help children work through deep emotional problems and conflicts. However, she parted from the traditional psychoanalytic approach, because she believed that play had an educational and developmental function. Isaacs proposed that play helped children to control their behaviour through developing a sense of self and a social conscience.

Isaacs did not believe that play was the only way for children to discover and learn. She felt it had a very important role in bringing balance to children's emotions during the early years of childhood. She wrote that 'play is indeed the children's work, and the means by which he or she grows and develops' (*The Nursery Years*, 1929, Routledge and Kegan Paul).

✔ PROGRESS CHECK

1. **Give three examples of learning through play in children's own homes from earlier than the twentieth century.**
2. **In what ways do the ideas of Froebel, Montessori or McMillan differ from 'learning through play' as we would understand it now?**
3. **Explain briefly the different tradition in which Isaacs worked.**

THE TRADITION OF OUTDOOR PLAY IN EARLY YEARS

The work of Margaret McMillan established a strong tradition in the UK, not just England, of the value of outdoor experience and play for young children. Play outdoors and hands-on learning was the central focus of nursery education and part of a rounded approach that did not divide concerns about children's health from their capacity to learn. This focus continued for many years but began to slip from sight in the last decades of the twentieth century.

The downgrading of outdoor play

There were several reasons that probably explain how outdoor play, physical development and related physical play became the poor relations in discussion about learning through play.

The focus on intellectual development

From the 1970s onwards, discussion about children's learning within early childhood settings became more and more focused on children's intellectual development and their communication as it supported thinking.

This discussion was especially focused on concern for children from socially disadvantaged backgrounds who were likely to have difficulties when they went to school. Relatively short special programmes, set up to compensate for disadvantage, placed more energy on promoting intellectual development than recognising the value of physical play. Better funded programmes, stretching over years rather than months, were more likely to take account of all the aspects of children's development, health and wellbeing.

The belief that learning happens indoors

Helen Bilton (1998) tracks how early childhood education became linked with the movement to counteract social disadvantage. She described how a simplistic view then developed, that it was enough for children to attend nursery and that indoor activities were the most appropriate to support learning.

Children's outdoor and physical play in many early years settings came to be seen as more and more divorced from valued learning. Proper learning was assumed to take place indoors, under peaceful circumstances and probably sitting at a table.

A low status for physical play

Physical play and the use of the outdoor space was steadily relegated in many settings to short bursts. Outdoor play was seen as a break from the 'real work' of nursery or school and a necessary allowance for children to let off steam. Excuses about how long it took to set up equipment or problems with the weather could then stop or severely restrict children's time outside.

Marjorie Ouvry (2000) also suggests that outdoor play in the early years and primary schools has been unhelpfully linked with physical education. PE has had a low status in the school curriculum and the value of outdoor play has suffered by association.

Risk from limited physical play

There are sound reasons to be concerned if physical play is downgraded, along with outdoor and energetic play for children. Apart from the great importance of physical skills in their own right for children, many of the more valued intellectual activities are highly dependent on confidence and practice in physical skills.

Sally Goddard Blythe (2000) has pointed out the dangers of failing to appreciate what babies and toddlers learn through movement, but the importance does not end with toddlerhood. Goddard Blythe's observations of very young children are linked with her work with older children. She has specialised in working with children with co-ordination difficulties and when physical factors seem to underpin dyslexia and attention deficit disorder. Her focus on the value of **physical play** has important implications for work with three- to five-year-olds who may be pushed too fast into pencil control and early writing. She also identified predictable difficulties for young school-age children who are expected to sit and concentrate for too long and without physical breaks. Goddard Blythe makes a strong case that adults are being unrealistic in demanding this kind of behaviour from five- and six-year-olds.

Physical play can also be the vehicle for a great deal of social interaction and rich communication. Children develop such skills precisely because they are on the move and enabled to plan, carry out and then admire large-scale projects. Researchers who study children's play in school grounds also identify the value of **outdoor play** (see page 83).

DEFINITIONS

physical play activities and opportunities that especially help children to use, practise and apply the full range of their physical skills

outdoor play opportunities for children to learn in the outdoors, in a garden or other open air space

Having fun together outdoors promotes children's all-round development

The potential of outdoor play

Marjorie Ouvry (2000) makes a strong case for learning through outdoor play, supported by case studies and her wide practical experience, including some years as head of the Rachel McMillan Nursery School. She describes how making the most of the outdoor space in an early years setting can promote every aspect of children's development. Outdoor experience directly supports the language and intellectual development that are so often linked with indoors and sit-down activities.

Rich potential for learning

Ouvry, like other informed observers such as Jacqui Cousins (see page 61), points out that children engaged in outdoor activity and games will promote their own learning in every aspect of development. A few examples follow.

- Children, who are enthused by projects, will talk together with energy. They engage in planning, raising ideas and problem solving.
- Children learn, with wise adult support, to handle negotiation, turn taking and delegation.
- In their projects they make informed judgements, decisions and learn from the consequences of their experimentation with materials.
- Outdoor space allows larger scale projects such as creating a den, transporting material about the garden and spreading out with a project. There are greater opportunities than indoors, even when the garden is not substantial.
- Lively pretend play can expand in the outdoors, although should not be banned inside (see page 111).
- Garden projects and helping out with garden maintenance can be undertaken even by young children. This activity promotes their understanding of the world and early science. Children's self-esteem is also boosted by being a trusted partner to adults.
- The work of Wendy Titman (see page 63) has shown that children have sensible ideas, when they are consulted, about making the most of the shared outdoor area.

The need for generous outdoor access

Helen Bilton (1998) challenges the relatively common assumption that important learning can only happen for children when they are indoors. From observation in nurseries and schools, she notes the problems that can arise from timetabled outdoor play. When the doors to the garden are opened, children may simply drop what they are doing and rush outside. Vivian Paley (1984) noted the change when she increased the amount of free playtime and spread it over a longer period in the day. The boys became more willing to go to the table-top activities and to do more work-oriented tasks.

In a 1993 study, Bilton observed the changes in children's behaviour when a short fifteen-minute timetabled outdoor session was altered to a flexible movement for children between indoors and the garden when they chose. The 'mad dash' to the outside stopped when children keen to play in the garden realised there was no time limit; they could relax. The play outside became less manic and more sustained when children were no longer trying to pack all their favourites into fifteen minutes.

You can take the indoors outside – even in wintertime

GOOD PRACTICE

It is crucial that early years teams value the importance of physical activity for babies, toddlers and children.

- Look at your indoor space – can the children move about easily?
- Look also at how you expect them to play and do activities. Is there an over-emphasis on sitting up to the table, working in a small space or not using the floor?
- If the children become fidgety and unable to concentrate in group time, perhaps they are not ready yet for this kind of exchange. How can you shift the pattern?
- Certainly think beyond the explanation of 'the children have problems with concentration'. Perhaps adult expectations are unrealistic.
- Value your outdoor area and look for ways to improve it, with the children's help. Work to create spaces so the children can move about easily on their feet or with wheeled vehicles, trolleys and wheelbarrows.
- Provide simple yet versatile materials like crates, tyres, logs, planks. All of these can be moved about by the children and made to serve different purposes.
- Natural materials like sand, earth and water can easily be handled outside and do not necessarily have to be in a conventional wheeled tray.
- Children need simple areas for digging and earthworks. They can be cleaned up or help with their own cleaning later.
- They need permanent and temporary shelters, dens or the material to make a den and large cardboard boxes.
- Outdoor areas can provide treasure trails and obstacle courses, some of which the children can help in designing.
- Look for how to make differences in levels, gradients and different surfaces for children to enjoy and explore.
- Have a range of outdoor games and equipment and show that you enjoy playing with them with the children.

On reflection, Bilton and the nursery team realised that the very short outdoor period had been a self-fulfilling prophecy. With a limited outdoor time, the children had wanted to rush about and let off steam. However, this wild activity was all they could manage in the allowed time.

Long-term advantages of physical play

There is now genuine cause for concern about what can happen in the long term when children have serious limitations on their physical play.

- They may fail to build up the necessary muscle strength that can only be achieved by plenty of happy and energetic play.
- Children whose physical play is curtailed may become lethargic and no longer bother to be physically energetic. Through no fault of their own the children are en route to become 'couch potatoes'. As Ouvry (2000) says, you want instead to encourage children to be 'runner beans'.
- On the other hand, some children become ever keener to manage some exciting physical activity. Prevented from legitimate outlets, some children may seem to have 'behaviour problems'. Adults may even consider that children, who are pressured to be too still, may have attention problems or a hyperactivity condition.
- Even the less physical children can become fidgety and unable to sit still, and genuinely find it hard to concentrate.
- Children may also develop the more inactive or passive pursuits. They may fail to develop any interest in physical activities, games and healthful pursuits later in childhood.

TRY THIS!

- Look at the developmental records that you use in your setting. You will have a range of physical skills and developmental 'milestones'.
- Do you show in your records how children use their skills, how they enjoy sheer practice and application of skills in different kinds of play?
- Crawling, climbing, jumping or balancing are not of interest just as single, one-off achievements. How do they feature in play?

The forest school movement

The Forest School in Bridgwater, Somerset (linked with the Children's Centre at Bridgwater College) was developed following a visit in 1995 to Denmark. In that country, the outdoors experience is a highly valued part of their nursery education. Special Danish forest schools (*skovbornehaver*) have also been developed to give children experience of the countryside.

The Bridgwater team developed an English version of the **forest school** idea. Children as young as four years old were enabled to learn practical skills in a natural outdoor environment, not a landscaped garden. In many ways the children's activities could be described as play in the outdoors and much of what they do has a playful look to it. However, the children often have a serious and intent look. They are absorbed in very practical activities and learning directly from adults' careful coaching. Watching the children is a timely reminder that children relish and learn from a broader range of activities than are usually included under the term 'play'.

DEFINITION

forest school an English development from the Danish focus on play and learning in a open air space. The forest school experience offers familiarity with a natural outdoors environment and coaching of appropriate outdoors and safety skills.

The Bridgwater Forest School team has a carefully considered philosophy and methods, that they have shared with interested practitioners. The practical approach is firmly based on building children's self-esteem and their wish for independence. Trust is central: that children (and young people who are also involved in the project) learn to trust the adults and the adults in turn learn to trust the children and let them show their competence.

The forest school has also tackled the practical issues of safety that concern many teams involved with young children. In contrast with the

Children are fascinated by 'creepy-crawlies'

TRY THIS!

If you and your team are interested in this aspect to outdoor play, contact the Forest School through the Children's Centre at Bridgwater College, Bath Road, Bridgwater, Somerset TA6 4PZ
Tel: 01278 455464
E-mail: frood@bridgwater.ac.uk
Web site: www.earlyexcellence.org

policy in many early years settings, children are coached to understand and practise safe behaviour near an open fire and handling sharp tools. The Forest School approach has more in common with the playwork philosophy developed in adventure playgrounds (see page 135).

✔ PROGRESS CHECK

1. **Suggest three reasons why outdoor play for children has been undervalued in many early years settings.**
2. **Give three disadvantages for children when their outdoor or physical play is seriously limited.**
3. **Explain three ways in which children's learning within their development can be promoted through outdoor play.**

DEFINITION

medical model dominant view that people, including children, in hospital are to be seen only through their illness and their stay must be managed with maximum convenience to the medical team

DEVELOPMENT OF PLAY IN HOSPITALS

A separate tradition has developed for the importance of play for children in hospital, although there are many links with early years learning. The movement to bring play into children's wards was part of a more child-centred approach to the whole experience of children in hospital and a challenge to the **medical model**.

Challenge to the medical model

The dominant medical approach, until changes in the 1950s and 60s, was to view children only as small patients, who tended to cry at the outset. The fact that children gave up crying was seen as proof that they were no longer upset and did not miss their mothers at all. The belief of medical professionals was that children had short memories, so there could be no lasting effects on children who had been separated from their family.

Hospital practice was unresponsive to children's need for emotional support and staff viewed parents as a source of infection. Parents were also viewed as people who upset their children, so family contact was best restricted. It was hardly likely that staff working in that professional atmosphere would consider that the ward routines should be disrupted for play.

The work of James and Joyce Robertson

James Robertson made two films: *A Two-year-old Goes to Hospital* in 1953 and *Going to Hospital with Mother* in 1958. Robertson's moving documentaries show the genuine distress felt by children on separation from their family combined with the strange situation of a hospital stay.

Robertson's work focused most on children's separation from their mother. The view now would be that children had been separated from a network of relationships within the whole family. A shift away now from the exclusive focus on the mother-child relationship does not reduce the importance of the work of the Robertsons. They did not just make the films, but were active in using the material to try to change hospital practice.

A Department of Health report in 1959, known as the Platt report, made many recommendations that recognised children's need to be treated as children and not as sick bodies. The report recommended, but could not insist, that medical practice should recognise the full emotional and social needs of sick children. The recommendation includes easy visiting arrangements for children's families, especially their mothers. Many hospitals and their staff continued to be resistant to change. Then community action developed in the 1960s, when excerpts of the Robertsons' films were shown on television.

Bringing play into hospitals

A group of mothers in Battersea, South London formed Mother Care for Children in Hospital (later called the National Association for the Welfare of Children in Hospital and most recently Action for Sick Children). This organisation gathered information of what was actually happening in hospitals around the country and offered information and advice to parents.

During the 1960s, the movement to promote play for children in hospital also gathered force. David Morris, a consultant paediatrician, had observed the aimlessness of children in the Brook Hospital where he worked. With Susan Harvey, an advisor to Save the Children and their community playgroups, Morris established the first SCF playscheme in the Brook Hospital. Hospital playschemes grew in number over the 1960s and 1970s, run by SCF, the Pre-School Playgroups Association (now the Pre-school Learning Alliance) and local health authorities.

The insensitive approach to children and their needs was gradually undermined over the second half of the twentieth century. Play with children in hospital has developed to achieve the following two equally important purposes:

- to meet children's continuing need for play and enjoyable recreational activities, a need that is not removed by being ill
- to draw on the possibilities of play as therapeutic. Play can be used to explore and reassure children in their anxiety about their condition and medical procedures. Play can be a means to help children gain vital knowledge and understanding of their experience of ill health or the need for medical intervention.

Hospital play specialists

This profession offers a wide range of play activities and materials appropriate to the age of children. Within any limits to the play space available, the objective is to enable children to play. Practitioners — the **hospital play specialist** and the **play therapist** — are also alert to creative ways to modify and offer play to children who may be in bed, immobilised or with periods of feeling too ill to do much at all.

Hospital play practitioners are especially experienced in using play and play materials to help children understand and explore medical procedures. Pretend play with teddies or dolls and small versions of medical equipment is supported by conversation in which practitioners encourage and answer

DEFINITIONS

hospital play specialist a trained practitioner who has specialised in bringing play to children in hospital and sometimes in home visiting to children who are long-term sick and cared for at home

play therapist someone who has trained in using play and play materials to support children in expressing and resolving anxieties and stress

Teddy is given an injection

children's questions. The play basis for younger children stretches naturally into recreational activities for older children and teenagers. Conversation can support older children and some like to express their concerns in words, perhaps by writing a story. When hospital play specialists are regarded as part of the whole team, they have valuable insights to share with medical staff about individual children, their worries and state of mind.

CASE STUDY

Jasmine

Jasmin has worked for several years as a hospital play specialist. Before this post, she had experience working in early years settings. Jasmin uses her broad play experience as well as her understanding of children who are sick, worried and perhaps also in pain. In this current post, she has used play and story telling in many different ways.

- It is very common for children to be fearful about needles and injections. They feel a little more in control by giving injections to dolls and teddies. Jasmin has a range of play materials that enable children to play out simple medical procedures with dolls and to care for sick dolls.
- Like her colleagues, Jasmin has found that therapeutic play is best done one-to-one when children are anxious. They can ask her questions and voice anxieties that are personal to them. Jasmin has found that even small group work with children does not encourage them to speak out as well.
- More general play and arts or crafts can happen in a group and children like the company. Sometimes Jasmin brings play materials, books and a companion to a child who has to remain in bed.
- Jasmin never makes assumptions about what will worry or frighten a child, although she is knowledgeable about some of the common fears. For example, it is not unusual that children, who are to have their tonsils removed, believe that this can only be achieved by cutting their throat. The children can be very scared and need reassurance.
- As well as play activities, Jasmin uses music and song. Music can be calming and reassuring for young and older children.

1. See if you can make contact with your local hospital to talk with one of the hospital play therapists.
2. Discuss how the team works and, if possible observe some of the play sessions. Check that the children are happy for an unknown person to be present. If they wish to talk about personal worries, it will not be appropriate for you to be there.

Links to play as therapy

Hospital play specialists include a therapeutic and supportive role with their work. They help children to face and understand worrying or pot tially painful procedures. They may work alongside and in consultation play therapists in the support of children who face life-threatening or terminal illness.

The use of play, story telling and all the resources of pretend play can be a way for children to explore and cope with strong feelings. The play setting gives some protection to children since they feel at a psychological distance from their worries. Children may of course talk directly about their concerns. They also have the choice to express their fear, confusion or anger through the play vehicle of a pretend character, story telling, music or painting.

Play after an accident

Since children run many experiences through play, practitioners in early years settings can find links with the kind of play support that is undertaken in hospitals. Children often re-run upsetting incidents and accidents through their play. Sometimes, the play experience seems to be a way to take the sting out the child's distress and sometimes the incident is run in play with a different ending.

Troyna (1998) reports the research of the Child Accident Prevention Trust. CAPT undertook a study of children's experiences after an accident and highlighted how much children need emotional support. Their concerns and continuing fears can emerge through their play as well as general behaviour. The project noted that children need to express and work through their anxiety. This need can be overlooked, especially when children's physical injuries are minor or they were the witness to an accident in which a friend or sibling was injured. Children can still be very distressed and scared, even when they are not coping with the aftermath of injury

Play therapists will usually be the professional to offer support for children who continue to be distressed. Parents, early years practitioners and playworkers have an important role as well. CAPT published a series of leaflets in 1998 that offer practical advice to all adults involved with children. The same project also drafted booklets for children of different ages.

TRY THIS!

Send for the booklet written by the Child Accident Prevention Trust for parents and carers on helping children get over an accident. Discuss the suggestions with your colleagues and consider how you could offer appropriate support within your setting.

CAPT can be contacted at 18—20 Farringdon Lane, London EC1R 3HA
Tel: 0207 608 3828
E-mail: safe@capt.demon.co.uk.

✔ PROGRESS CHECK

1. **Explain briefly the sources of resistance to offering play to children in hospital.**
2. **Outline the three advantages for children when play opportunities are made available before or during a hospital stay.**
3. **Suggest ways in which children might express and resolve anxieties through play.**

THE PLAYWORK TRADITION

Compared with day care or early childhood education, playwork is a relatively young tradition.

DEFINITIONS

playwork the professional area focused on play opportunities for children of school age and older

junk playground the original Danish adventure playground

adventure play and **adventure playground** play and play settings that focus on children's opportunity to experience physical and related emotional challenges

Adventure play

The **playwork** tradition really started in the middle of the twentieth century with the open space playgrounds developed by the Danish architect C.T. Sorenson. He wanted to provide children with freedom for exploration and choice in a setting that belonged to the children and provided a rich array of materials. Sorenson's first facility, called a **junk playground**, opened in Copenhagen in 1943. The idea spread within Denmark and to neighbouring European countries. Lady Allen of Hurtwood brought the idea to England in the late 1940s.

The playwork tradition developed for slightly older children, usually those of statutory school age. The philosophy was, and in many ways has remained, one of freely chosen play that provides a contrast with schooling. The junk playgrounds grew in number and in the UK became known as **adventure playgrounds**. The individual details vary, but the pattern has usually included some fixed structures. These structures can be modified on a regular basis by the children supported by the playworkers. There will also be a wide choice of building materials.

The philosophy of play and the role of the adult are in contrast to some ideas in the early years tradition of learning through play. In the **adventure play** tradition, the adult is a facilitator, an enabler who supports children. Adults do not in any sense direct play towards particular learning goals.

Children love the challenge of an adventure playground

Lady Allen of Hurtwood was also an important figure in the development of adventure play for disabled children. She was the founder of Kidsactive (first known as HAPA, the Handicapped Adventure Playground Association). For 30 years, this organisation has promoted the importance and good practice in adventure play for disabled children and the value of inclusive play facilities.

Adventure playgrounds are by their nature **open access**: children can come and go as they choose. Playworkers are responsible for play and reasonable boundaries to safety on the site but have not taken responsibility for individual children. This commitment to open access created difficulties when the Children Act 1989 brought most settings with any under-eights within the requirements of the Act. These playwork settings have found ways to adjust and compromise but the idea of limits to children's freedom of access, and leaving, was contrary to the values of such settings.

DEFINITIONS

open access play in a setting that allows children to come and go as they wish

playcare a development of the playwork tradition in which children's opportunities to play are offered within a setting that takes responsibility for them within agreed time boundaries

The development of playcare

Over the 1990s, there was a significant growth in after-school clubs and holiday playschemes. Playworkers in these settings take specific responsibility for named children for agreed times and days. They are not open access settings.

Kids' Clubs Network was at the forefront of these developments to merge the playwork tradition with reliable out-of-school care for children whose parents were working. What has become known as **playcare** does not always blend comfortably with the earlier playwork traditions. The playcare tradition does, however, have a long historical tradition at least in the UK. Supervised play centres started in the 1860s with the Settlement Movement.

The tensions between the two areas of practice arise because of the more organised nature of after-school clubs and playschemes.

- Children are the responsibility of the playworkers between times agreed with the parents and the children have to stay on site.
- Disagreement about the nature of appropriate play also arises from the requirements on registered settings. Safety guidelines are likely to restrict the more exciting opportunities of the adventure play concept.
- Concerns arise from a perceived reduction in choice for children about how they play and use materials.
- There is also professional sensitivity about any moves towards an adult-driven learning agenda. Playworkers are especially wary about moves towards making after-school facilities effectively an extension of the school day.

Some of the concerns in the playwork field echo discussions that are ongoing in the early years sector.

Play in the playwork tradition

The range of play opportunities within playwork settings share much in common with many early years settings, although variation results from the older age range. The shared values of playwork are central to the National Occupational Standards that apply to the training of playworkers. These include that play:

Tidying up can be part of an activity in any setting

DEFINITIONS

empowerment the process of enabling people, in this case children, to make their own choices and decisions

facilitator a role in play that means an adult gives support and guidance but does not direct or take over children's activities and choices

THINK ABOUT IT

- In what ways do the core values of playwork have links with concerns and priorities in the early years sector?
- In what ways may they diverge? Does it matter?
- Gather your own ideas and consult with colleagues.

- is a child-centred process that should start with children's needs, extending their current experience through flexible play opportunities
- offers an experience of **empowerment** to children, where the adult is the **facilitator** affirming and supporting the children's right to make their own choices, discover solutions for themselves and play in their own way and at their own pace
- is not controlled by adults or it no longer is real play. Children's play can be enriched by the involvement of adults. However, playworkers should always be sensitive to children's needs
- offers stimulation and challenge to children, including reasonable risk and the chance to grow in confidence and self-esteem
- remains within safe boundaries, respecting children's right to be safe, to have access to play environments that do not endanger and offer creative play in which children can feel personally safe
- offers children an experience of respect for them as individuals, confident that their individuality and identity are valued by adults
- involves care and consideration for children and their families, as a visible part of playwork all the time
- is available within a framework that ensures equal opportunities on the basis of social and cultural background and disability, and is therefore accessible to all children and parents locally
- is offered within the current legislative framework.

✔ PROGRESS CHECK

1. In what ways is the adventure play tradition different from playcare?
2. Describe three ways in which good practice in playwork should create a child-centred process in play.
3. Explain two concerns about play within the developing playcare tradition.

KEY TERMS

You need to know the meaning of the following words and phrases. Go back through the chapter to make sure you understand them:

adventure play
adventure playground
didactic apparatus
empowerment
facilitator
forest school
gifts
hospital play specialist
junk playground
medical model
play therapist
playcare
playwork
physical play
occupations
open access
outdoor play

FURTHER READING

Belsen, Peg (1993) 'The care of children in hospital' in Gillian Pugh (ed) *30 Years of Change for Children*, National Children's Bureau

A useful chapter that describes the dramatic changes that have taken place in the view and treatment of children in hospital.

Best Play Project Team (2000) *Best Play: What Play Provision Should do for Children*, National Playing Fields Association

A clear statement, from a playwork perspective, about the value of play in childhood and the obligations of good quality play provision.

Bilton, Helen (1998) *Outdoor Play in the Early Years: Management and Innovation*, David Fulton

Good coverage of the importance of outdoor play in early years settings.

Bonel, Paul and Lindon, Jennie (2000, second edition) *Playwork: A Guide to Good Practice*, Nelson Thornes

A useful book to understand playwork history, values and good practice. Early chapters will give an insight for readers who are not playworkers.

Evans, Russell (2000) *Helping Children to Overcome Fear: The Healing Power of Play*, Hawthorn Press

A description of the work of Jean Evans, the author's wife, in her role of hospital play leader, working with children who were seriously ill or with terminal conditions.

Goddard Blythe, Sally (2000) 'Mind and body' in *Nursery World* 15 June

An accessible explanation of why children need to use their physical skills.

Kidsactive (2000) *Side By Side: Guidelines for Inclusive Play*

Explains the principles and practice of making an inclusive play setting work for children.

Ouvry, Marjorie (2000) *Exercising Muscles and Minds: Outdoor Play and the Early Years Curriculum National*, Early Years Network

A practical book that considers the potential of working outdoors with children whatever the size of the outdoor space.

Paley, Vivian (1984) *Boys and Girls: Superheroes in the Doll Corner*, University of Chicago Press.

One of Paley's insightful records of a nursery year. In this book she addresses the issues that arise from energetic play, often that of the boys.

Steedman, Carolyn (1990) *Childhood, Culture and Class in Britain: Margaret McMillan 1860—1931*, Virago

A biography of Margaret McMillan that places her work on nursery education in the broader context of her social and political ideals.

Troyna, Alexandra (1998) *Providing Emotional Support to Children and Their Families After an Accident: Guidelines to Professionals*, Child Accident Prevention Trust

A practical description of good practice in supporting children and their families.

Learning through play in practice

PREVIEW

The key topics covered in this chapter are:

- Developing the importance of play
- Evaluation of children's play
- Different sources of learning
- Play and learning in the foundation stage.

The proposal that 'children learn through play' has long been part of early years philosophy and daily practice. This chapter takes a step back to consider what researchers and practitioners usually mean by saying that children learn through their play. The discussion moves on to explore the possible consequences of a narrow outlook that may restrict such learning to particular age groups and settings. Children can learn through play but the question arises whether their best, or only, route to early learning is within play. The chapter also considers the pressures on early years and school practitioners that can undermine a commitment to play.

DEVELOPING THE IMPORTANCE OF PLAY

The stance that young children 'learn through play' now has a long history within early years practice. It is useful to recall that innovators, such as Froebel or Montessori, who are often credited with this transformation, actually developed rather structured systems (see page 120). Nevertheless, the support for learning through play has such a well-established tradition in early years practice that it can seem obvious.

Reflective practice

The aim of this section is to challenge some of the unspoken assumptions about play and to identify possible risks of an unreflective approach. Many other sections of this book promote the positive consequences for children of enjoyable play. So there should be no risk that readers take this section as a call to abandon play as a support to children's learning.

Good practice needs thought as well as action. So it is important to discuss play and learning and not just regard it as accepted wisdom that needs no explanation. Some questions to consider include the following.

- Do children learn through play? What do they learn? Can this be demonstrated? Do we have to prove that play supports learning?
- Do children learn only through play? Do they have other sources of significant learning? What may happen if adults overlook those sources?
- Do young children learn only through play in specialist settings and with trained professionals? Can they learn at home?
- Is it appropriate to seek to define 'quality' in play? What are the potential problems once adults seek to evaluate children's chosen play?

Are there drawbacks to the 'learning through play' philosophy?

Children's play is valuable

It seems a self-evident truth within early years and playwork professional circles that children's play is the vehicle for much valuable learning. Yet, as soon as you start conversations outside this boundary, it becomes clear that many people within our society do not agree. For many adults, play is what unsupervised children get up to and it has limited value except to keep them occupied.

Parents are likely to be more positive, especially those who still have younger children. Yet, many still feel that proper learning occurs outside a play

Patient adults can track broad learning through play

context and that play will distract children from more important educational tasks. The focus on learning through play is also a particularly Western European view. Families from non-European cultures may be perplexed by the idea that playful activities will promote recognisable learning.

Development of the play ethos

DEFINITION

play ethos an approach that stresses the crucial importance of children's play within their development

The focus on the value of spontaneous play grew in Western Europe from the 1930s to become established by about the 1970s.

Peter Smith (1994) describes the development of what he calls the **play ethos**. Spontaneous play was regarded not just as important and pleasurable for the children themselves. It was also promoted as an essential component of their social, intellectual, creative and personal development. This outlook became established by the Plowden report for the DES in 1967 with the statement that:

> We now know that play – in the sense of 'messing about' either with material objects or with other children, and of creating fantasies – is vital to children's learning and therefore vital in school. Adults who criticise teachers for allowing children to play are unaware that play is the principal means of learning in early childhood.

Sources of the play ethos

Smith suggests that this play ethos had several strands that came together over the central decades of the twentieth century.

- Theoretical perspectives from the psychodynamic tradition (see page 36) had stressed how play was vital for children to express their emotions and resolve the inevitable conflicts of childhood.
- Studies from evolutionary biology (see page 26) proposed that playing was an important part of the way that the young of any mammal species learn skills during their years of immaturity. This argument is the reason that some books on play start with descriptions of play among young mammals.
- Socio-economic changes within Western Europe, along with smaller families, led to a separation of work from home life. There was less need for children as workers and a growth in the toy industry followed a longer childhood (see the historical descriptions in Chapter 1).

All these changes created a focus on children as a distinct group with needs separate from those of adults. Play as an occupation for children became important in adult eyes, especially within the context of early childhood education. An approach of learning through play, within a curriculum shaped by play activities, developed as a stark contrast with more formal, rote-learning approaches to the education of young children.

Adult interest in children's play

The consequence of a powerful play ethos has been that adults, in their varied professional roles, have become highly involved in defining, promoting and researching children's play. The potential disadvantages of this development have been recognised by some researchers and practitioners. Once adults' self-esteem, absorbing interests and career progression become involved, the tradition of children learning through play has sometimes been distorted. It is frankly hard to 'see' the children any more in some academic discussions about the purposes of play or the need to plan and supervise play in order to achieve quality.

Do children learn through play?

Observation of children in different settings, including their own home supports the proposal that they learn through their play. Children practise existing skills and develop new ones. Attentive observation shows how even very young children build in and extend their current knowledge. Children learn through freely chosen play activities and in play where adults are closely involved as well. Much of this research is discussed in Chapters 3 and 4. The fact that children can and do learn through play is not in question. One needs to challenge the contention that play is children's only or main route to valuable learning.

Is learning through play specific to early years settings?

Many books and articles focus on the play of children and not of babies or toddlers. Some limit the framework even further and stay within the context of nursery education and therefore the age span of three to five years of age.

There are disadvantages to saying 'play and learning' but actually meaning 'play and learning activities in a nursery educational setting'.

- Play becomes defined in practice as what is possible with three-, four- and five-year-olds. There is then a temptation to perceive the play of babies and toddlers as a less full or proper version in comparison with what comes later. (See also page 73.)
- The most valued play may be seen as what happens in early childhood settings, with the guidance of trained practitioners.
- Professionals can then be tempted to judge children's play along a quality dimension. Some activities, games and play resources, important to children, may be undervalued or criticised.
- There is a risk of sidelining how children can and do learn within the family home and with their own parents and siblings.
- Partnership with parents to support learning at home then risks becoming a one-way exercise, in which parents are persuaded to become more like early years practitioners.

THINK ABOUT IT

- **Read through this list of ideas a couple of times.**
- **Think about what has been said and how it might apply to your own practice.**
- **Discuss the ideas with colleagues or fellow students.**

Good practice in early childhood settings can be immensely supportive of children, a source of enjoyment and learning to them and great satisfaction to adults. However, this is not the sum total of what, how, when and where children learn, and it is important that we recall this fact. It is also crucial to recognise that not all children's activities, of intrinsic value to them and their learning, would be classified as play by some early years researchers and professionals.

✔ PROGRESS CHECK

1. **Explain two sources of the play ethos.**
2. **Describe two disadvantages of assuming that children learn only through play in specialist settings.**

EVALUATION OF CHILDREN'S PLAY

Adult concerns about the purposes of play and issues of quality have led to some attempts to evaluate play.

Demanding expectations for play?

A problem has arisen because children's play has often been idealised and portrayed as the best way of learning. Adults within early childhood education have been properly concerned with children's learning. Supported by the play ethos, they have therefore looked towards children's play to create opportunities and promote learning valued by those adults. The problem arises that sometimes children's play, left to its own devices, apparently fails to meet exacting adult goals and standards.

Tina Bruce (1996) expresses doubts that children's play will be of quality unless adults intervene:

> From the research that has been done on children playing, it seems that play cannot be left to just natural development. If it is, children do not learn to play well. Some researchers believe it is best to teach children directly to play. Others prefer an indirect approach in helping children to play. (Page 3.)

It is important to note that Bruce is not referring to children who need compensatory educational experiences (see page 145) because of social disadvantage. She is talking about children within the normal developmental range in mainstream nursery classes and schools.

Wood and Attfield (1996) discuss the dilemma that can arise when adults become invested in the value of play for their own professional purposes. They explain their goal of linking play closely to the task of teaching and the early childhood curriculum as:

> ... a direct response to the fact that play has too often been found as limiting, stereotypical, unchallenging and occupying rather than extending. The claims made for play do not seem to be realised in practice. (Page x.)

It is important not to take this quotation out of context. Wood and Attfield explore play in early years settings in a productive and thought-provoking way. However, their comments pinpoint the adult-dominated nature of the debate on children's play and learning.

You could well ask:

- who has found play to be 'limiting' and all the other negative descriptive words
- who has made 'claims' for play that remain unproven?

Not the children it would seem, who may be perfectly content with their play themes and actions. Their only claim is likely to be that their play is enjoyable. They may use the justification of 'We're only playing' when adults criticise the content of their play. It is adults who judge children's play and find it wanting.

Proving specific links between play and learning

THINK ABOUT IT

Some of the strands of research on the impact of play are described in this section. But, as you read it, consider the following as well.

- **Why, once adults were involved in the play, did it seem so important to prove specific consequences for learning?**
- **Why was it not enough to say that children were content, absorbed, happily involved in their play? Or that adults could observe and track some areas of learning?**
- **Early years practitioners often feel under greater pressure to justify their work than teachers. Why might they feel this way?**

The high value assigned to children's play led steadily to a greater adult involvement in the content and assumed outcomes of play. Difficulties arose over the 1960s and 1970s as researchers claimed, and then tried to prove, that play or certain kinds of play had a measurable impact on specific areas of children's development.

Adults can support children's keenness to explore and learn

There have been claims that spontaneous play is more beneficial than structured activities for children's development. Smith (1994) and Wood and Attfield (1996) are some of the reviewers who conclude that there is no reliable evidence to support this claim. None of these researchers are saying that spontaneous play is without value, just that one cannot prove it supports certain kinds of learning.

Sylva (1994) describes the lasting positive impact on children of some early years programmes in the United States. These programmes were well funded, highly supportive of children and their families and the changes can be seen well into adult life. Children from disadvantaged families experienced more than an early years play curriculum. The programmes, whose children were tracked long-term, were detailed projects that included extensive partnership with parents. There was also careful consideration of how to support children's long-term confidence and interest in learning. The consequence has been that children from such programmes were more likely to stay in school, achieve well and gain employment than children who did not experience this early intervention.

Play, or certain kinds of play, were proposed to make a significant difference to children's intellectual development. Peter Smith and Helen Cowrie (1991) reviewed the research studies. They concluded that there was no convincing evidence from any research method that play delivers clear-cut and strong benefits to children's intellectual development. If anything, the evidence was stronger that play enhances children's social skills and competence. The complexity of building a link between certain types of play and intellectual development is also demonstrated in the play tutoring research (see page 108).

It is not necessarily a problem that play does not obviously boost intellectual development in particular. Judy Dunn has made a strong case that intellectual development is not separate from social development (see page 52). Furthermore, the most recent practice developments in England with the Early Learning Goals have stressed that social and emotional development underpins children's learning.

Research studies try to prove definite links between a measurable cause and observable effect. It seems likely that children's learning at any age does not follow a set pattern and there are many contributing factors. It is very possible that no single approach will work effectively for all young children. So, the varied research results do not show a failure in early years provision, nor of the capacity of children to learn. After all, the statutory school system fails to teach some children to read, write and be confident with numbers. Few people suggest that the entire educational system should be abandoned.

Attempts to classify children's play

Problems arise in academic studies, because researchers need clear-cut categories of play if they are to test their research predictions. They often want to focus on only one area of development, perhaps intellectual or social and emotional. The firm boundaries required by research can then restrict the view of play. When children play in ordinary settings, they move with ease between play categories or adult-defined areas of development and learning. This raises problems for researchers, but also limits the usefulness of typologies of play (see page 40).

Are some kinds of play better?

Wood and Attfield (1996) comment on the risks of adult over-involvement, including the wish to judge play in an evaluative way. They explain how play is regarded as part of the private world of children and perhaps as a result, adults have:

> ... sought to control and manipulate play both inside and outside the home and to make it educationally worthwhile. A further problem is that we often make value judgements about 'good' and 'bad' play and potential learning outcomes. (Page 6.)

CASE STUDY

A fire-station corner

Drummond Road after-school club had a very successful half-term trip to the local fire station. The five- and six-year-olds in the setting were then keen to set up their own fire station in one corner of the room.

- The playworkers helped clear a space and collect materials, but then let the children organise what they wanted. The team expected that the fire station area would probably support complex pretend play and made informal observations over the next few days. They noticed the following.
- The fire station did indeed give a lively focus for boys and some girls who had been less interested in the existing pretend play resources.
- However, observation highlighted that the children also used and extended their constructional skills, working on large cardboard boxes for the fire engines.
- They engaged in conversation to thrash out ideas and resolve technical difficulties with making fire hoses and ways to produce something like the fire station pole they had seen.
- Negotiation and recall were involved in sorting out roles and draft 'scripts' for the fire emergencies.
- Several children, who had not previously been very enthusiastic about reading, asked for help in finding information books. They were motivated to explore any other resources about fire engines and discover how fire officers would attack different kinds of fires.

1. What types of learning can you identify in the children's play?
2. What could be lost in the richness of the children's experience, if adult observers homed in only on the pretend play theme?
3. In your own setting, assign some time to observe a play focus that enthuses children. How might you classify the different kinds of play and how do these link together in real play?

DEFINITION

free flow play the kind of play that Tina Bruce proposes is most supportive of children's learning in early educational settings. This play allows them to 'wallow' in the play and bring in skills managed elsewhere

The concept of free flow play

Tina Bruce (1991) proposed the superior value of activities she defined as **free flow play**, emphasising that, 'If I had my way nothing else would be referred to as play'. Bruce's ideal of free flow play can be achieved in a range of play activities, indoors or outside. The defining characteristic is that activities should allow children to 'wallow' in ideas, feelings and relationships. Play should, in Bruce's view, enable children to apply the competence and technical prowess that they have already achieved.

Defining quality play

Bruce (1996) proposed twelve indicators of 'quality free flow play'. She advised that if seven or more of these indicators are present, then the observer was probably watching quality play. These indicators are brief descriptions of what play might be or might achieve. The indicators are grouped below (the numbers in brackets are the order number given by Bruce). Some indicators could be observed but others express advice to adults.

- Bruce proposes that quality play is indicated when play uses a child's first-hand experience (1) and children show their skills and what they already know in their play (11).
- There are options about who is involved, because children may play alone (7) but might also play together in pairs or groups (8).
- Children should be in charge of their play since children make up rules in order to keep control of their play (2). They choose to play and cannot be made to play (4). Adults can play with children but must not take over (9).
- Quality play brings in real life since play encourages children to make play props or mime things or people (3). Children rehearse adult roles and life as they play (5) and they pretend when they play and transform real life (6).
- Quality play is also shown by children's focus because children at play can be deeply involved and concentrating hard (10).
- Play co-ordinates ideas, feelings and relationships and promotes development and learning (12).

Bruce suggests that adults support quality play by finding a positive balance between giving too little help and overloading children. Her view is that low-quality play results, when children are either left to themselves to play or when adults control the play. She believes deep-quality play develops when adults help children to sustain roles and themes. It is an adult role to ensure that children have enough equipment, are enabled to negotiate and learn social skills in order to enter play. Adults also need to ensure that children's play productions, such as construction work, are protected.

Reservations about free flow play

Bruce (1991) places some forms of play outside valued free flow play. Her view is that quality play does not include, 'structured play, guided play, games play, practice play or exploratory play. (Page 7.) It is hard to reconcile the exclusion of these forms of play from the experience of learning for children. The boundaries of quality free flow play do not acknowledge the extent to which children learn through routines and direct skills coaching from adults (see page 152).

The definition of quality free flow play also seems to be focused on the over-threes. The importance of exploratory play, especially for young children, should not be overlooked (see page 72). Bruce's advice to carers of children under three years is to give them everyday experiences such as meals, sleeping and shopping. However, her expressed objective is that these experiences can be fed in as raw material for play. There seems to be limited recognition that children learn directly through mealtimes or being involved in shopping, although in another context Bruce (1994) appears positive about domestic chores (see page 14).

THINK ABOUT IT

- In practice, early childhood settings that value the idea of free flow play do not automatically exclude routines and direct skills sharing as valued learning activities.
- From your experience of children, what could be the drawbacks to a strict interpretation of quality free flow play?
- What could be the problem with a belief that more valued learning only occurs when real-life experiences are recycled through play?

Are some play resources more valuable?

Wood and Attfield (1996) acknowledge the importance to many children of collectible figures and the themes of television programmes as resource material for play. They note that these sources are often belittled and undermined by adults. They also question, 'Sometimes it is useful to look at issues through a different lens. In elevating the status of play within early childhood, are we being patronising to children? (Page 8.)

Young children are flexible about learning resources

THINK ABOUT IT

- Consider how you and your colleagues react when a child brings a fashionable collectible figure to your setting.
- What happens about pretend play themes inspired by television programmes?
- Are you and your colleagues interested, do you watch the programme to understand the child's interest?
- Are there any toys or play themes that are banned in your setting?
- How do you think the children feel about this adult reaction? (Look also at the discussion on page 113.)

Gunilla Dahlberg (1999) described how a visit to the Reggio Emilia region of Italy made her think deeply about her own assumptions. She was surprised to see He-Man™ toys and My Little Pony™ in the Italian pre-school. These toys were firmly discouraged in Swedish centres in favour of wooden play materials. Dahlberg talked with the Italian practitioners and understood that they had reflected on their own practice. The Italian team has recognised the importance of the play figures to the children and that the adults had no business to dismiss play items valued by the children.

The pre-school team had undertaken personal research: watching the relevant television programmes and really listening to what the children had to say. This attention led to a far better understanding of the significance of the toys and related stories for the children in their pretend play. As a consequence, the Italian team, in a way that is typical of the pedagogical approach in the region, started a project with the children on modern fairy tale figures. They built in children's own experiences, ideas and stories. The example has links with the approach of Vivian Paley in the United States (see page 102).

A balanced adult role

The approach that children learn through play needs early years practitioners to consider carefully how they develop their adult role. Children's learning seems to be limited when adults take extremes in their role. Children can be left floundering if adults withdraw, worried that they might interfere in the play. On the other hand, adults can become overbearing, when they are so concerned about the purpose of play that they drive the content far away from the children's own choices.

You will find examples of adult judgement and related issues in other sections of the book:

- pretend play themes felt to be dubious by adults (page 110)
- the potential downgrading of physical and outdoor play (page 125)
- the view that school children do not play proper traditional games any more (page 82)
- the problem of play fighting and genuine aggression (page 172).

CASE STUDY

A play-based approach to learning

The nursery and reception teams of Croft primary school have talked at length about how to build links between the two classes in a proper foundation stage approach to children's learning. The practitioners recognise that they all still feel a lot of pressure to show evidence for children's learning. Nevertheless they are committed to a flexible, play-based approach.

The team work hard to observe and support children's learning wherever it happens. A team phrase becomes, 'Graphics doesn't just happen in the graphics area'. Once staff are alert, it becomes clear that children are keen to use early literacy skills in different areas of the nursery and reception class. Some information books are moved out of the book corner and spread around the setting, for example art books are placed close to the art materials. Activities that had previously been regarded as indoors are taken outside in reasonable weather. Children can move easily between sitting down and more physical play. Practitioners focus on alerting children to their skills at the time they use them. On a local trip, children who recognise the names of roads or shops are encouraged with, 'Good reading'.

The team move away from a single technology area and offer children different ways to explore these skills. Children can work on computers in one area but a play-office area also has non-working computers. Children can get used to the keyboard through play without being constantly reminded to be gentle. Another table offers old equipment like tape recorders that children can take apart with screwdrivers and discover what is inside.

1. The Croft team are committed to children's learning and have worked to be flexible about means to an end. In what ways can you make your planning unobtrusive, so that children can learn throughout the early years environment and have genuine choice?
2. How can you ensure that play with a purpose remains as much the children's purpose as the adults'?

✔ PROGRESS CHECK

1. Give two reasons why some early years practitioners or researchers might judge children's play as limited or of poor quality.
2. Describe an example of how children's real play may cross over the boundaries of categories of types of play.
3. What are the possible risks if adults judge and dismiss children's preferred play themes or materials?

DIFFERENT SOURCES OF LEARNING

It is often said that 'Parents are their children's first teachers (or educators)'. Beyond that statement, at least some settings and early years practitioners have worked in practice as if parents have far more to learn from the professionals than could happen in the reverse direction. Some models of partnership are genuinely two-way, but many are not.

Learning at home

The observational work of Judy Dunn has frequently highlighted the ways in which children, even very young ones, learn within their own family home, both through play but also in social interaction and communication with parents and siblings (see page 52). Children respond to their environment, so it is not surprising when their behaviour is noticeably different between their own home and an early years setting.

Barbara Tizard and Martin Hughes (1984) observed conversations held by four-year-old girls with their mother at home and in their nursery class. The research was a small-scale study and did not include boys, so it is important not to generalise too widely from the results, as interesting as they are. Tizard and Hughes challenged the assumptions of some nursery staff that, of course, the children's language and intellectual development must be best served within the nursery curriculum. In many instances the girls had longer and more complex conversations at home (see page 169).

The study encouraged some rethinking of assumptions within daily early years practice. It has also provoked some defensive professional reactions. Tina Bruce (1991) is critical of this specific research, and similar studies on the grounds that it:

> ... has contributed to a serious undermining of confidence amongst early years professionals, of their intuitive knowledge that free flow play is important for young children. It has always been difficult to articulate what those close to young children sense is good for them and these research studies have not furthered their ability to find a voice for free flow play.(Page 16.)

THINK ABOUT IT

- What do you think about Tina Bruce's criticism?
- Should the intuitive understanding of early years professionals be accepted as given?
- Is the kind of challenge offered by Tizard and Hughes really unacceptable? And if so, on what grounds?

Tizard, Mortimore and Burchell (1981) explored models of partnership with parents. They noted that early years practitioners frequently judged that parents needed advice and direction to make them become involved in their children's learning. Yet, partnership is less often deemed to work in the opposite direction, that practitioners could learn from parents and that the latter were often already very involved with their children's learning.

The studies led by Tizard were definitely not an attack on early years practitioners. The research redressed the balance by showing that children do learn at home and nursery methods are not necessarily appropriate for the home setting.

What about very young children?

Margaret Henry (1996) was especially interested in how very young children learn. She noted that nurseries who cared for babies and toddlers needed to look towards the home and family-based learning for a developmentally appropriate approach. Following a review of number of approaches, Henry identified three dimensions of direct relevance:

- ***responsiveness***: a warm and affectionate relationship with children demonstrates an adult's high regard for babies and toddlers. Adults need to be closely engaged with and attentive towards the children
- ***involvement***: an active support of very young children's learning, that encourages exploration and achievement at the level of a baby or toddler
- ***control***: a positive approach to guidance and direction, characterised by adult consistency and giving explanations. Positive control encourages children to independent action and works through both responsiveness and involvement.

Henry emphasises the importance of what she calls 'by the way' teaching of young children, that much of their learning arises from daily events and domestic routine, rather than planned play activities with a clear adult purpose. Other writers concerned about appropriate practice with very young children have highlighted similar themes.

In my own overview of approaches to the learning of very young children (Lindon 2000), it was possible to identify several aspects of good practice with under-threes in particular. Some main points follow.

- A 'very early years curriculum' based on play has to reflect what can be learned from contented home-based learning. Suitable approaches for three- and four-year-olds do not simply transfer to younger children.
- Serious problems also arise in practice from the long-term artificial split between 'care' and 'education' in early years. Babies and very young children learn a great deal during the care routines that are so essential for them.
- Research into early communication (see page 57) has highlighted how much close contact and affectionate communication is a vehicle for detailed early learning.
- Children under three are active participants in their own learning but they seek meaning very much through the responses of key and familiar adults. This form of social behaviour is called **social referencing**.
- The daily experiences of babies and very young children are just as important as the later developmental outcomes of those experiences. An approach of learning through play geared to older children can far too

DEFINITION

social referencing the idea that babies and very young children look towards a familiar adult, to see that person's reaction and expression, in order to make some sense of a new or ambiguous situation

CASE STUDY

Learning through original experiences

In Fairham day nursery, the team places a high value on play. But they are equally aware of how much children can learn through activities that would not be classified as play. The following are some examples.

- The mobile one-year-olds have been thrilled to watch the weekly rubbish collection from the bay window. They wave to the collectors who do some dramatic staggering with the bins to make the toddlers giggle.
- Today, several two-year-olds have been fascinated by and involved in watering the large plant pots in the garden and sweeping away the surplus water.
- An enthusiastic group of three- and four-year-olds have been discussing possible plans for reorganising the home corner with one practitioner. The conversation flows to and fro as different possibilities are weighed in the balance.
- Mealtimes are important social occasions at which children are keen to take turns in the routine. They are ready and willing to use their counting skills to ensure that there is sufficient crockery and cutlery for everyone.

1. Some of these activities may be recycled in the children's play, but the original experience is equally important for their learning. Collect some examples from your own setting that show how much children are motivated to have a trusted part to play in the routines.
2. Make brief notes on what you feel they learn through this experience.

Play between siblings starts at an early age

Play between siblings grows over the years

easily overlook how much learning is ongoing, because the more recognisable developmental milestones are way into the distance.

Do children learn only through play?

It is important to question an excessive learning through play philosophy. This challenge is not the same as devaluing play or promoting a return to highly formal instructional methods for young children. The problems have arisen because so much has been claimed for play by adults. Children can learn a very great deal through play, but they do not learn only through play. Children's opportunities to learn through conversation are covered on page 169. The value of involvement in routine is discussed now.

Learning through involvement in daily routine

Children find it very enjoyable to be involved in real-life activities like cooking or mending, with adults who are patient and share skills. They learn skills, make connections with other experiences and often talk and listen while involved in the activity. There is no basis for implying that such activities gain significance only if recycled through play. Such an approach can also undermine parents' sense of confidence, leading them to wonder if their children can learn only in specialist settings.

Wood and Attfield (1996) voice concerns shared by a range of early years professionals when they challenge an over-reliance on child-sized versions of domestic equipment and home corners for pretend play. Is there a real risk of

Children learn through involvement in daily routines

creating an unreal world and failing to recognise the skills and competencies learned in a family home? The point was made on page 13 about Western observers of non-Western cultures noting the lack of pretend domestic and baby-care play in some rural communities. Yet the children had family responsibilities that gave them direct skills training and they also engaged in pretend play as well.

Children with access to child-sized home corners are often enchanted and delight in the pretend play and social interaction that results. However, this source of learning through play can and should co-exist with opportunities to be part of real cooking, domestic responsibilities, helping safely with DIY and gardening.

Some curriculum documents, including that on the Early Learning Goals, have now shown a greater awareness of the rich sources of learning outside the boundaries of what is usually called play. Children learn from involvement in daily routines and having a trusted part in what makes a nursery, pre-school or family home run smoothly.

The apprenticeship role

Children also want and need to learn directly from adults. An exclusive learning through play approach, combined with insistence that children discover for themselves, can sideline the importance of demonstration and direct coaching from adults. Undoubtedly the task of helpful adults, at home or in early years settings, is to find a supportive balance between over-direction of children, in their play or conversational exchanges and a distance that reduces children's learning opportunities.

Donaldson (1992) points out that, although children enjoy solving problems and making discoveries, they can manage this only within the framework that they understand currently. A genuinely child-centred learning environment is not one that leaves children to re-invent the wheel. She explains that:

> (children) like to make discoveries and it is good to challenge them to do so, but they also enjoy and benefit from having things explained to them. They ask questions and they want clear, honest answers, which, of course, if these are well-judged, need not close the inquiry but may provoke a further desire to know. (Page 257.)

Interested children will do their 'work'

✔ PROGRESS CHECK

1. **What could be the risks for children if parents believe that they cannot support learning at home?**
2. **Explain why a framework of learning through play designed for children over three years of age could fail to support the learning of younger children.**
3. **Suggest three ways that children could learn through involvement in daily routines.**

PLAY AND LEARNING IN THE FOUNDATION STAGE

A foundation stage within the framework of the Early Learning Goals was established in autumn 2000 in England. This development created a first stage of children's education to last from three years to the end of the reception year in primary school, when children will be five or six years of age. The ideal of a coherent foundation stage offers a framework to reflect on what is meant by play for children in a learning environment shaped by adults.

Children's play – adult purposes?

Mari Guha (1996) suggests that perhaps a distinction should be made between what she calls 'play as such' and 'play in schools'. As she explains:

> The kind of play we seek educational justification for is the meeting ground where children and teachers *share intentions* [italics in original]. (Page 70.)

Guha makes a strong case for giving play a place in schools, by which she means both the nursery and early primary years. Her suggestion addresses some of the problems that arise when discussion of 'children learn through play' fails to acknowledge related assumptions about where the play takes place and to whose purpose.

Guha suggests that teachers should look with care at the messages they give children about play. One question has to be whether play is used as an incentive, that children can play only when they have finished their work. Guha argues for an explicit value of play in schools, but stresses that play opportunities are not a substitute for well-planned and detailed instruction. She proposes that play can enhance the curriculum, bringing in children's energy and enthusiasm, but only when adults remain honest and generous with information. She is also wary of possible misuse of a discovery play approach. Guha observes that some teachers counter too many requests for help from children with the instruction to 'work it out for yourself'.

Rhetoric or actual practice?

Joy Roberts (2000) expressed similar concerns to Guha and reports that the expressed philosophy that children learn through play is not necessarily shown in daily practice in reception classes.

Roberts is aware of the pressures on reception teams to show measurable learning for young children at the beginning of their schooling. Roberts and her colleagues interviewed headteachers, teachers, classroom assistants, children and parents from ten primary schools in north-west England. They identified three main approaches to play in the reception class.

- Children exercised free choice within a learning environment structured by the adults. However, this openness was only for the first term.
- Children could choose from teacher-selected activities before or after a focused teaching session.
- Groups of children were directed by the teacher to a succession of play activities throughout the school day.

The reception class teams described the dilemma they faced. They wanted children to exercise genuine choice and direct their own learning. Yet they felt great pressure to ensure that children covered the full curriculum and could be seen to learn in all areas. The consequence was often that greater adult attention was paid to the more formal activities. More freely chosen play was an option once children had completed directed tasks, often worksheets. Children who struggled more with the paper and pencil or more structured activities were therefore likely to have less time for self-chosen play. The children themselves recognised the difference with comments like, 'You have to do work like colouring and then you can play' and 'now I'm in reception, you just learn that you can't play 'cos Mrs B wants me to do my work'.

Roberts points to the key issues: that teachers are at risk of over-directing the more formal 'work' for children and being under-involved in play. Despite the rhetoric, children are not being enabled to learn through play and they recognise the differential evaluation of 'work' and 'play' in the reception class. The change from autumn 2000 to the Foundation Stage within the framework of the Early Learning Goals may be the opportunity for reception teams to rediscover their professional trust in children's learning through play.

Roberts offers a personal reminiscence from her own first years as a teacher, which highlights the key issues. She felt committed to learning through play but, in order to teach language about position and colour:

> I had carefully prepared an activity sheet of a road with cars in a line and I spent 15 minutes sitting at a table asking children to colour the first car red, the second car blue and so on. The children willingly completed the task and I assessed their understanding by asking them individually, 'Which car is blue?' 'Which car is second?' Later in the session, I observed some of the same children playing with a variety of vehicles on the play mat. They were using a range of positional language confidently, talking about cars that were 'in front of', 'between', 'behind'; cars that were 'first', 'last'; cars that were 'fast' and 'slow', cars that were 'turquoise' and 'silver'. They were using language to compare sizes, shape and quantity too.

With this example, Roberts effectively highlights the importance of trusting that children will learn and using adult skills of observation to track that experience.

THINK ABOUT IT

- The example given by Joy Roberts shows that early years practitioners often need to trust that children will learn through play.
- Problems arise from believing that proper learning can only really happen at a table and probably with paper and pencil and a pre-structured worksheet.
- In what ways can you see these issues at work in your own practice?
- In what ways can you and your colleagues, or fellow students, resolve the dilemma?

Anxiety undermines learning

Jacqui Cousins (1999 and personal communication) expressed serious concerns about what can happen to children's learning environment when adults become highly anxious about measurable learning.

When adults become anxious

Cousins describes the negative consequences on children's experiences and learning when adults feel both under great pressure and doubt their skills.

- Cousins spent time in playgroups and pre-schools where she observed highly varied play. The children were closely involved, playing in a relaxed way and using rich language in conversation together.

- Yet, some early years practitioners seemed to have lost their confidence in children's ability to learn through play and conversation. They withdrew four-year-olds for formal work and interrupted the play.
- The children were made to complete separate activities that appeared to match the requirements of the desirable learning outcomes applicable at the time, and to produce evidence of learning.
- These alternative, sit-down activities were usually paper and pencil worksheet-type sessions. The children seemed to tolerate these sessions as 'work' that had to be done in order to be released for more enjoyable activities.

Such an approach is almost certain to undervalue the outdoors environment as a source of learning for children (see page 125). Cousins observed that some of children's highest quality language emerged naturally in their play and conversation when they were outside, engaged enjoyably in outdoor activities and relaxed. Their explorations in the outdoor environment led children to many of the discoveries that practitioners wanted for learning outcomes.

Ideas are learned through play

Worried children

Cousins observed the consequence of pressure on children as well as the adults. One four-year-old explained to her, 'I can't talk now, 'cos Mum said I got to do all my de ... serious de ... lerious somefins' (desirable learning outcomes). Cousins noted that in several settings children would imitate the adults and stress the importance of getting 'on with your work'. She described a child explaining in detail to her about the metamorphosis of a butterfly. Then, 'a younger child interrupted him and said to me, "He's big now... got to get on with his proper work"'. The children seemed to have accepted a low valuation of conversation, that it was not proper work.

Part of the anxiety communicated to children was that time was at a premium. Play could be interrupted in some settings and longer-term projects were not even attempted, because children knew they would be stopped. Cousins described the insights brought to one nursery by Sonnyboy, a four-year-old from a traditional traveller family. Sonnyboy's teacher was able to reflect on what she could learn from the child's differences, rather than viewing him as a child who ought to fit into the existing pattern. The boy's sense of the importance of taking time to do something properly threw into sharp relief the impact of pressure on this nursery setting. Jacqui Cousins uses Sonnyboy's phrase, 'Time's as long as it takes' on the back cover of her book.

GOOD PRACTICE

Play is valuable for children as a means of exploration, learning and enjoyable occupations on their own or with friends. You can promote the value of play without getting over-specific or unrealistic about exactly what play will deliver and in what way. A team needs to talk and reflect together. You need to be ready to observe your own practice as well as children's play.

- Try hard to avoid narrow definitions of play or valuing some activities more than others.
- Look for the learning potential when children are part of daily routines.
- Children do not have to discover everything themselves. Look out for their chance to learn directly from adults who share their skills with children.
- Children can and do learn early literacy and numeracy through play and involvement in daily routines. Watch out for the temptation in your team to slip towards structured and formal methods that risk losing children's interest and enthusiasm.
- Be ready to talk and listen to each other in the team. You may need to discuss your own worries about whether children are really learning and how to document the changes.
- Children who are rushed will not learn; remember the phrase, 'Time is as long as it takes'.
- Ask yourself some key questions. Does your team value children's work in progress? Can they return to a longer project? Do you all go with the flow of children's absorbing interests? Over time, you will find that the different areas of learning are covered.

Enthusiastic children

Cousins offers many examples of children who develop positive attitudes to learning through play, social interaction and conversation. Children were keen to show her their books, to explain why the garden was so wonderful, how they liked to climb and what fun it was to do real cooking. The practitioners in such settings did not appear to have different qualifications or beliefs to those in other settings. They did put into practice a genuine commitment to learning through play and conversation and they refused to be tyrannised by time.

✔ PROGRESS CHECK

1. In what ways are the skills of observation crucial to support the confidence of early years practitioners that children will learn within the context of play and social interaction?
2. In what way is the use of time relevant to supporting children's learning?
3. Suggest two ways in which anxiety can block children's learning through play or any other route.

KEY TERMS

You need to know the meaning of the following words and phrases. Go back through the chapter to make sure you understand them:

free flow play
play ethos
social referencing

FURTHER READING

Bruce, Tina (1991) *Time to Play in Early Childhood Education* and (1996) *Helping Young Children to Play*, Hodder and Stoughton
The books explain Bruce's approach to free-flow play and ways to establish what she regards as quality in children's play.

Cousins, Jacqui (1999) *Listening to Four-year-olds*, National Early Years Network
Observations of children in nurseries and playgroups that highlight how they learn and the blocks created by anxiety, in children and adults.

Dahlberg, Gunilla, Moss, Peter and Pence, Alan (1999) *Beyond Quality in Early Childhood Education and Care: Postmodern Perspectives*, Falmer Press
Generally a more academic than practical book, but the authors share a valuable European perspective.

Donaldson, Margaret (1992) *Human Minds: An Exploration*, Allen Lane
A book that ranges widely over ideas of how children think and learn, with practical ideas about the adult role.

Guha, Mari (1996) 'Play in school' in G.Blenkin and A.V. Kelly (eds) *Early Childhood Education: A Developmental Curriculum*, Paul Chapman
Guha explores ideas and practice following a distinction between what she calls 'play as such' and 'play in schools'.

Lindon, Jennie (2000) *Helping Babies and Toddlers Learn: A Guide to Good Practice with Under-Threes*, National Early Years Network
A discussion of developmentally appropriate practice in settings with very young children, with consideration of the great importance of care.

Qualifications and Curriculum Authority (2000) *Curriculum Guidance for the Foundation Stage*
The detailed guidance for practitioners working with children aged from three to six years old.

Roberts, Joy (2000) 'The rhetoric must match the practice' in *Early Years Educator* Vol. 2 no. 5, September
Roberts explores that the expressed philosophy of children learning through play is not necessarily shown in daily practice in reception classes.

Smith, Peter and Cowrie, Helen (1991) *Understanding Children's Development*, Blackwell
A general book explaining children's development that also describes key research.
Sylva, Kathy (1994) 'The impact of early learning on later development' in Christopher Ball *Start Right: The Importance of Early Learning*, Royal Society of the Arts
Sylva explains the subtle impact of effective early years programmes and what can be learned about how to support children's learning.
Tizard, Barbara and Hughes, Martin (1984) *Young Children Learning. Talking and Thinking at Home and at School*, Fontana
Research undertaken in the 1980s that is still relevant now. A comparative study of girls at home and at nursery class.
Tizard, Barbara, Mortimore, Jo and Burchell, Bebb (1981) *Involving Parents in Nursery and Infant Schools: A Source Book for Teachers*, Grant McIntyre
Reflection on the underlying assumptions about partnership with parents that are still relevant a couple of decades after the original study.
Wood, Elizabeth and Attfield, Jane (1996) *Play, Learning and the Early Childhood Curriculum*, Paul Chapman
A careful consideration of the dilemmas raised when play is of professional interest to adults.

CHAPTER 8

Adult roles in children's play

PREVIEW

The key topics covered in this chapter are:

- Adult involvement in children's play
- Adult judgements on play
- Supporting play at school
- Support for social skills.

Discussion about how children learn through play inevitably moves on to the role of the adult in supporting children's play opportunities and the potential learning that can result. This chapter considers a positive adult role and the need to be a reflective practitioner in early years, playwork and school settings. Boys and girls sometimes play in different ways and these patterns are considered. Concerns that boys' play choices may sometimes be restricted has led to some rethinking. There is also an awareness that early experience can have an impact on children's attitudes to learning during their school years. The link is made between social skills and play, with implications for an adult role that can support children.

ADULT INVOLVEMENT IN CHILDREN'S PLAY

Practitioners do not agree on the details of how best to relate to children's play as it unfolds in early years and playwork settings. A general theme of agreement is that adults of any professional background have to find a balanced middle course between a very low level of involvement and such a high level that their actions operate as interference. However, a considerable amount of discussion, and disagreement, goes on around what would be an appropriate balance, and how this might vary with children of different ages.

Possible roles

Several broad themes emerge in terms of possible adult roles.

The adult as companion in play

Adults are not simply big children and they definitely have responsibilities to meet. Children themselves will often look towards early years or playwork practitioners and teachers to step in and help. However, this adult responsibility still leaves wide scope to be a play companion.

Helpful adults can be fully part of an activity

Children often invite adults to join in or may direct them to take a particular action to support play. You may be requested to find something, hold an item, push a swing or take a clear role in pretend play. Some of the play in school grounds is eased when adults will join in (see page 174) as someone who also enjoys the game or who takes a vital part such as holding the end of a skipping rope.

The adult as learner and observer

Adults can take a positive role in play as someone who can still learn and be excited about new ideas and perspectives. Such a role can link with good practice in observation skills and the importance of being a reflective practitioner. Adults as observers are discussed further from page 166.

The adult as admirer

Children welcome the attention of an adult. They often call out, 'Look, look', when they are negotiating a complex climb on outdoor apparatus or are confident in a tricky manoeuvre with the bike. Jacqui Cousins (1999) reports how four- year-olds in many of the settings she visited wanted to show her the special parts of their nursery or playgroup. The children were keen to talk her through with great excitement why the books, the woodwork materials or the garden were so enjoyable. The children in the Mosaic project (see page 62) did not have to be persuaded to document and share their views. They wanted to show adults the important places and objects in their nursery.

THINK ABOUT IT

Children sometimes want help, but how often do children on the slide or climbing frame call out, 'Look!' to encourage you to admire their physical prowess?

Consider times that the children in your setting want you just to come and look at something that they find intriguing. They do not necessarily want to talk about this sight or ask questions, although children may, but they simply want to share their intrigue or excitement with you.

The adult as facilitator

This role focuses on the adult ability to ease play, to give an appropriate nudge, without taking over the direction of the play or making the children passive. An adult role as facilitator, or enabler, recognises that children's playful activities happen within a learning environment shaped to an extent by the adults. Facilitating and encouraging play can also happen through positive use of conversation. Adult skills in this area are discussed from page 168.

Adults are responsible for organising children's environment

Empowerment of children

Adults who facilitate without taking over play may also envisage their role as one form of empowerment of children. Empowerment is a key value in playwork but is a far less familiar word in early years or primary school teams. The objectives are broadly that children are treated more as equal partners, that they have a genuine choice in how their play develops and a real voice in decisions about the setting. Adults still retain responsibility, but aim to share elements appropriately with children.

The adult as a model

In different ways adults may offer a lead in play that still leaves children with choices about how and what to follow. When children are inexperienced in use of some play materials, then adults may show ways that these can be used. Careful consideration of social skills has highlighted how much children need to be set a good example by adults, who behave in the way they wish children to follow (see also page 180).

> **DEFINITION**
>
> **mediator** someone who uses skills of communication and problem solving to enable two or more people to face and resolve a situation of disagreement or conflict

The adult as mediator

Children look towards adults to take a fair and impartial role in their play and related issues of life in any setting. Adult involvement as a **mediator** at times of disagreement or conflict can also blend with a role of model (showing children ways of problem solving in action) and peacekeeper (when children need help to stop and calm themselves). The role of mediator may also merge with appropriate sharing of skills by adults, discussed in Lindon (1999).

The adult as responsible judge

A possible role for adults in children's play can be to direct play themes and expression towards what adults regard to be more acceptable directions. Adults have responsibilities towards children's physical and emotional wellbeing, so utterly free play in terms of content and themes may not be a safe option. However, the potential problems of adult evaluation of children's play were discussed on page 144. Key issues are also covered in this chapter from page 170.

The adult as safety officer

Part of adult responsibility is to keep children safe from harm. Yet this protection needs to be balanced with sufficient challenge and excitement for children to learn. Over-anxious and agitated adults can make play boring or even unsafe, as children have to work ever harder to bring some spark to play activities.

The organisation Kidsactive (see also page 136) gives serious consideration to safety in the play of disabled children. Their outlook has been that careful risk assessment needs to identify any steps appropriate for the special needs of children. Thereafter, disabled children need freedom to play and will get bumps and scrapes like any other children, who are enabled to enjoy themselves. Lindon (1999) discusses the difficult balance for adults and the risks that arise when they aim for an unrealistic one hundred per cent risk-free environment.

The adult as observer-learner

Good practice in early years and playwork emphasises observation skills. Used positively in everyday practice, observation of children can support the crucial role of being a reflective practitioner. Observation of children in play needs to be:

- open-minded and taking the child's perspective as well as adult views
- guided by adult values, but open to a range of possible interpretations
- free of fixed assumptions about more valued play activities and restrictive views of quality play.

Supportive adults are interested in what fascinates young children

Using schemas with observation

Chris Athey's development of Piaget's concept of schemas emerged from her project during the 1970s at what was then the Froebel Institute in Roehampton, South London. The use of schemas is also discussed on page 34.

The approach encourages practitioners and parents to look really carefully at what very young children are doing and to focus on toddlers' current interest themes. The schema approach in action in nurseries has also supported early years practitioners to respect the play of very young children. Adults become more able to watch and wait and to resist over-shaping children's experience towards what might be regarded as more 'proper' play.

THINK ABOUT IT

- Consider the phrase used by Vivian Paley: 'It did not occur to me that the distractions might be the sounds of the children thinking'.
- Reflect on your own practice, especially when you are tempted to pull children back onto what seems like the 'right' track for their involvement in an activity.
- Sometimes it may be appropriate to guide the children back on task, but sometimes will it be more supportive to follow their lead?

Observation and reflection

Vivian Paley has documented many years of observation and close involvement as a nursery teacher (see also page 58). In *Bad Guys Don't Have Birthdays: Fantasy Play at Four* (1988), Paley explains how she changed in her perception of how to be a genuinely helpful teacher:

> ... I became a kindergarten teacher and had curriculum guides ... (I) believed it was my job to fill the time quickly with a minimum of distractions, and the appearance of a correct answer gave me the surest feeling that I was teaching. It did not occur to me that the distractions might be the sounds of the children thinking. (Page 7.)

Vivian Paley describes how she reflected on her role in the classroom and how she learned to draw on children's play. She stresses the importance not only of listening to children but also using their ideas in ways that really make sense to the children. This respectful approach was an alternative to forever adapting children's ideas to what she, as the nursery teacher, wanted to fit her pre-organised adult plans.

Initially, Paley had viewed circle time as a way for her to raise issues that seemed important for the group and she tape-recorded these sessions. Then she realised that the themes the children were motivated to discuss were those that arose in their play:

> When anything was mentioned that had occurred during play, everyone snapped to attention. If an argument was recalled, or a scene of loss and despair was described, the class became unified in purposefulness. Annie complains that Kathy always has to be the mother, which reminds Sam that he doesn't like the mother pig because she made her children go into the woods where the wolf was. And, speaking of wolves, how come Paul every day tells Simon to be the bad guy, or else he can't play? Is that fair? (Page 12.)

Following her recognition of what really made children enthusiastic, Paley started to leave her tape recorder on after the end of circle time and so built up her observational material on children's play.

Adults as partners in conversation

Children learn through relaxed conversation, where they take the lead at least as often as the adult.

Children wanting to know

The work of Tizard and Hughes and of Margaret Donaldson and her team highlighted the learning task from the perspective of the children. Their thinking progresses along two related tracks.

Children appreciate hands-on help

- Children need to learn details and they are hungry for information. Children, whose queries bring a positive adult reaction and sensible answers, go on to ask many questions, when they are ready.
- However, young children are also developing an intellectual framework in order to make sense of new and old information. So, their questions sometimes show their recognition that something is confusing. They make comments like, 'But that can't be right because … ' or ask persistent 'Why?' questions.

Sometimes children make mistakes because they are missing vital bits of information, but sometimes they are struggling with the ideas. Several of the home conversations quoted by Tizard and Hughes (1984) demonstrated how four-year-olds show through their questions that they have not yet grasped a key idea. Some ideas are so obvious to adults that the latter have not understood that the child is confused.

Jacqui Cousins' (1999) observations (see also page 160) and her reflections on them also show that children are interested in what goes on. Children want and try to make meaning. Their learning is not restricted to what adults would define as play. One child who listened to her tape recording of his conversation, commented, 'I never knew I asked so many questions. Do they stretch my thinking brain?' The children themselves observed, commented and offered interpretations. They were very interested in what 'OFSTED ladies' did and why (this material came from Cousins' time as an inspector). Their searching questions showed how children wanted to make sense of an event that did not easily relate to other ideas already familiar in their experience. Cousins also reports how a few children made their own notebooks and proceeded to observe her actions and reactions.

Questions and answers

Children also learn through relaxed conversation with adults, that may or may not be focused on their play. Barbara Tizard with Martin Hughes described how question and answer exchanges between an adult and a child can be very different. It depends on whether this conversation occurs naturally or is an adult-initiated exchange with a definite adult learning purpose.

Tizard and Hughes contrasted the conversations of four-year-old girls at home and at their half-day nursery school. The researchers were constructively critical of a form of adult driven conversation that can still be observed in early years settings. They highlight the risks in any exchange in which the adult, parents as well, are too concerned about their own learning objectives. The main points to consider are as follows.

- When adults explore and attempt to guide children's learning (most often in schools or nurseries), they tend to ask children questions to which the adults already have the answer.
- Adults want the children's replies to demonstrate whether those children know or understand, or do not.
- In contrast, children's questions are usually, although not always, a request for information. Children are not usually checking out whether the adult knows something. They do not usually ask the kind of **testing question** used by many adults.

DEFINITION

testing questions the type of question asked by adults who know the answer and want to check whether children are aware

- Even the familiar opening phrase used by some children of 'Do you know?' is most often a way to start a conversation. The child intends to tell the adult interesting nuggets of information.
- Replies to questions and given explanations in normal conversation tend to have a function and purpose of sharing information and suggestions. In the more **didactic model**, children's explanations in reply to adult questions have a display function: the replies show children's knowledge, or lack of it.

DEFINITION

didactic model an approach in which adult learning objectives are to the fore and may override learning opportunities approached from the children's perspective

✔ PROGRESS CHECK

1. **Describe three possible roles for adults in children's play.**
2. **What are the drawbacks to using testing questions with children?**
3. **Suggest two ways for adults to behave in order to have useful conversations with children.**

GOOD PRACTICE

Early years practitioners can and do hold open-ended conversations with children. Reflective professional practice within a team needs to acknowledge different ways of running a question and answer exchange.

The Saplings group of nurseries in South London has a guiding framework for their teams that includes four simple queries to guide reflection.

- Is the question you are asking the child a genuine question?
- Do you really want to know the answer?
- Does the child have the answer and you do not?
- Would you ask an adult this question?

Consider using these reflective questions to support you and your colleagues in exploring how you use questions with the children as they play.

ADULT JUDGEMENTS ON PLAY

There seem to be some broad differences in the play of boys and girls, starting in early childhood. There are, of course, many common features as well. Historically girls and boys have been treated differently (see page 118) and their play and learning seen as a means to train them in skills and outlooks appropriate to later adult life. The main thrust of equal opportunities in play and gender has tended to be on equalising opportunities for girls. The focus of this section is to consider how both the visible differences and social pressures in early years have exerted an impact on adult reactions to boys' play. It is time to reflect on the possible negative impact of practice as well as identify positive approaches for boys and girls.

Wider play opportunities for all

Careful observation and reflection can bring early years practitioners to a more genuinely equal stance on the play of boys and girls. Pretend play was discussed on page 110 and the issues are revisited here with a particular focus on the role of the adult.

Boys are keen to use their imagination but some will not be attracted to domestic scenarios such as the home corner. Transport and construction scenarios, adventure, re-enacting scenes from admired television and video characters – all of these can engage boys, and some girls as well. Early years teams who have organised different spaces and learning areas have observed the absorbed involvement of children, whose attention is not captured so well by the home corner.

Boys, on balance, also seem to need more physical space. Genuine attention to their needs often alerts practitioners to the immense value of using the outdoor space and taking the curriculum into the garden (see also page 125). The girls benefit as well from this opening up of possibilities.

Neither sex benefits from a narrow view of 'proper play', but it seems very likely that the boys' learning will be particularly limited, for now and with negative consequences for their future.

Research for The Qualifications and Curriculum Association's *Could Do Better* report in 1998 pointed out that there were negative consequences when mainly female nursery and primary school staff stopped the action-packed play more typical of boys. The negative approach seemed to risk further disaffection of boys from school life. The report was concerned about holding onto boys' potential enthusiasm especially in the area of literacy. In contrast, staff who listened to the boys and encouraged them to explain and develop their play actions found that the boys had invented complex story lines and it was not all 'bash and crash'.

THINK ABOUT IT

Responsible teams are reflective. Children's play and learning needs will not be met by adults who are resistant to genuine observation and rethinking practice on gender equal opportunities. In your team you could discuss and consider the following

- **Have equal opportunities on gender in any way left the boys on the sidelines?**
- **Can it ever be appropriate to treat girls and boys as if there is no difference?**
- **How should adults intervene sensitively in play that appears to follow very strict gender stereotypes?**
- **What about genuine respect for parents' views on how they wish it is appropriate to raise boys and girls? Some parents are very concerned if their sons dress up or play with tea sets.**
- **In what ways can a genuine opening of all children's opportunities sit comfortably with partnership with parents?**

Rough and tumble and play fighting

Early years practitioners and parents encounter **play fighting**. The term is used to mean very physical games involving struggles between children, usually boys rather than girls, in which the play develops into wrestling and close body contact. Some play fighting occurs in the context of pretend play themes that concern adults. **Rough and tumble** is a phrase sometimes used interchangeably with play fighting. However, rough and tumble is usually more a form of physical play for younger children, often both girls and boys. They enjoy the energetic use of their skills, sometimes with an adult, who may enable them to perform some of the livelier movements in safety.

Play fighting provokes mixed reactions in early years settings and it is relevant that nursery and playgroup teams are overwhelmingly female. Helpful discussion is emerging from research and a concern to make gender equal opportunities properly inclusive of boys. Practitioners need to talk about the nature of play fighting and consider alternatives to a straightforward ban in settings.

DEFINITIONS

play fighting a form of play activity, more usual with boys, in which close physical contact and struggles form part of the action and may also be integrated into pretend play themes

rough and tumble a form of physical play in which children enjoy energetic use of their skills, sometimes with an adult

A number of research projects have observed play fighting in primary school playgrounds and asked adults and children to comment on what has happened. The pattern that emerges supports a more sophisticated approach than deciding play fighting is always aggressive and has to be stopped.

Playful or aggressive?

Children are generally confident that they can tell the difference between play fighting and proper fighting. Mechthild Schafer and Peter Smith (1996) showed children and primary school teachers video footage of play fighting incidents. They reported that there was broad agreement between the children and teachers on how to tell the difference between play fighting and real fights. The cues included facial expressions and the detail of actions.

David Brown (1994) also confirmed that children who watched his videoed exchanges showed a high degree of agreement among themselves. They could point out in detail how observers should use the change in gestures and expressions of the participants to identify the point at which a play fight turned into a bullying incident. Brown reported that the adults who viewed the videos were far less able to read the body language.

Michael Boulton (1994) also noted that it was harder for adults, even males, to read the subtle clues in play fighting than the children who were actually involved. If one takes the reasonable line that children know if a play activity has turned nasty, then this observation has practical implications for playground supervision. Boulton's observations suggest a cautious approach by all adults, since adult males are not necessarily more attuned to particular incidents. He reported that, in contrast with children's views, adult males were more likely to classify an aggressive incident as playful and the females to judge a playful fight as aggressive. The crucial practical implication seems to be that all adults should listen to the children's analysis, before they exercise their adult responsibilities of protection, rule reminding or boundary setting.

Does play fighting slip into real?

Schafer and Smith found that children and teachers agreed that play fights could turn into real ones, but their views then diverged.

- The teachers estimated that about sixty per cent of fights were play and over a third real and that up a third of play fights would turn into real ones.
- This concern then supported an outlook that play fighting as a whole was unwise, because of the high risk.
- In contrast, the children's estimates were that the overwhelming majority of fights were play and that very few turned into real ones.
- The intriguing rider was that the researchers' objective observations and counting up of incidents supported the children's claims.

Schafer and Smith suggest that teachers generalised from the small number of children whose behaviour was habitually aggressive. Their play fighting often turned into real fights and teachers had to deal with the resulting mayhem. However, these children's behaviour was not typical of playground life in general and the other children knew this fact from daily observation and experience.

The situation around play fighting is not straightforward. It is one of those areas in which adults have a responsibility to understand what is really happening and not to wade in on the grounds of keeping children safe. Since play fighting is overwhelmingly an activity of the boys, one can also argue that the principle of equal opportunity should be seriously considered.

The value of play fighting

Careful observers of play fighting, like Schafer, Smith, Brown and Boulton view play fighting as potentially positive. They stress that play fighting is one way that relationships are formed and friendships gel, especially with boys. It is an enjoyable activity and, in the main, low risk. It does not lead to increased aggression as a matter of course. Peter Smith has also undertaken extensive studies of bullying. So, he is a researcher who is well aware of the significance of genuine playground troubles to children.

There does not seem to be any sound basis for simply claiming that all play fighting is potentially aggressive and should be stopped. Perhaps practitioners need another descriptive phrase that is less value-laden. Vivian Paley also faced the issues of boys' games and ways to deal with energy rather than banning play themes (see also page 60). She discussed where games could be played and addressed the issues in a problem solving context with the children themselves. Penny Holland (see page 111) explored ways for adults to join and add to the play, moving well away from a limited adult role as nagger, with 'stop it', 'play more quietly' and 'do be careful of the others!'

TRY THIS!

Consider how you handle play fighting and vigorous rough and tumble in your setting. Ideally, discuss some of the issues with colleagues or fellow students. Try also to have a conversation with practitioners from different settings in early years or playwork.

- Look through the above section, do you think you may assume play fighting is aggressive without careful observation? Be honest! How much do you really watch and listen?
- What are the possibilities for setting boundaries of time and place for energetic rough and tumble?
- Early years settings and primary schools are staffed mainly by women. In what ways can females work to understand play fighting and offer the same level of respect that is rightly expected for more female play activities?
- If you have a mixed staff or student group, then explore this issue with male colleagues. Listen and be sensitive to the fact that they, or just he, will be in the minority.
- Consider ways in which your own setting could apply some of the ideas in this chapter. How could you build on and show respect for the more energetic and lively physical play?

✔ PROGRESS CHECK

1. **Explain how equal opportunities on gender and play may have developed an imbalance, although with good intentions.**
2. **Describe two ways in which adults' and children's perceptions may differ on the activity called play fighting.**
3. **Suggest three practical ways to support physical play of this kind.**

SUPPORTING PLAY AT SCHOOL

Several research projects have observed children's play in the breaktimes at primary school. Some aspects of this research are described in Chapter 4, as an insight into the play of older children. The studies are also important for discussion about possible adult roles to support and encourage play in school breaktimes.

Break times as problematic

Peter Blatchford and Sonia Sharp (1994) explored the perspectives on play in the primary school through the activities within breaktimes in the school playground. They point out that much of the public discussion about school breaktimes has been driven by adult concerns. There has been proportionately far less consideration of how children view this time, its opportunities and limitations.

Primary school teachers tend to perceive breaktime mainly in terms of problems rather than offering potential for play. Blatchford and Sharp highlight the focus on:

- concerns about bullying and aggression
- problems when children are perceived to be 'just hanging about' or 'don't know how to play'
- risks for the youngest and littlest ones in a primary playground
- domination of space by larger children or football playing boys.

Some of these playground issues are very real and concern is also felt by the children. However, Blatchford and Sharp emphasise the great risks of leaving children out of the discussion:

> If teachers are the main recipients of problems arising during playtime, children are the main participants. They are the experts on life in the playground. They have privileged knowledge, and in many cases may well be the only witnesses to what takes place there. What is more, any schemes seeking to improve playtime will need to build on their views about playtime. (Page 4.)

An additional concern is that primary school teams under great pressure on educational outcomes have also seriously considered, and in many cases made changes to reduce children's playtime. The objective has been to increase contact during classroom time. Playtime for children is seen effectively as lost time, as optional recreation rather than purposeful and

Childred have ideas on how to develop school grounds

valued learning. Peter Blatchford (1998) reported a national survey from the 1990s that over a half of primary schools had reduced the children's breaks within the school day by decreasing the time given for lunch break and stopping any afternoon break.

Children's views of break time play

The observations of researchers who have studied play in school share a similar focus on the importance of considering the children's perspective.

- Play is a time valued by children. They recognise some of the problems and want effective adult help that includes proper consultation with children as users of school grounds.
- The quality of school grounds matters a great deal. Children have informed views on what helps and what does not help to make the grounds a welcoming environment for play and social contact.
- Having friends and supportive friendships seem to be a key issue for children. Being without friends in the playground is a serious problem. Happy breaktimes depend on social skills of getting into games and dealing with any problems from feeling isolated.
- Equipment is not everything, but can make a difference to the range of possible games.
- Children appreciate the friendly involvement of playground staff. However, children are only too aware of when these adults are not valued members of the school team. Primary schools need to treat the playground staff with respect, value them and offer appropriate training.
- Children dislike the heavy teasing, name calling and other verbal bullying that can go on in a playground. Fighting is an issue, as is use of space, but children are not always content with the way that adults handle these issues. They do not appreciate non-consultative bans and heavy-footed adult 'solutions' that fail to recognise the complexity of a situation.
- Children, especially the youngest and smallest can find breaktime in the main primary playground a daunting experience. They can be perplexed about what they are supposed to do. Supportive playground staff and careful consideration about use of the space, can make a major difference to children's experiences.

The problem with bans

One of the frustrations experienced by primary school children is that problems in the playground are sometimes 'solved' by adults imposing a ban on an activity. Anecdotal evidence from children, practitioners and parents generates a range of blunt prohibitions on play activities enjoyed by children. Bans have been imposed on football, games of tag, temporary crazes such as yo-yos and play equipment like milk crates and large tyres when there have been one or two accidents.

Undoubtedly there are pressures on some nursery or primary teams, especially following any accidents, but there are also serious disadvantages to bans. Lindon (1999) points out that children are very annoyed by bans, especially since these are usually imposed without any discussion of alternatives. Adults have also lost a vital opportunity to take a problem-solving approach with children. Children can learn through being properly involved in the process of discussing problems and possible solutions in a calm and open-minded way.

It is not only the children who are frustrated. Many parents are increasingly unhappy about bans being used as the first and only approach to deal with lively physical games or favourite play items for children. Practitioners are also frustrated, when the pressure to ban has come from more senior staff or advisors concerned about the slightest possible risk.

It is also noticeable that bans in primary or nursery are usually only applied to activities or play materials that adults feel are of little educational value. Lindon points out that staff tend not to consider bans for activities or equipment that are regarded as a legitimate part of the learning environment. Trouble around the sand tray or misuse of crayons are dealt with as a problem around the behaviour of individual children. Teams do not usually exert a ban on what are regarded as educational resources.

TRY THIS!

Being a reflective practitioner means some thought about the consequences of action. Adults in early years, playwork and schools are often keen that children should 'think about what you're doing'. Adults have a responsibility to do the same. Children, even of nursery age, can be sensible participants in a conversation about 'How do we solve the problem with the bikes?' or 'Football is exciting but people are getting knocked over'.

Children can feel respected in a proper discussion and also learn skills of problem solving and negotiation. The five basic steps in effective problem-solving are to:

- enable a full discussion about the nature of the problem
- generate a range of possible solutions to the problem
- decide on the best solution out of those discussed
- put the proposed solution into action for long enough to see how it works
- monitor and evaluate the situation and discuss again as necessary.

Consider in what you already undertake this kind of discussion with the children and to what extent you could strengthen the work.

A positive role for adults

Wendy Titman (1992 and 1994) puts a constructive case for the value of play and recognises the importance of school environments. She supports a non-banning approach and proper consultation with the children as school grounds users:

> Children can, or should, be able to play without being organised by adults. But children need adults to **enable** play [bold in original]. Positive play experiences cannot happen in a vacuum, however ingenious and creative children may be. Children need time to play, access to environments of quality to play in and other people to play with. They need adults to provide those opportunities. (1992, page 5.)

In both reports, Titman describes how children appreciated adults in the playground who got involved in their play, as a partner and not to order them about. Children notice adult behaviour and it was symbolic in one school that the headteacher was regularly present in the playground. A child commented, 'Our headteacher skips so if you've got nothing to do you can play with her. She's always there and she sees everything' (1994, page 121). Other aspects of the positive adult role and involving children in proper consultation are covered from page 63.

Children's persistence

When children are regularly blocked in their preferred play choices, they sometimes become more creative. Children do not always passively accept the adult ban. The keenness felt by children to pursue their play interests and activities becomes clear when they confide in adults whom they feel will appreciate their efforts.

Wendy Titman (personal communication) shares a telling anecdote in her presentations about the importance of making mud pies. In the grounds of one primary school she heard a strange retching sound and looked to see what was happening. Some children appeared to be spitting water out of their mouths onto the ground. The children explained to Titman that they needed water to make the mud pies. First of all they used buckets, but 'they', being the school adults, stopped that. The children then creatively used empty crisp packets, followed by sodden paper towels that they wrung out onto the earth. But 'they' stopped that too. So now children managed by the strategy that they ran from the toilets having taken a mouth full of water and emptied it into the hole. A new strand of play had developed since the boys laid in wait and tickled the girls to try to make them lose the water.

The support of other children

The importance of having friends in school grounds was recognised by the organisation Learning Through Landscapes. They developed the idea of the Friendship Stop and the Friendship Squad. The aim is that an agreed welcoming location is established in a school playground. It may be a tree or an area with seating rather like a bus stop. Children who are without companionship can stop at this location. The named members of the Friendship Squad ensure that they notice and go across to keep the child company. Children choose to become part of the squad and they are available for any children who find themselves alone.

The friendship stop is a welcoming location

The ability of children to support their peers is an untapped resource in many schools. The practical ideas of the Friendship Squad require some adult support, but then the children undertake the befriending. Hilary Stacey and Pat Robinson (1997) describe how children can be taught the skills of mediation to apply in the playground. Conflict resolution skills have successfully been taught to children as part of the personal and social education element of the primary school curriculum. Children as young as nine and ten years old have become effective playground supporters, enabling their peers to deal with conflict in a non-aggressive way.

CASE STUDY

Improving breaktime

The team of Croft Primary School became aware that many of the children complained they were bored in the playground. The problem was worse in the winter when they were not allowed on the grass area. Children were also getting chilled from standing about. Several actions developed in response to the problem.

- The PTA offered a small fund for buying simple breaktime equipment. A range of skipping ropes, hoops, soft balls and bean bags were then made available in part of the playground.
- Discussions with the playground supervisors stressed that their role was to play with any children who wanted some support.
- More money was found to have some markings done for hopscotch and circles for a jumping game.
- Children expressed an interest in more organised team games but everybody did not want to play football. A rota was discussed and set up in which individual teachers and assistants signed up to lead different games each day. They also worked to mobilise the children in the care and tidying up of the equipment.

A review was held after three months and the discussion involved representatives from each class. Two main issues arose that the staff team recognised needed further attention. The status of the non-teacher playground supervisors was still an issue. They were on the receiving end of a lot of cheek from a minority of the children. The children identified a continuing problem for their peers who had trouble making friends or who were 'rubbish' at team games.

1. In what way could you address any lack of play resources in your setting?
2. What could be possible routes to resolving the outstanding issues for Croft School?

TRY THIS!

Turn to your own memories of primary school experience.

- How did you and your friends spend your time in the playground?
- What other activities went on that you can remember, but that did not involve you?
- Were there some games or ways of playing that you and your friends liked but were curtailed in some way by the adults in the playground?
- Were there any activities – play or otherwise – that caused you trouble from other children?
- Did the adults help and in what way? If not, what would you have liked the adults to do for you and your friends?

If possible, share these memories with colleagues or fellow students. What picture emerges and how much variety? Of course, you are dealing with your own selective childhood memories. But what insights does this offer for your approach to children now?

✔ PROGRESS CHECK

1 **Suggest two disadvantages for children when adults see school breaktime mainly as a source of problems.**

2 **Describe briefly why breaktime can be so important to primary school children.**

3 **Explain the advantages of involving children in plans to make changes to school grounds and how play is organised.**

SUPPORT FOR SOCIAL SKILLS

DEFINITION

social skills a range of behaviours that can be learned and practised that enable children, or adults, to become more attuned to those with whom they interact

Objective observation of children's play by adults often highlights the social complexities of playing together. The necessary **social skills** of happy play include patterns of co-operative interaction such as sharing. Adults, parents as well as practitioners often promote sharing as an ideal for group life, but they often have not thought in detail about what it means in practice for young children or how adults can help.

Social skills and under-threes

Sonia Jackson and Elinor Goldschmied (1994) were especially interested in very young children, but their comments on the social tasks are applicable to the slightly older ones as well. Adults often underestimate the social complexities for children of nursery or primary school life.

Even very young children are ready to make contact

Jackson and Goldschmied described how young children need to learn and often appreciate help in all of the following.

- Ways to approach an existing group of playing children and how to join the group and the activity, ideally without being told to go away or rejected by other means.
- Socially acceptable ways to behave in a group with other children. It is not easy sometimes for children to find the middle course. How do you lead without being regarded as bossy? What does it feel like to be part of a group?

TRY THIS!

Choose two social skills that support children in a group from the Jackson and Goldschmied list of bullet points on pages 179–180. Watch out for this kind of situation as it arises for children in your setting.

- What happens? How do some children seem to manage this skill and how do some have struggles?
- Consider the ways in which you, perhaps with your colleagues, help children deliberately to cope and learn this social skill. Could you help in more effective ways?
- In what ways does your setting actively support and make it easier for children to take turns in play and to be considerate of others? How might you improve the situation?

- Sometimes children have troubles in finding out how to leave a group. They may want to move onto something else, because they want a change or the play has become uninteresting.
- There are different strategies for joining the existing play of another child. Some ways to make contact tend to promote conflict rather than shared playfulness. Pushing into the other child's personal space, or seizing play materials, does not usually go down well.
- Children often find difficulties in coping with children who want to play with them more often than is reciprocated. Children sometimes also want to play on their own for the time being.

Adult support for children's social skills

Once adults focus on what is likely to be the children's perspective, it becomes clear that the social skills that support happy play in group life need to be learned. A helpful adult role extends well beyond simply telling children they 'must share' or they 'ought to be nice to each other'.

Some practical projects have highlighted that adults can be genuinely helpful once they pay careful attention to children's real choices in behaviour. Adults need to observe how the setting supports or works against their efforts. Some of these projects have been specifically concerned to reduce children's more aggressive ways of coping. The practical suggestions also highlight the kinds of behaviour adults wish to encourage and how this guidance could work.

Sue Finch (1998) describes the positive impact when staff observe the regular conflict points within the day. Rather than assuming the problem is all about children's behaviour, staff consider how changes in the routine could mean children find it easier to co-operate. One example was the problem that arose because young children had to wait around at snack time. Self-service milk and snack tables promoted less irritation and more conversation, because children chose when to take their snack break,

Ronald Slaby and his team (1995) looked in detail at adult responsibilities in helping children to learn co-operative behaviour over nursery resources. They especially considered the real meaning of sharing: what adults meant in practice and what children thought was expected of them. One example is that the team recognised taking turns should not have to mean that children simply handed over an important item. The adults helped children to feel confident in saying phrases like, 'You can have it when I've finished' or 'I'll trade you the big bricks for those smaller ones'.

Social skills in primary school

David Brown's (1994) observations highlighted that social skills matter in playground interactions, just as much as in the play of younger children. He made the following observations.

- Conflicts can arise when isolated children try to enter games and are rejected, either verbally or physically. Children may need sensitive support from playground staff, when they find it hard to enter play.

- Observation of those children, who are distanced from their peers, shows that these individuals seem to find difficulty in using accepted techniques to ask to join groups or to establish partnerships over time.
- Other children, who are on the sidelines, may be rejected because their performance at the chosen activity is judged unsatisfactory by the group. Certainly, team games will depend on a minimal level of skill and adults need to support children in learning appropriate skills.
- Some children are ejected from an on-going game because of their repeated breaking of the rules. Other children have probably explained the rules more than once, so further inappropriate behaviour is unacceptable.

Children learn the skills to discuss and negotiate

Brown noticed that children who were temporarily out of the play action showed their situation by varied body posture. Some children who wanted to regain entry might adopt a searching or questing posture. Other children implied through their body language that they did not care about being uninvolved. Others would use verbal ridicule of the game and its participants.

Ejection from play may be temporary or children may find other playmates. Some children find themselves rejected over the long term and for a range of reasons. They may stay isolated, but some form a sub-group whose play activity develops into disruption of other games or bullying to establish a status and focus to their playground time.

Learning from autistic children

Children within the autistic spectrum have disabilities that affect thinking, but also exert an impact on communication and social development.

Children who are autistic do not play like their peers. Their problems in relating to other children, as well as adults, highlight the amount of development we take for granted in 'normal' childhood. Children with autistic range disabilities do not learn the social skills of play and this difference highlights just how much subtle learning and practice occurs with children who are not disabled in this way.

When social skills are hard to learn

Autism is a broad developmental disorder that disrupts children's social development and their ability to form and maintain relationships. Learning about language is as much a development of social communication as a technical task of learning words and grammar. Children with autism have difficulties with verbal and non-verbal communication, both of which are necessary to support the development of relationships with other children or adults.

Children with autism have an intense need for a rigid routine. Their intolerance of change or even mild variation and their frequent obsessive interest in particular objects means that they are not easy companions for other children. Autistic children 'break' too many of the social rules of interaction and play. You may be hardly aware of these important rules, until you observe the reaction of children when an autistic child has no idea how to behave 'properly' in play. Most play activities that are regarded as normal within early childhood require both practical playing skills and social skills.

Learning social cues

Jannik Beyer and Lone Gammeltoft (2000) highlight that autistic children have difficulties in three main areas: the skills of social interaction, communication and imagination. All these areas are crucial for the development of play relationships. Beyer and Gammeltoft have explored possible ways to coach autistic children in strategies that create enough social competence that they may be able to play with other children. Of course, the work depends on a full understanding by adults of the social rules governing children's play.

The struggles of autistic children highlight what their peers are learning or have already learned. Many playful exchanges between children depend on the ability to pick up the social cues that distinguish between something that is fun or serious, words that are a joke or a telling off. Cause and effect and the working of intentions in social behaviour are highly confusing to autistic children. They have great difficulty in grasping social rules to apply in similar situations. It is as if they have to memorise and understand each social situation anew. Of course, non-autistic children or adults can misread a situation, but there is nothing like the confusion that autistic children experience every day. For instance, did the baby cry because somebody is yelling or is somebody yelling because the baby cried?

The growth of social skills in play

By nine or ten months of age babies recognise the experience of joint attention with an adult on an object of interest. You will sometimes see this shared focus with younger babies. There is an expression on the baby's face, combined with deliberate looking at the adult, or older sibling, that communicates 'we are doing this together'. Autistic children have great difficulty in this essential aspect to play. They also find it hard to recognise that their own image of what is happening is not the same as that of another person.

Two-, three- and four-year-olds usually show through their play that they have expectations of how different people they know are likely to behave. They have formed what Beyer and Gammeltoft call a **script**. Scripts are flexible working models of what normally happens in everyday situations. Non-autistic children incorporate this understanding into their play. Children act upon and create further play around those observations, especially in their pretend themes. Pretend play requires a deliberate disregard for reality. Children at play are, at the same time, aware of the real situation and able to create an image of it as being something else of their own choice.

DEFINITION

script a term used to describe an understanding by children of how normal everyday situations unfold. Autistic children have great difficulty in learning such patterns

THINK ABOUT IT

Observation of, or reading about, autistic children shows just how much most children understand and the sophistication of their thinking.

Autistic children have great difficulty in picking out the meaningful aspects to the behaviour of others and so have little to guide them in advance each day. It is understandable that they are often so anxious and develop coping strategies that create anything from mild to chaotic disruption.

In what ways can a greater understanding of autistic children highlight what many children manage in their play?

Autistic children at play

Observations of the play of autistic children shows the following features.

- The children tend to use objects in an inflexible way, without the variety that can be seen in the exploration of their peers. Perhaps a child requires that the bricks always make exactly the same tower. A child may be intrigued by finding and looking at wheel-like objects, but does not want to play with them once they are found.
- Intentional play with objects is less spontaneous and tends to follow set patterns for this individual child. A child may insist on climbing up any structure, not just acceptable climbing apparatus.
- Pretend play is rare and, if it is observed, tends to be fixed around this child's specific interests or television programmes that preoccupy him (more boys are autistic than girls).

Beyer and Gammeltoft describe practical approaches to autistic children that aim to coach them in the strategies they need to play and so to make some social contact. The work focuses on:

- coaching and practising attention, expectation and shared focus on objects of interest
- how to imitate a play partner and how to mirror what that partner is doing
- how to play alongside in parallel play and how to sustain a simple dialogue in play

TRY THIS!

It is useful to reflect on the links between social behaviour and play for all children.

- Do you observe children in your setting who have not yet learned or who 'break' the social rules of childhood groups?
- Perhaps their struggles are related to lack of play experience. The children will not necessarily be autistic.
- In what ways could you and your colleagues help the children to address their difficulties and become more integrated within the group of children?
- Observe the children individually and use the ideas in this section to make simple plans to help their learning step by step.

- talking through simple everyday scripts of what happens and what follows what, including simple stories. This activity aims to help children grasp the rules of social interaction
- how to make the shift in order to take turns
- simple games and the rules of playing.

Autistic children will continue to have problems with social patterns and how one experience can connect with and support another. They continue to struggle to make sense of social interaction, but the coaching system seems to give them more understanding.

Nurture groups

The importance of play, learning and related social skills was shown through the work of Marjorie Boxall (1996). The ability of older children to cope in primary school is built through earlier experiences with their peers and the support of caring and attentive adults.

Young children learn with supportive adult contact

As an educational psychologist during the 1970s, Boxall dealt with many referrals of children whom teachers judged to be hard to manage in the classroom. Her observations led her to develop small **nurture groups** for these children in order to develop the skills and outlook that they needed in order to manage in the ordinary primary school class. A revival of interest in the 1990s led to some re-development of the ideas.

DEFINITION

nurture groups an idea developed by Marjorie Boxall, in which deliberately planned play and social experiences were offered in a small and safe group for children who found an ordinary primary class hard to manage

In the nurture groups, the aim was that children were enabled to experience early years learning activities that they had largely missed. However, the way in which the group was run was equally important as the activities. The children needed a regular routine in which they could learn about predictability, as well as variety in daily events. A key feature of the group was that the teacher warned children of any changes and visitors were kept to a minimum. The overriding aim was to combine a nurturing approach derived from family life (an explicit link made by Boxall) with a supportive daily structure. Children were enabled to learn social skills crucial to group life, such as taking turns, making choices and seeing an activity through to completion. The adults' interaction with thc children was also planned to encourage unsure children to develop self-esteem. Children needed to see adults as a useful resource and as trustworthy.

Playing 'Peek-a-boo' is fun

✔ PROGRESS CHECK

1. Describe three social skills that can be observed as necessary to support children's play.
2. Suggest two ways in which the struggles of autistic children can highlight the social skills that are an integral part of play.
3. Explain two ways that adults can effectively support social skills in children's play.

KEY TERMS

You need to know the meaning of the following words and phrases. Go back through the chapter to make sure you understand them:

didactic model
mediator
nurture groups
play fighting
rough and tumble
script
social skills
testing questions

FURTHER READING

Bennathan, Marion and Boxall, Marjorie (1996) *Effective Intervention in Primary Schools: Nurture Groups*, David Fulton
Detailed description of the ideas and practice of nurture groups for children who need special support in primary school.

Beyer, Jannik and Gammeltoft, Lone (2000) *Autism and Play*, Jessica Kingsley
The practical ways to support autistic children also highlight the social skills needed for all children's play.

Boulton, Michael (1994) 'Playful and aggressive fighting in the middle school playground' in Blatchford, Peter and Sharp, Sonia (eds) *Breaktime and the School: Understanding and Changing Playground Behaviour*, Routledge
Useful insights into children's play that adults believe is aggressive.

Brown, David (1994) 'Play, the playground and the culture of childhood' in
Moyles, Janet (ed) (1994) *The Excellence of Play*, Open University Press
Useful observation of children's play in primary school and the sense that they make of what is happening.

Finch, Sue (1998) *An Eye for an Eye Leaves Everyone Blind: Teaching Young Children to Settle Conflicts Without Violence*, National Early Years Network
Plenty of practical ideas and examples to guide young children towards co-operative behaviour.

Hislam, Jane (1994) 'Sex differentiated play experiences and children's choices' in Moyles, Janet (op cit)
A practical chapter that raises some of the dilemmas in responding well to boys and girls, especially in mainly female early years teams.

Jackson, Sonia and Goldschmied, Elinor (1994) *People Under Three: Young Children and Day Care*, (Routledge)
Consideration of the needs of very young children in day care settings.

Schafer, Mechthild and Smith, Peter (1996) 'Teachers' perceptions of play fighting and real fighting in primary school' in *Educational Research*, Vol. 38
An intriguing study that highlights the issues involved in adult and children's judgements.

Slaby, Ronald, Roedell, Wendy, Arezzo, Diana and Hendrix, Kate (1995) *Early Violence Prevention: Tools for Teachers of Young Children*, National Association for the Education of Young Children, available in the UK from the National Early Years Network
Detailed consideration on how adults can help children behave in socially acceptable ways, including sharing. The team consider the importance of adult behaviour and how the setting is organised.

Stacey, Hilary and Robinson, Pat (1997) *Let's Mediate*, Lucky Duck Publishing
Description of how primary school children can learn conflict resolution skills.

Titman, Wendy (1992) Play, *Playtime and Playgrounds*, Learning Through Landscapes/WWF UK)
Written from the children's perspective as well as from the adults', this book has a wealth of ideas to improve play at school.

Titman, Wendy (1994) *Special Places; Special People: The Hidden Curriculum of School Grounds*, Learning Through Landscapes/WWF UK
Report of an early 1990s project to explore children's views of school grounds and how consultation can improve their play environment.

Glossary

adventure play and **adventure playgrounds** play and play settings that focus on children's opportunity to experience physical and related emotional challenge

cognitive competence a focus on what children can understand and how their thinking operates at a given time

didactic apparatus the set of learning materials developed by Maria Montessori to support children's physical and sensory abilities

didactic model an approach in which adult learning objectives are to the fore and may override learning opportunities approached from children's perspective

empowerment the concept of sharing control and choice, in this case with children, and enabling them to make their own decisions in a more equal relationship with adults

experimental method a planned approach, in this case to the study of children's play, when a situation is set up and questions asked of children in order to prove or disprove the researcher's hypothesis

facilitator a role in play that means an adult gives support and guidance but does not direct or take over children's activities and choices

fantasy play the term often used to describe pretend play in which the characters are drawn from fiction, television or video stories

forest school an English development from the Danish focus on play and learning in a open air space. The forest school experience offers familiarity with a natural outdoors environment and coaching of appropriate outdoors and safety skills

free flow play the kind of play that Tina Bruce proposes is most supportive of children's learning in early educational settings. This play allows children to 'wallow' in the play and bring in skills managed elsewhere

gender word used to describe the social role taken by boys and girls, men and women. Gender differences are shaped by children's learning and cannot all be explained by the biological sex difference of being male or female

gender-stereotyped behaviour that follows social expectations about how males and females should behave. Children learn ideas about how boys and girls should play as well as their own expectations about what older children and adults can do

gifts the term used by Froebel to describe learning materials designed to support children in exploring the structured nature of the world

hospital play specialist a trained practitioner who has specialised in bringing play to children in hospital and sometimes in home visiting to children who are long-term sick and cared for at home

hypothesis the detailed prediction made before an experiment. The hypothesis states what researchers expect to happen following particular events within the study. A hypothesis is developed from a theory; it is not the theory itself

incompetence or **deficit model** of early development is the approach of defining young children in terms of the skills they have not yet managed, rather than what they can do. Sometimes called a top-down approach in contrast to a bottom-up perspective

interpretation the process of making sense of what is observed, finding meaning or explanation of reasons or motivations for actions. Adult values may also influence interpretations of play in terms of ideas of quality or acceptability

heuristic play a form of exploratory or discovery play, with suggested materials developed by Elinor Goldschmied

inclusion the approach that disabled children should, as far as possible and with careful consideration of their disability, be enabled to attend mainstream early years and school provision

junk playground the original Danish adventure playground

mediator someone who uses skills of communication and problem solving to enable two or more people to face and resolve a situation of disagreement or conflict

medical model dominant view that people, including children, in hospital are to be seen only through their illness and their stay must be managed with maximum convenience to the medical team

medical model of disability an approach, now largely discredited, that treated disabled children as medical cases. Children's individuality and their play and social needs in childhood risked being lost in specialist treatment of their condition

metamemory means the deliberate transfer of strategies and skills between different tasks and problems. It is a skill of active use of ideas and ways of thinking already stored in the memory

metacognition means children's aware and conscious work on problem solving and their use of existing ideas and knowledge

non-directive play therapy using play to support and help children express their concerns or confusions but with an adult role that does not assume a particular theoretical underpinning to play behaviour

nurture groups an idea developed by Marjorie Boxall, in which deliberately planned play and social experiences were offered in a small and safe group for children who found an ordinary primary class hard to manage

objectivity a presumed characteristic of the experimental method. An objective outlook is shown when researchers remain detached from personal preferences and assumptions about results and interpretations

observational method an approach that focuses on watching and listening to children's chosen play. The ideal is that observers remain open-minded and allow the observations to shape the sense made of what children can do

occupations the sixteen activities that Friedrich Froebel designed to interest children and support their learning

open access play in a setting that allows children to come and go as they wish

outdoor play opportunities for children to learn in the outdoors, in a garden or other open air space

playcare a development of the playwork tradition in which children's opportunities to play are offered within a setting that takes responsibility for them within agreed time boundaries

playwork the professional area focused on play opportunities for children of school age and older

physical play activities and opportunities that especially help children to use, practise and apply the full range of their physical skills

play ethos an approach that stresses the crucial importance of children's play within their development

play fighting a form of play activity, more usual with boys, in which close physical contact and struggles form part of the action and may also be integrated into pretend play themes

play therapy an approach to supporting children and helping them with concerns or problems through the medium of their play

play tutoring an intervention programme designed by Sara Smilansky in which adults helped children to learn the skills necessary for sociodramatic play

play therapist someone who has trained in using play and play materials to support children in expressing and resolving anxieties and stress

pretend play the play of children from very young characterised by the presence of imagination and that children act as if something or someone is other than is the case in reality

proprioception the skills and bodily awareness that enable a child to recognise what it feels like to be in balance or about to lose their balance. They are learning to interpret the messages of sensation sent from the body into the brain

psychodynamic play therapy using children's play to resolve conflicts that are believed to arise in childhood and to share the psychodynamic interpretation of play with the child

reflective practitioner a phrase that describes alert professionals, in early years and playwork, who are willing to think as well as act. Reflective practitioners are ready to re-consider as well as explain their current approach, values and priorities in work with children

rough and tumble a form of physical play in which children enjoy energetic use of their skills, sometimes with an adult

schemas are patterns of behaviour linked to a broad theme. A schema describes a child's way, often their favourite way, of exploring the world at a given time. Schemas include a combination of actions and ideas that shape a child's current approach to learning

script a term used to describe an understanding by children of how normal everyday situations unfold. Autistic children have great difficulty in learning such patterns

sixth sense Elinor Goldschmied's focus on children's awareness of bodily movement and use of physical skills. An idea similar to proprioception

small world play the term sometimes used to describe pretend play with miniature people, animals and settings made to scale with the figures

spiral curriculum the idea that children will revisit play materials and activities over the years, but then use them differently because their development has progressed

socio-dramatic play the pretend play of children older than 3–4 years in which they develop make-believe games with agreed roles and plans for actions and words

social construction of childhood the idea that there is neither an absolute, nor a universal image of a child and childhood. The image is created by social attitudes

socialisation the process by which children learn what is expected of them in terms of behaviour and attitudes within their society, or social and cultural group

social referencing the idea that babies and very young children look towards a familiar adult, to see that person's reaction and expression, in order to make some sense of a new or ambiguous situation

social skills a range of behaviours that can be learned and practised that enable children, or adults, to become more attuned to those with whom they interact

sociology of childhood a branch of the discipline of sociology that has focused on children and childhood in the context of social groups and society as a whole

testing questions the type of question asked by adults who know the answer and want to check whether children are aware

values perspectives and priorities that adults hold as important, using them as a source of judgement and choice

Vygotskian tutorial the helping approach offered by an adult to a child that is sensitive to that child's current zone of proximal development

zone of proximal development the area of potential learning for an individual child at a given time

Resources

Action for Sick Children
300 Kingston Road
Wimbledon Chase
London SW20 8LX
Tel: 020 8542 4848
Fax: 020 8542 2424
Works to ensure that health services are responsive to the needs of children and parents.

Bethnal Green Museum of Childhood
Cambridge Heath Road
London E2 9PA
Tel: 020 8980 2415
A free museum with a substantial collection of play materials and information about play and childhood.

Children's Play Council
8 Wakley Street
London EC1V 7QE
Tel: 020 7843 6016
Fax: 020 7278 9512
E-mail: cpc@ncb.org.uk
Brings together national voluntary organisations, working to promote children's play.

Children's Play Information Service
8 Wakley Street
London EC1V 7QE
Tel: 020 7843 6303
Provides a library and information service on all aspects to play and playwork. Visits by appointment.

Daycare Trust
Shoreditch Town Hall Annexe
21 St George's Road
London SE1 6ES
Tel: 020 7840 3350
Fas: 020 7840 3355
Email:info@daycaretrust.org.uk
Website:www.daycaretrust.org.uk
Consultancy and publications on many aspects to quality in childcare, including consultation with children.

Early Education
111 City View House
463 Bethnal Green Road
London E2 9QY
Tel: 020 7739 7594
An organisation concerned about all aspects of young children's learning, with a particular focus on early educational settings.

Kidsactive
Pryor's Bank
Bishop's Park
London SW6 3LA

Tel: 020 7731 1435
Fax: 020 7731 4426
Email:ntis@kidsactive.org.uk
Website:www.kidsactive.org.uk
Promotes play and opportunities for children and young people with physical and learning disabilities.

Kids' Clubs Network
Bellerive House
3 Muirfield Crescent
London E14 9SZ
Tel: 020 7512 2112
Fax: 020 7512 2010
Email:info.office@kidsclubs.co.uk
Website:www.kidsclubs.com
Promotes after-school and holiday playschemes for children. Offers consultancy and advice on services for 5–15s.

Learning Through Landscapes
3rd Floor
Southside Offices
The Law Courts
Winchester
S023 9DL
Tel: 01962 846258
Website:www.ltl.org.uk
Promotes support for children's play through development of schools grounds and consultation of children in this process.

National Association of Hospital Play Staff
c/o Mrs J.Ellis, Information Officer
Fladgate
Forty Green
Beaconsfield
HP9 1XS
Organises training and experience to anyone who wishes to specialise in playwork with children in hospital.

National Children's Bureau
8 Wakley Street
London
EC1V 7QE
Tel: 020 7843 6000 (main) 020 7843 6008 (library)
The valuable resource collection of the Early Childhood Unit is now part of the main library.

National Early Years Network
77 Holloway Road
London
N7 8JZ
Tel: 020 7607 9573
Fax: 020 7770 1105
Email:neyn.org@virgin.net
Offers training, information and publications relevant to children and their families, including learning, play and good practice.

Planet
C/o Warwickshire College
Moreton Morrell Centre
Moreton Morrell, Warwickshire
CV35 9BL
Tel; 01926 650195
Part of Action for Leisure, Planet promotes play and leisure for disabled children, young people and adults.

Index